THE MUSIC FORUM

Volume I

THE MUSIC FORUM

Volume I

Edited by WILLIAM J. MITCHELL *and* FELIX SALZER

Columbia University Press   1967   New York and London

The editors are most grateful for the expert autography of
Thames Hickman and the editorial assistance of Hedi Siegel.

THE MUSIC FORUM ADVISORY BOARD

Sydney Beck, *New York Public Library*
Lewis Lockwood, *Princeton University*
Alfred Mann, *Rutgers University*
Saul Novack, *Queens College of the City University of New York*
Claude Palisca, *Yale University*
George Perle, *Queens College of the City University of New York*
Carl Schachter, *The Mannes College of Music*
Roy Travis, *University of California in Los Angeles*
Robert Trotter, *University of Oregon*

Statement of Aims

*I*N PUBLISHING the first volume of *The Music Forum*, we present with some diffidence a statement of our purposes and aims. We know that it is as easy as it is meaningless to announce high-sounding goals. Only the articles themselves, their hoped-for value and interest, and the challenges that they express will justify the need for their presentation. Nevertheless it should be possible to stress some specific points which may explain the purpose of this new venture.

A token of an age of specialization is to be found in the number of periodicals of limited, concentrated scope, whether it be serial or other specialized music, musicology, ethnomusicology, concert reviews, theory, or mathematics. Some of these are limited in coverage by the societies they represent, the houses they serve, or the purposefully restricted aims of the editors. It is our contention that such separation is not good, that a better purpose is served, by cutting across restrictive interests, however justified they might be, and giving representation to provocative articles from the many fields dedicated to music. The reader will thereby be kept abreast of significant activities in many areas as reported in a variety of vital articles. Some of these will be in opposition to or extension of existing trends in our musical scene, more specifically, to present-day approaches to theory, analysis, and musicology. Such articles need a special forum, not only because of the support they require from a favorably disposed editorial policy, but also because of the space demanded by a detailed treatment of certain topics, combined with a number of musical illustrations.

It is our belief that there is need for a publication which will attempt to come to terms with a variety of problems and issues not taken up elsewhere because they are off-limits, or are considered "unpopular," controversial, or lacking in general interest. Since *The Music Forum* is independent in the true meaning of the term, it plans to present and to discuss just such issues. As to our contributors, it should be stressed that we are not interested in "names" per se. The only deciding factors in accepting an article will be the relevance of its subject and the quality of its treatment.

Although we shall deal with a great variety of topics and will give the authors all possible individual leeway, a definite and unifying point of view will be noticeable. In various articles, especially in those of an analytical nature, the influence of Heinrich Schenker's ideas, teachings, and theories will be evident. Such a stress is called for at a time when the efficacy of Rameau's theories comes increasingly in doubt, when linear views are in an ascendant position, when the dissemination of Schenker's views is clearly in evidence, some hundred years after his birth. Schenker was among the first to break with conventional harmonic systems and was in the fore-front of those who placed a major stress on the structural and generative force of linear-horizontal factors. So far as the dissemination of his ideas is concerned, information and misinformation are badly commingled. When it is asserted that he recognized only descending lines, had difficulty with ascending lines, or rejected the concept of modulation, we are deal-ing clearly with misinformation. When it is asserted that Schenker was interested only in a segment of music within a tightly defined period, it is difficult to know whether Schenker the man, or the analytic approach created by him, is being criticized. It is planned to examine such issues carefully.

In the meantime, let it be said that among our contributors may be those who have applied his approach rigorously to a literature of limited historic scope with highly insightful results. There will also be others who recognize the more universal values that lie dormant in his ideas and are capable of providing valuable insights into earlier and later music. These latter views are clearly in evidence in the present issue. Certainly, if these analyses prove valid, it would not be the first time that ideas with seemingly limited application initially grew far beyond their original intent.

Nevertheless, *The Music Forum* will not be an exclusively Schenkerian publication. We shall present topics which were not within Schenker's sphere of immediate interest, e.g., articles on contemporary music and historical musicology. We shall also publish views which contrast not only with those of Heinrich Schenker, but also with those held by the editors. Our unifying function will be expressed without imposing a single philosophy upon all the articles.

Heinrich Schenker was among the first to point to faulty editions of masterworks—some of them still widely distributed even today—as a cause of faulty interpretation, and to draw the attention of the musical world to the manuscript or first edition as the main sources for correct interpretation. We hope to make contributions to this ever acute problem and to illustrate such articles with manuscript facsimiles of entire pieces or movements. It is planned also to present analytical studies by him not heretofore translated or not heretofore published, and to reprint in translation, if necessary, important writings of the past which are now out of print.

It is our belief that general musical experience and maturity have reached a stage where these stated aims can find an interested public, ready to support our constant efforts to seek out issues of basic and enduring significance.

WILLIAM J. MITCHELL

FELIX SALZER

Contents

Contributors

Peter Bergquist is Assistant Professor of Music at the University of Oregon

Hans Neumann taught at the Mannes College of Music

William J. Mitchell is Professor of Music at Columbia University

George Perle is Professor of Music at Queens College of the City University of New York

Felix Salzer is Professor of Music at Queens College of the City University of New York

Carl Schachter teaches at the Mannes College of Music

THE MUSIC FORUM

Volume I

The Two Versions of Mozart's Rondo K.494

HANS NEUMANN
revised and completed by
CARL SCHACHTER

EDITORS' NOTE. When *The Music Forum* was first planned, it was decided to include in the first issue the facsimile of the autograph of Mozart's Rondo for piano, K.494. The late Hans Neumann was asked to contribute an article about the appearance, history, and editorial implications of the autograph. In investigating references to the Rondo in the Mozart literature, Neumann was struck by the divergent and even contradictory views held by scholars and biographers. These views impinge upon substantive issues of biography and of editorial policy. Neumann therefore expanded the article to include a critical survey of the relevant literature.

Before his untimely death in February, 1963, Neumann had sketched out the main lines of his article and had written about two-thirds of it. Approximately half of the written material was in connected sequence; the rest was in the form of separate but carefully worked out paragraphs and short sections. Mrs. Sheila Aldendorff, a student of Neumann's who had assisted him in some of his research, was kind enough to assemble these notes into as coherent a draft as possible, in view of the inevitable gaps.

Carl Schachter had been in close touch with Neumann and had frequently discussed the article with him; the editors therefore asked Schachter to complete the article for publication. Schachter has been able to refer to a number of works that have appeared since Neumann's death—notably to the recent revision of the Köchel catalogue and to Alexander Weinmann's catalogue of the Vienna publications of F. A. Hoffmeister. Because of some important new findings, Schachter has had to change a few of Neumann's emphases; most of his conclusions, however, remain untouched.

Schachter had originally intended to identify his own contributions by brackets or footnotes; this has proved impossible. The process of completing the article has dictated many changes in organization and sequence. Because of these changes, Neumann's work and Schachter's have become so intermixed that accurate identification would make the article unreadable. In its present form the first section of the article is mainly Schachter's; the description of the autograph, however, embodies many of Neumann's observations. The second and third sections are mainly Neumann's work, although the inclusion of new material has required some revisions. The fourth section begins with an attempt to settle some of the controversies surrounding the Rondo; Neumann's views and wording have been retained with only minor changes. The latter part of this final section compares the autograph version of the Rondo with the edition published by Hoffmeister; Schachter has written most of this.

I

ᴘᴇʀʜᴀᴘs none of Mozart's works for piano has given rise to so many
divergent opinions and conclusions among biographers and scholars
as have the Rondo in F major K.494 and the Allegro and Andante (F major
and B♮ major) K.533. According to Mozart's thematic catalogue the
Rondo dates from June 10, 1786, and the Allegro and Andante from
January 3, 1788. Early in the latter year—probably in late January or
February—all three movements were published together as a sonata; the
Rondo was enlarged by the addition of a cadenza of which the composition
date is unknown.[1] In the sonata publication, the tempo indication of the
Rondo was changed from the original andante to allegretto. During the
same year, 1788, two publishers, one in England and the other in Germany,
brought out the Rondo in its original version of 1786—that is, as an independent piece in andante tempo and without the cadenza.

The many conflicting opinions about K.494 and K.533 result in large
measure from two causes. First, we do not know the precise circumstances
surrounding the publication of the three movements as a sonata. Secondly,
almost none of the relevant source material—autograph or first edition—
was available to the earlier Mozart scholars. Indeed, the manuscript of the
sonata has never come to light. At present the only autograph sources
available are Mozart's entries in his own thematic catalogue—three bars
of the Rondo and four of the Allegro—and the complete autograph of the
Rondo as Mozart wrote it in 1786. This autograph, presented in facsimile
on pp. 6–8, forms the subject of the first section of this article; the
second and third sections will survey the treatment of the Rondo in various
biographical, critical, and scholarly works; in the fourth section we shall
present our views and conclusions.

We know little of the early history of the autograph. For several years
after Mozart's death, it almost certainly remained in the possession of his

---

[1] Until quite recently it was generally believed
that the sonata publication (by Hoffmeister of
Vienna) dated from circa 1790. Alexander
Weinmann's catalogue of Hoffmeister's Viennese
publications gives a date of circa January-Feb-
ruary, 1788. See Alexander Weinmann, *Die
Wiener Verlagswerke von Franz Anton Hoffmeister*
(Vienna, Universal Edition, 1964), p. 84.

widow, Constanze. Two curiously contradictory references to the Rondo occur in Constanze's published correspondence with the publishers Breitkopf and Härtel in Leipzig and André in Offenbach.[2] The first appears in a letter to Breitkopf and Härtel dated June 15, 1799.[3] The Leipzig publishers were then bringing out the first large-scale edition of Mozart's works, the so-called "Oeuvres Complettes." Constanze had been sending them autographs (and some copies) of works that were unknown, unpublished, or not available for other reasons; the publishers paid her a modest sum of money for those manuscripts they decided to use.

In the letter Constanze acknowledges receipt of a number of manuscripts that she had sent to Leipzig on March 25. Breitkopf and Härtel had not needed these autographs and had sent them back. Among them are "Nr. 15 Einsam bin ich meine Liebe und ein Rondo Andante mit folgendem Anfang." There follows an incipit of two bars of the right-hand part of the Rondo exactly as it appears in our autograph (notated in soprano clef, rather than in treble as in Mozart's thematic catalogue). If he refers to the facsimile, the reader will note that "N.15" appears, crossed out, above bars 2 and 3; presumably Constanze was referring to this classification number.

The letter to André dates from May 31, 1800.[4] André had purchased all of the Mozart autographs in Constanze's possession. He wrote to her asking why he had not received the manuscripts of a number of works known to him through Mozart's thematic catalogue. Included among these works are the Rondo as well as the Allegro and Andante. In her answer, Constanze states that the Rondo belongs to the Allegro and Andante and that Artaria has published the whole sonata; she implies, therefore, that the autographs are in Artaria's possession. Constanze must have confused Artaria with Hoffmeister, for it was the latter who had published the first edition of the sonata. (Artaria was responsible for a later publication;

2 It is convenient to refer to the correspondence as Constanze's. Most of the letters to publishers were written for her by Georg von Nissen, later her second husband.

3 Reprinted in *Mozart Briefe und Aufzeichnungen*, Wilhelm A. Bauer and Otto Erich Deutsch, eds. (Kassel, Bärenreiter 1963), IV, 244–53; reference to K.494 on p. 247. Earlier reprinted in abridged form in Hermann Abert, "Konstanze Mozarts Briefe an Breitkopf und Härtel," *Mozart-Jahrbuch* (Augsburg, Benno Filser, 1929), III, 173.

4 The letter is printed in Bauer and Deutsch, IV, 352–59; reference to K.494 on p. 355. It had previously appeared in English abridged and translated by C. B. Oldman in Emily Anderson, *Letters of Mozart and His Family* (London, Macmillan, 1938), III, 1477.

as this was printed from Hoffmeister's plates with only the title page changed, Artaria would have had no use for the autographs.)

So far as we know, André never acquired the manuscript of the Rondo. In 1841 he published a thematic catalogue of the Mozart autographs in his collection; the Rondo is not listed among them. As we have seen from the correspondence with Breitkopf, the autograph had been in Constanze's hands in June, 1799; her reference to the filing number 15 almost eliminates the possibility that she had sent a copy rather than the original. Why, then, did she not deliver the autograph to André, who had bought her entire collection? We can only guess. Perhaps she had already sold or given it to someone else before the negotiations with André were completed. Or she might have deliberately misled André in order to keep the autograph for herself. Although she had agreed to dispose of her entire collection of autographs, Constanze seems to have withheld some items. In 1835, for instance, she presented Schubert's friend Albert Stadler with a Mozart autograph (two early songs) "which I had firmly resolved never to part with."[5]

During most of the nineteenth century the autograph had disappeared from view. Köchel's catalogue of 1862 lists it as missing. At some time before 1878 Joseph Joachim acquired the manuscript. He placed it at the disposal of Breitkopf for the Mozart *Gesamtausgabe*; the volume containing the Rondo appeared in 1878.[6] The autograph remained in Joachim's collection in Berlin for a number of years, probably until his death in 1907. Later it passed into the hands of the Wittgenstein family in Vienna and, after World War II, found its way into the collection of Felix Salzer in New York. During the present century the autograph must have been inaccessible during periods of war and political unrest. The writings of Saint-Foix and of Einstein would indicate that they had not seen it. However, Kurt Soldan, Walther Lampe, and Eva and Paul Badura-Skoda have been able to use the photostat owned by the Hoboken Collection of the Austrian National Library.

The Rondo is 160 bars in length and is written on Mozart's customary

[5] Letter to Albert Stadler of December 12, 1835 in Bauer and Deutsch, IV, 512. It had previously appeared in English translation in C. B. Oldman, "Constanze Nissen: four unpublished letters from Mozart's widow," *The Music Review*, XVII (February, 1956), 69–70.

[6] See *Revisionsbericht* to W. A. Mozart, *Werke*, Serie XXII (Leipzig, Breitkopf and Härtel, 1888).

AUTOGRAPH OF RONDO K.494, W. A. MOZART

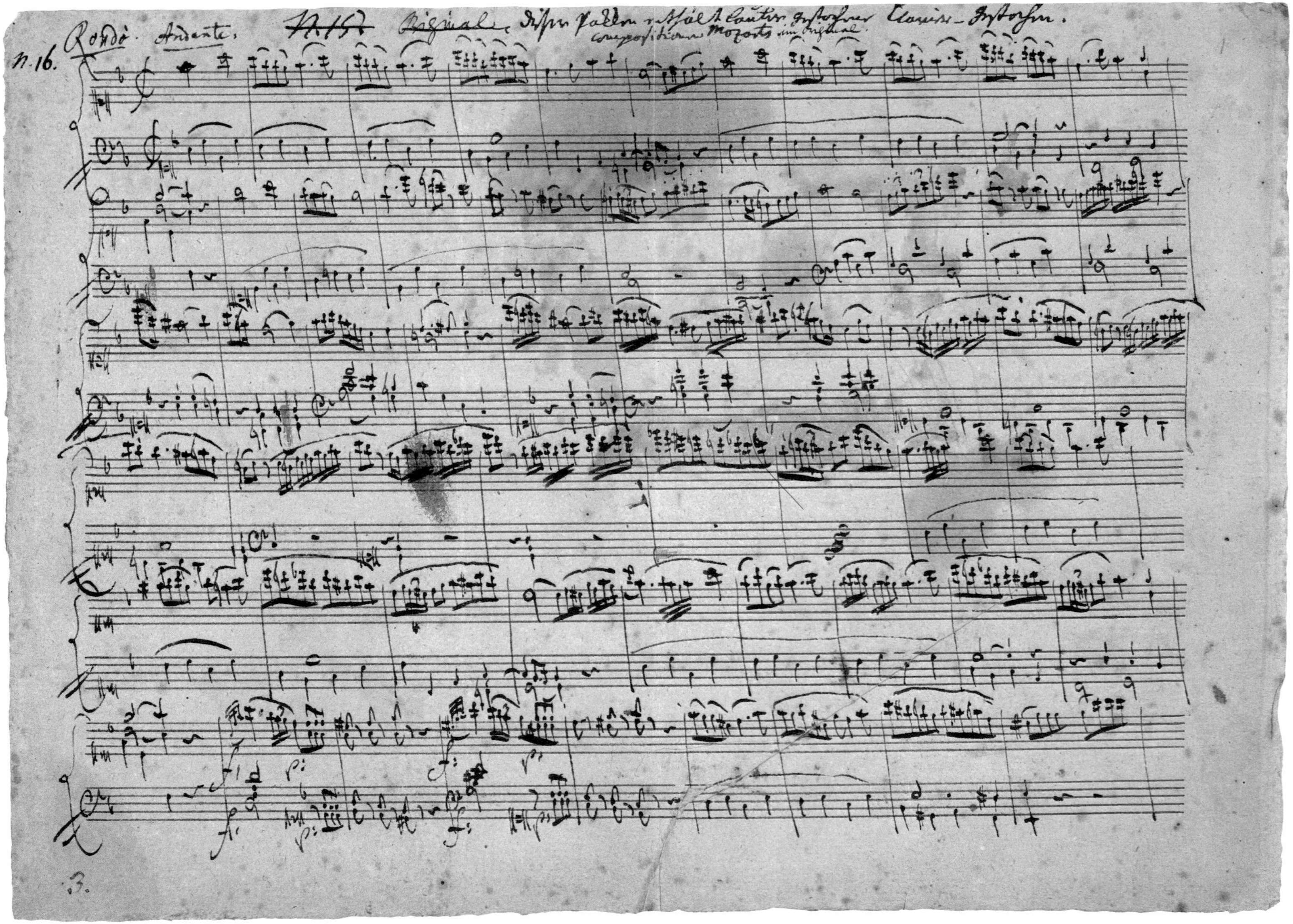

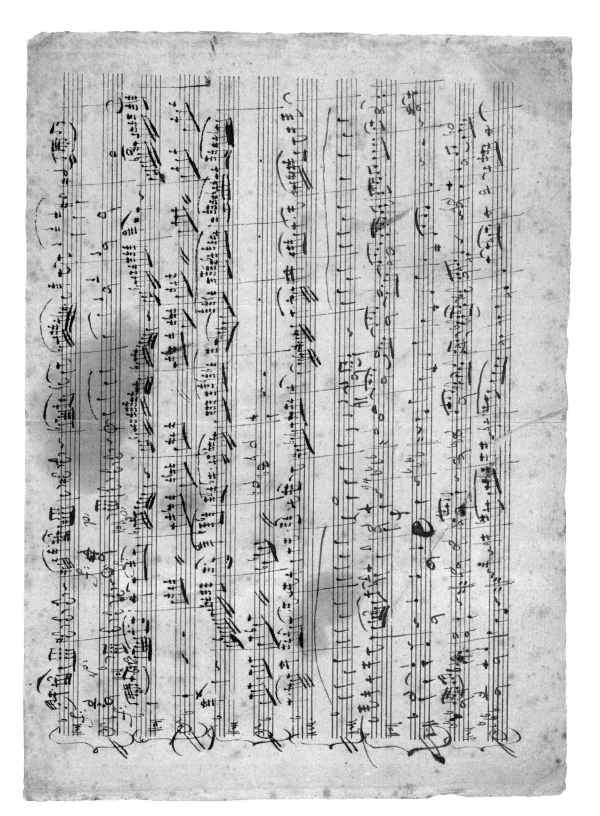

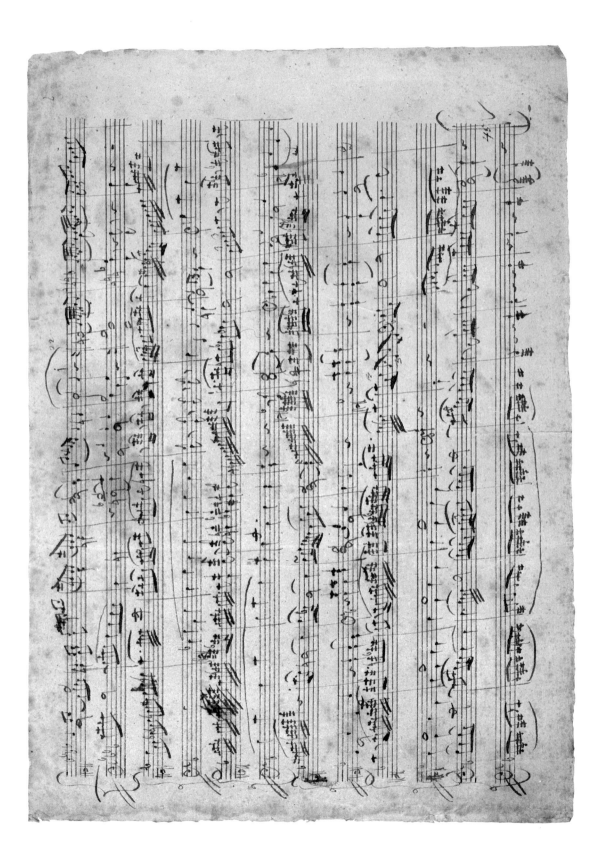

12-staff oblong paper measuring 31.1 by 23 centimetres. His signature and the date, often found in the upper right-hand corner of Mozart's autographs, are absent. The date of composition, therefore, is established not by the autograph but by Mozart's thematic catalogue. There the Rondo is dated June 10, 1786, under the title "*Ein kleines Rondo* für das Klavier allein." In the autograph, the words "Rondo" and "Andante" are in Mozart's own hand. The soprano clef is used for the right hand until bar 148 and for the left hand as well whenever the latter plays in a high register.

To facilitate study of the fascimile, we give here the measure number of the first bar of each system.

Page 1	Page 2	Page 3
1	59	111
12	67	119
23	75	127
33	83	135
41	92	143
50	101	151

The beauty of the manuscript speaks for itself. It clearly reveals Mozart's ability to complete a masterpiece mentally and later write it down from memory, as it were, with the utmost fluency and assurance. Few signs of hesitation or correction occur. Two legato slurs appear to have been lengthened (in bars 28 and 32); a superfluous natural sign seems to have been scratched out in bar 101, fourth quarter; a slip of the pen is discernible in bar 127. The notes are clearly and easily legible throughout despite the fact that the space between staves is sometimes very crowded. The crowding results from the unusually large number of ledger lines arising from the use of the soprano clef for a right-hand part of predominantly high register. As in other Mozart autographs, the precise length of some legato slurs is difficult to determine. This problem, of course, is well known to readers of Mozart's handwriting and to editors of his works. We shall discuss an interesting and important instance at a later point.

The autograph helps to shed some light on several apparent inconsistencies of Mozart's articulation. For example, a legato slur is missing over the sixteenth notes at the beginning of bar 140, although the parallel passage in bar 27 contains the slur. This omission is probably due to the lack of writing space caused by the high register. Lack of space also may have caused Mozart to omit in bar 22 the slur he employed over the corresponding notes in bar 135. Crowded space, however, cannot account for all the missing slurs. They are lacking, for example, over F and A in bar 40; over the entire left-hand part of bar 132; over the last half of the right-hand part of bar 142; and over the last three quarters of the right-hand part of bar 144. Slurs are present over the corresponding notes of bars 3, 19, 29, and 31.

The autograph contains instances of inconsistency and notational variation other than those caused by missing slurs. In bar 154, a slur covers the triplet sixteenths although a larger slur extends over the half measure that contains the triplet group; this represents the only use in the entire piece of two slurs at one time. In bar 45, the slur clearly extends over the whole measure; in similar situations (e.g., bar 39), the slur covers only the first half of the measure. In the F-minor section (bars 98, 99, and 112), Mozart writes a group of two sixteenths preceded by an appoggiatura. For similar melodic patterns through the piece (e.g., bar 17), triplet sixteenths are employed. The staccato dots of bar 20 do not recur over the corresponding tones of bar 133.

The autograph distinguishes clearly between staccato dots and dashes. Dots are employed for a row of light unaccented tones in bars 17 and 20. Dashes occur over single notes for stronger separation and phrase division. In this autograph, "wedges" and "dashes" have the same meaning, or at least they appear in similar contexts. For example, bars 31 and 33 have wedges over the second eighth notes, while the parallel bars 144 and 146 have dashes. The visual dissimilarity between the two signs seems to be due to a different angle of Mozart's quill. When the quill is held at approximately a right angle to the staff, a wedge results; when the quill is parallel to the staff, a thin dash is produced.

Bar 157 presents a puzzle. In the left-hand part, the fourth quarter seems to contain a three-note chord, C–E–B♭. The E creates a doubled leading tone with the right-hand part. The doubling is highly inappropriate to the thin texture and clearly defined part-writing of the conclusion of the piece; moreover it does not recur when the chord is restruck in the two following measures. Perhaps the E results from an ink blot formed by the writing of the upward stem through the still wet ledger line. In any case, modern editions omit the doubled E; this procedure is undoubtedly correct, although an explanatory note might be in order. The doubled leading tone does occur in the two editions published in 1788 of the Rondo as an independent piece: by Birchall and Andrews in London and by Bossler in Speier. The presence of this anomalous note would indicate that both editions were engraved from copies of our present autograph.

To the right of bar 142 of the facsimile (third page, end of fourth system), the reader will note three squiggles somewhat resembling mordents in shape. These are examples of the *custos musicus*, a notational sign of great antiquity. The *custos* indicates the first tone (or, if there are several *custodes*, the first chord) of the following line or system. Leopold Mozart explains the *custos* as a reading aid particularly appropriate to pieces in quick tempo.[7] The sign still occurs, sporadically but by no means infrequently, in Wolfgang's autographs (and in printed music of the time). Mozart tends to use the *custos* where the end of the line or system visually interrupts a close rhythmic, harmonic, or melodic connection. In the Rondo Andante of 1786, Mozart employs the *custodes*—signs indicating uninterrupted continuity— at the very spot where, in the sonata finale of 1788, the cadenza breaks in with such unexpected force. This is no more than an interesting coincidence. There is no reason to assume that the *custodes* were intended to indicate to a copyist or engraver the place where the cadenza begins.

The following inscriptions appear in Georg von Nissen's hand, undoubtedly for filing purposes: "N.15" crossed out and presumably replaced by "N.16" in the left-hand margin; at the top of the page, "Dieser Pakken enthält lauter gestochene Clavier-compositionen Mozarts im Original" meaning "This package contains only engraved piano compositions of Mozart in the original." The last two words "im Original" seem to have been added later to replace the word "Original" which is crossed out. To the right of the inscription but independent of it is the word "gestochen" (engraved), also in Nissen's handwriting. The reference to the composition having been engraved relates to the market value of the autographs in the late eighteenth century. It is clear from Constanze's correspondence with

---

[7] Leopold Mozart, *Gründliche Violinschule* (3d ed.; Augsburg, 1787); printed in facsimile, Hans Joachim Moser, ed. (Leipzig, Breitkopf and Härtel, 1956), p. 48.

Breitkopf that she was paid less for manuscripts of compositions already engraved than for unpublished works. These inscriptions date from the period when Constanze was trying to dispose of her collection of autographs, first to Breitkopf, and then, successfully, to André.

Other inscriptions in a foreign hand are three figures: 94, 22, and 45. These represent the numbering of bars by sections possibly for purposes of copying or engraving; they appear at the beginning of the F-minor section, at the end of that section, and at the end of the piece. The three figures add up to a total of 161 measures, a sum arrived at by counting the *prima volta* and *seconda volta* measures at the end of the F-minor section as two separate bars. If the two measures are counted as one, in accordance with the usual modern procedure, the total is 160 measures.

When Mozart quotes the beginning of the Rondo in his thematic catalogue, he diverges from the autograph in some respects. Four changes occur: the notation is in treble clef rather than soprano, the beginning is marked "P:" and a single slur covers bars 2 and 3 of the left hand. The most important difference, however, is a legato slur which connects the first two tones F and A of the right hand. This legato, which is absent from the autograph, creates a problem of considerable complexity which will be discussed below (see pp. 32–33).

As to the Allegro and Andante, K.533, and the cadenza to the Rondo, the most authentic source is generally considered to be the edition of Hoffmeister, Vienna. The publication date of the sonata was for a long time believed to have been circa 1790. Alexander Weinmann's catalogue of Hoffmeister's Vienna publications has established a date of circa January —February, 1788.[8] Weinmann's redating is confirmed by Otto Erich Deutsch's revised listing of plate numbers.[9] The autographs of the Allegro and Andante and of the cadenza are lost. The composition date of January 3, 1788, for K.533 is established by Mozart's thematic catalogue.

II

SCRUTINIZING the statements of some of the important Mozart scholars on the subject of K.494 and K. 533, we discover an astonishing array of

8 See footnote 1.
9 Otto Erich Deutsch, *Musikverlagsnummern: Eine Auswahl von 40 datierten Listen 1710–1900* (Berlin, Merseburger, 1961), p. 14.

contradictions and ambiguities. These contradictions mainly revolve around three questions. First, a historical problem: did Mozart initiate or authorize the publication of the Rondo as a sonata finale to K.533, and did he write the cadenza for the sonata publication? Second, an esthetic issue: does a stylistic or other imbalance exist between K.533 and the Rondo, weakening the unity of the composition as a sonata? Finally, a problem of text: is the Hoffmeister edition of the Rondo more authoritative than the autograph? We shall deal with the first two questions in this section, reserving for the third part of the article a discussion of the question of text.

Doubts about Mozart's authorization of the sonata publication would probably never have arisen had the relevant source material been available to mid-nineteenth-century scholars. Neither Jahn nor Köchel seem to have known of the Hoffmeister publication. Jahn states categorically that the sonata scheme is not Mozart's.[10] Köchel lists several sonata publications of K.533 and the Rondo; as these were not issued in Mozart's lifetime, they have no bearing on Mozart's intentions. Not until the Waldersee revision of 1905 does the Hoffmeister publication appear in the Köchel catalogue under 533. Köchel and Jahn must have based their judgments largely upon Mozart's thematic catalogue. As we have seen, Mozart lists both the Rondo and the Allegro and Andante; nowhere does he state that he intends to combine the three movements into a sonata.

The mistaken judgments of early scholars often perpetuate themselves in the works of their successors. Hermann Abert's revision of Jahn offers a case in point. In one place he states that the cadenza, lacking in the autograph, was written for the first edition.[11] At a later point he writes that the sonata publication was not authorized by Mozart.[12] These two statements are, of course, mutually exclusive, as the cadenza was published for the first time as part of the whole sonata. Any listing of scholars who doubt Mozart's authorship of the sonata scheme must include those editors who have published K.533 and K.494 separately; the editors of the Breitkopf and Härtel *Gesamtausgabe* (and they had many followers) would figure prominently among these.

---

[10] Otto Jahn, *W. A. Mozart* (Leipzig, Breitkopf and Härtel, 1856–1859), IV, 14.
[11] Hermann Abert, *W. A. Mozart* (Leipzig, Breitkopf and Härtel, 1923–1924), II, 373, footnote 1.
[12] Abert, II, 427, footnote 8.

Saint-Foix discusses at length the issue of Mozart's authorization of the sonata scheme. He considers the various possibilities but, because of the lack of evidence, avoids drawing definite conclusions about Mozart's intentions. He allows himself to speculate that Mozart might have written the cadenza specifically for the sonata publication. However, his general tone is one of doubt that Mozart approved the sonata combination, and he declares firmly that the Allegro and Andante are in no way musically related to the Rondo.[13]

The majority of twentieth-century scholars and editors agree implicitly or explicitly that Mozart authorized the sonata publication.[14] Many of them, however, believe that the Rondo does not form an appropriate finale to the Allegro and Andante. Some writers, like Saint-Foix, raise the issue of stylistic imbalance, pointing out the contrast between the largely polyphonic first two movements and the mostly homophonic Rondo. Others believe the Rondo to be musically inferior to the Allegro and Andante. Eric Blom, for example, does not comment on the issue of Mozart's intentions. He notes without objection the use of the Rondo as a sonata finale, but nonetheless finds it less excellent than the Allegro and Andante.[15] Hyatt-King believes that Mozart "apparently" sanctioned the sonata publication. However, he considers the style of K.533 to be entirely different from the Rondo and states that the F-major Rondo, like the one in D major, lacks depth of feeling despite its fluency and charm.[16] Girdlestone goes even further in criticizing the combination of K.533 with K.494. He ascribes the sonata publication to a "counsel of laziness" on Mozart's part and recommends the omission of the Rondo altogether because of its inferiority and lack of connection.[17]

Einstein's treatment of K.494 and K.533 contains serious shortcomings. At a later point, we shall have occasion to refer to the Einstein revision of the Köchel catalogue. In the present context, a paragraph from this eminent scholar's monograph on Mozart is pertinent.

---

13 Georges de Saint-Foix, *Wolfgang Amédée Mozart*, IV (Paris, Desclée de Brouwer, 1939), 175–76.

14 Among them are Einstein, Haas, Paumgartner, the Badura-Skodas, Dennerlein, Broder, Lampe, and Martienssen-Weisman.

15 Eric Blom, *Mozart* (New York, Dutton, 1935), p. 271.

16 A. Hyatt-King, "Mozart's Piano Music," *The Music Review*, V (1944), 182, 187.

17 C. M. Girdlestone, *Mozart's Piano Concertos* (London, Cassell, 1948), p. 301.

For another pupil he wrote on 10 June of the same year a "Little Rondo" in F major (K.494), which he provided on 3 January 1788 with an Allegro and an Andante (K.533), the three movements forming a sonata. He owed his friend and publisher Hoffmeister money at the time, and doubtless partly acquitted the debt with this sonata. In doing so he paid no attention to what is called unity of style. These movements composed later have a grandeur of harmonic and polyphonic conception, a depth of feeling, and a harmonic daring such as we find only in his last works; indeed they are conceived for an entirely different and more powerful instrument than the innocent rondo, which is written mostly for the middle register. (For Hoffmeister's engraved edition Mozart added a contrapuntal cadenza and a conclusion in a deeper register.) Yet even this rondo, with its lovely *minore* in three obbligato parts, is so rich and perfect that no uninitiated listener would observe any break in style. It is characteristic of the stodginess of many editors of the nineteenth and twentieth centuries that the rondo and the two preceding movements still appear separately.[18]

It would appear from Einstein's remarks that he had not seen the autograph. The conclusion in low register, added later according to Einstein, is plainly in the manuscript of 1786. The autograph also shows that Mozart used the full range of the keyboard, F^1 to f^3; Einstein was incorrect in maintaining that K.494 was written mostly for the middle register and for a less powerful and presumably smaller instrument than that intended for K.533. (Saint-Foix, incidentally, also mused about the kind of instrument for which K.494 had been conceived. He notes the wide range of registers and deduces that Mozart wrote the Rondo for the "new pianoforte"— almost the antithesis of Einstein's hunch.)[19]

Einstein's paragraph generates the feeling that Mozart, under pressure of his debt to Hoffmeister, waived the requirement of stylistic unity, but in a manner undetectable to anyone but an expert. No matter how highly Einstein praises the individual beauty of K.533 and of K.494, this is a serious charge. What evidence is there to substantiate it? The tragic vicissitudes of 1788 are well known to those familiar with the events of Mozart's life. In that year Mozart wrote a number of works based on earlier compositions: K.533/494, K.546, K.547a, and K.564. Was the revision of earlier work necessarily dictated by Mozart's need to have publishable

---

[18] Reprinted by permission from Alfred Einstein, *Mozart: His Character, His Work*, Arthur Mendel and Nathan Broder, trans. (New York, Oxford University Press, 1945), p. 248.

[19] Saint-Foix, IV, 176.

material ready because of financial pressure? Though it is possible, we cannot prove it.

One also wonders whether, at the beginning of January, 1788, Mozart was already particularly vulnerable to financial pressure. He had returned from the triumph of *Don Giovanni* in Prague but a short time before; he had just begun to earn his modest but secure salary in the service of the emperor; and, a few months before, he had collected his share of his father's estate. We shall present our views about the stylistic unity of the sonata in the fourth section; at this point we can already state that the biographical data do not provide conclusive evidence that the sonata scheme represents an artistic compromise caused by financial need.

The Adagio and Fugue, K.546, has never been the subject of such conjectures and doubts as we witness in connection with K.533/494. In the case of K.546, the Fugue for two pianos of 1783 was transformed into a piece for strings; like our sonata, K.546 was published by Hoffmeister. Although Einstein occasionally likes to refer to the financial needs of Mozart as having prompted the writing of some of the works for Hoffmeister, on the subject of K.546 he refrains from such comment. But K.546 was written almost half a year after K.533; by this time Mozart's pecuniary distress had become acute. If one follows Einstein's timing of events, this work rather than K.533/494 would seem to indicate Mozart's financial plight. However Mozart himself forestalled all possible speculation by mentioning in his thematic catalogue that he had written the Adagio for the previously composed Fugue.

The lack of a similar indication for K.533 makes it impossible to assign a date of composition to the cadenza of the Rondo finale. Those writers who maintain that Mozart did not authorize the sonata publication thereby imply that no causal connection exists between K.533 and the cadenza. And if this is so, the occasion for which Mozart wrote the cadenza, as well as the date of its composition, remain shrouded in mystery; the cadenza could date from any time between June 10, 1786, and Hoffmeister's publication of circa January–February, 1788. Even the scholars who take for granted Mozart's authorship of the sonata scheme do not agree about the sequence of events. For we do not know whether Mozart decided upon the sonata combination before, during, or after the composition of the Allegro and Andante. Until recently, it was believed that Hoffmeister published the sonata around 1790; with this dating, the composition of the cadenza would fall within a period of two or even three years between January 3, 1788, and the end of 1790. Alexander Weinmann's redating of the Hoffmeister print sets far narrower limits; if the sonata was published at the beginning of 1788, the composition date of the cadenza would have to be placed close to January 3, 1788.

III

IN DISCUSSING whether the autograph or the Hoffmeister edition takes precedence in establishing an authoritative text, we should naturally deal first with the Köchel listings. We can ignore the original catalogue of 1862, which cites neither the autograph nor Hoffmeister. The Waldersee revision lists both, but does not attempt to evaluate their relative importance. Waldersee does indicate that of the total of 187 measures of the Rondo, 160 are from the autograph. This information, although factually correct, can confuse the reader, for Waldersee fails to explain that the 160 measures represent the complete original version of the piece, while the twenty-seven measures not from the autograph comprise the cadenza written later. He thus creates the impression that the autograph is incomplete or mutilated. Einstein's third edition of Köchel adds to the confusion. Although he mentions the cadenza in an "Anmerkung" and continues to list the total number of measures as 187, Einstein attributes 161 to the autograph rather than 160. As a result, the unwary reader might conclude that only twenty-six measures fall to the cadenza instead of the correct twenty-seven.

Köchel-Einstein contains several items not found in the earlier editions of the catalogue. Among them is a remark to the effect that the Rondo constitutes one of those cases in which the first edition is more authoritative than the autograph. Einstein mentions that the autograph does not yet contain the cadenza, which fact apparently leads him to the conclusion that the Hoffmeister edition is the more complete and therefore definitive form of the Rondo, superseding and rendering obsolete the original version. Even if one could accept this reasoning (and we do not), Einstein's statement would not be sufficiently specific, for he fails to clarify whether the Hoffmeister text should take precedence in all other respects wherein it differs from the autograph. There are differences of tempo, articulation, dynamics, and ornamentation.

Köchel-Einstein also mentions an old British edition of the Rondo. Under 494 in the paragraph listing "Editions," there is an entry "B. and A., . . . 1788." Immediately preceding this, we find the listing of Hoffmeister's sonata publication (according to Einstein circa 1790) as the "first edition" of the Rondo. What explains this contradiction of dates? How could Hoffmeister's engraving be the first one if (according to Einstein's dating) it appeared some two years after the British edition? The publication date of this edition is not a printer's error; the date in Köchel-Einstein is consistent with other standard reference works. The full title of the British edition is "Storace's Collection of Original Harpsichord Music. Printed for S. Storace, N. 23, Howland Street, Rathbone Place, and sold by Messrs. Birchall and Andrews, N. 129, New Bond Street." "S. Storace," of course, is Mozart's friend and pupil Stephen.[20]

Why did Einstein not comment on this discrepancy of dates? His preference for the Hoffmeister sonata text over the autograph version of the Rondo may be one of the reasons Einstein failed properly to evaluate the significance of the British edition, for the Storace print is based on the autograph and presents the Rondo in its original version of 1786. More puzzling still is the fact that in his 1947 "Supplement" to Köchel, Einstein does list an edition of the original version of the Rondo, the publication of Bossler, Speier, 1788, which he calls the first edition of the autograph version.[21] Why is the Speier publication now called the first edition rather than the London? The British publication may very well be the earlier one. *Storace's Collection* was issued in several installments and contained pieces by ten composers (including Haydn and Clementi). Mozart was represented by six original works and one arrangement. The Mozart pieces came out between 1787 and 1789. Since the Rondo was part of the first volume (second installment) it probably appeared *early* in 1788. The Bossler *Archiv* appeared in twelve volumes, all of which were published in 1788;

20 See Edith B. Schnapper, ed., *The British Union Catalogue of Early Music printed before the year 1801* (London, Butterworth, 1957), II, 712.
21 Alfred Einstein, ed., *Chronologisch-thematisches Verzeichnis sämtlicher Tonwerke Wolfgang Amade Mozarts* (Ann Arbor, University of Michigan Press, 1947), p. 1022.

if they were issued consecutively, the Rondo probably came out in the *latter* part of the year, as it is included in the last of the twelve volumes.

The precise chronology of the two publications is of no great importance. Both editions exhibit the printing imperfections and carelessness in indications of articulation typical of the era. Highly significant, however, is the fact that both editions appeared in Mozart's lifetime and that both present the autograph version of 1786 in its entirety, unadorned and unabridged. They represent the first editions of the independent Rondo of 1786, just as the Hoffmeister publication represents the first edition of the later Rondo finale. To call the latter the final version ("endgültige Fassung"), as Einstein does, is to imply that it replaces and supersedes the earlier version. How then are we to explain the two editions of the Rondo in its original form? We can hardly assume that both the Bossler and the Storace editions were pirated. The Storace printing would seem to be particularly strong evidence of Mozart's approval of the publication of the Rondo in its original form. This is so because of Stephen Storace's devotion to and close friendship with Mozart; these make the possibility of a pirated printing seem very remote. It is noteworthy that the first two Mozart works published by Storace are the Piano Quartet K.493 and our Rondo; as Mozart's friend and student in 1786, he may well have witnessed their creation. Incidentally, Storace published the quartet in 1787, the same year in which Artaria brought out the Vienna edition. Storace's publication of Mozart works may have been part of the plan of Mozart's British friends who tried to pave his way to England. Storace undoubtedly took copies of Mozart's works to London when he returned there in 1787; however, he continued to publish Mozart pieces long after the plan of the journey to England had been abandoned.

Now that the "6th" edition of Köchel has appeared, it may seem pointless to discuss Einstein's treatment in such detail. We do so because the new Köchel retains many of Einstein's judgments. The editors have changed the date of the Hoffmeister printing from 1790 to 1788 and have listed the correct number of measures for the autograph. Otherwise the entry under 494 is substantially that of Einstein's catalogue as modified by the 1947 Supplement. The remark about the first edition's priority over the autograph is reproduced verbatim; although two first editions are now listed, the reader is evidently supposed to understand that Hoffmeister is meant rather than Bossler.

Some other scholars agree with Einstein in giving Hoffmeister priority over the autograph. The Badura-Skodas do so on the assumption that the addition of the cadenza was accompanied by other changes by Mozart. At any rate they feel that Hoffmeister's deviations from the autograph with respect to articulation are in no way inconsistent with Mozart's style of writing.[22] Nathan Broder also respects the Hoffmeister text, as we can see from his edition of the Mozart sonatas.

IV

THE WELTER of conflicting opinions and puzzling ambiguities which one encounters in dealing with this intriguing subject prompts us to state our own conclusions on the important issues.

We agree with the view of those authors who are convinced that Mozart wanted and authorized the publication of the sonata. Early scholars, unaware of the Hoffmeister edition, arrived at the mistaken conclusion that the sonata publication took place without Mozart's approval. Unfortunately this opinion has been perpetuated (or at least not refuted) in the work of such eminent twentieth-century writers and editors as Abert, Saint-Foix, Pauer, and Soldan. There is no evidence for the belief that Hoffmeister acted arbitrarily in undertaking the sonata publication. It is hard to imagine that Hoffmeister, who published ten other works of Mozart in the normal manner, would have departed so radically from usual business procedure in this instance.

Furthermore, the music itself contains a piece of confirming evidence. The cadenza is joined to bar 142 of the Rondo by the chord progression shown in Example 1, which recurs four measures later. The beginning of the cadenza bears a striking resemblance to a progression—a so-called deceptive cadence—that occurs three times in the Allegro, in bars 22, 82, and 219 (Example 2).

In the Allegro, the dominant chord progresses to a $\frac{6}{3}$ with raised sixth;

22 Eva and Paul Badura-Skoda, *Mozart-Interpretation* (Vienna, Eduard Wancura, 1957), p. 313.

EXAMPLE 1

EXAMPLE 2

in the cadenza to the Rondo, the dominant moves to a closely related chord, the $^6_3$ also with raised sixth. In general, one would not attempt to demonstrate a relationship between movements on the basis of a single chord progression. This progression, however, is striking in itself; its appearance at the beginning of a cadenza-like section is both unusual and unexpected. Furthermore, the progression occurs quite infrequently in Mozart's compositions. Similar instances appear in the Andante of the C major Quintet, K.515, bars 48, 51, 108, 111; the Variations for Piano, K.613, bar 10 of the final $^3_4$ section, etc. However, the investigator can read through several hundred pages of Mozart's music without coming upon a similar example; the progression is sufficiently unusual to impress itself distinctly upon the ear and memory of the listener. We do not adduce the similarity as a "unifying feature"—a term used all too frequently without any clear or precise meaning. We do maintain that the attentive and musically aware listener will remember the thrice-stated progression from the Allegro. Its reappearance in the Rondo, but slightly altered, produces in the listener's mind a strong associative link between the two movements.

On both biographical and musical grounds, we are firmly convinced of Mozart's authorship of the sonata scheme. However, we cannot offer a precise solution to the problem of the timing of the sonata idea and composition date of the cadenza. We strongly incline to the view that Mozart decided to base the sonata finale upon the Rondo of 1786 prior to January 3, 1788, when he entered the Allegro and Andante into his thematic catalogue. It is impossible to believe that Mozart could have considered the Allegro and Andante a complete, self-sufficient, work without a finale. It is equally unlikely that he could have contemplated abandoning these magnificent movements immediately after having written them. The very fact that he entered the Allegro and Andante into his catalogue suggests that he had already hit upon a scheme for their completion as a sonata. The publication of the sonata so soon after the composition of the first two movements tends to confirm our supposition.

Let us now turn to the esthetic issues. Does the sonata suffer from a stylistic imbalance between the first two movements on the one hand and the Rondo on the other? Doubts about the stylistic unity of the sonata have

arisen largely because of differences in texture. Unlike the first two movements, the Rondo is largely homophonic; the introduction of obbligato
voices does not occur before the F-minor section (bar 96), and returns only
briefly in the stretto section of the cadenza. This is no sympton of disunity.
The coexistence—indeed the blending—of polyphonic and homophonic
textures constitutes an important characteristic of Mozart's style. The
Andante of this very sonata illustrates the mixing of textures; a considerable amount of homophony already distinguishes it from the highly polyphonic Allegro. The issue of imbalance or disunity on these grounds can
therefore be dismissed. We might add in passing that some writers have
unduly emphasized the distinction between homophony and polyphony
in attempting to point out the importance of polyphonic procedures in
Mozart's mature works. Mozart does not treat the two kinds of texture as
polar opposites. He deploys polyphony within a stabilizing harmonic
framework of underlying chords unfolded in time. And he can endow a
seemingly conventional broken-chord accompaniment with sharply defined
linear profile; the left-hand part of our Rondo offers many cases in point.
Incidentally Jahn, who considered the sonata combination spurious,
thought the Rondo a not really inappropriate ("nicht eben unpassend")
finale to the Allegro and Andante.[23]

Is the unity of the sonata impaired because the Rondo is musically inferior to the two preceding movements? Blom, Hyatt-King, and Girdlestone think so. Saint-Foix and Einstein, although they doubt the stylistic
unity of the sonata, do not raise the issue of the quality of the Rondo as
such. Einstein calls it "rich and perfect" and Saint-Foix calls it a "magni-
fique morceau."[24] Contradictions among Mozart scholars reach an extreme
when subjective quality judgments are involved.

In this connection, our opinion coincides with those of Saint-Foix and
Einstein. The Rondo is a composition of a depth not revealed at first glance;
as in many of Mozart's works, uncanny mastery is cloaked in apparent
simplicity. The art of variation which Mozart applies to the several re-
capitulations of the Rondo theme is of the most refined logic and subtlety.
The unobtrusive and gradual unfolding of the variations can be compared
to Mozart's last masterpiece for piano, the Variations, K.613, in the same

23 Jahn, IV, 84.   24 Saint-Foix, IV, 176.

key as our Rondo. Also highly noteworthy is the suppleness of rhythm, in part the result of an exquisite balance between symmetric and asymmetric phrase organization. The wonderfully unified motivic design must also be cited. The episodes relate to the Rondo theme through motivic references at times explicit and at times disguised.

To offer only one example, we refer the reader to the D-minor section (bars 51–67), the beginning of which is reproduced as Example 3. Bars 55–57 present almost an exact transposition of bars 2–4; less obvious is the fact that bar 54 echoes the first bar of the Rondo. The opening bar is characterized by an ascent from tonic to third in the melody, counterpointed by a descent from third to tonic in the left-hand part. Bar 54 also outlines ascending and descending thirds (now in a D-minor context), but fills them in with passing tones. The disguised reference to the opening measure prepares the listener for the explicit quotation of the following measures. The reader will note the fascinating new light thrown on the figure of bar 2 by its altered rhythmic emphasis in bar 55. At the beginning of the Rondo, the figure occupies a "weak" measure in the middle of a six-bar phrase; in bar 55, it occurs in a rhythmically "strong" position at

EXAMPLE 3

the beginning of a four-bar phrase. This Rondo is neither "simple" nor "innocent" and the notion that it is in any way lacking seems to us absurd.

Our final issue, concerning the relative authority of the autograph and the Hoffmeister edition, divides into two questions. The first question deals with the compositional enlargement of the Hoffmeister version: does the expanded Rondo with cadenza take precedence over, and replace, the version of 1786? The second question involves details of articulation, ornamentation, dynamics, etc. Where the two sources differ, is preference automatically to be accorded one of them?

Our answer to the first question is a decided negative. We maintain that the two forms of the Rondo are equally valid versions of the piece; each is meant for a different purpose and setting; neither invalidates the other. The earlier version, represented by the autograph (and by the Storace and Bossler editions), is a complete and self-contained composition needing neither addition nor change. It has its own life as a "Kleines Rondo" in andante tempo and is neither nullified nor rendered obsolete by the existence of the sonata finale with cadenza. To indicate, like Einstein and others, that the sonata version with cadenza is the "final" one creates a confusing over-simplification. The transformation and enlargement of the Rondo was undertaken by Mozart in order to shape it into a sonata finale commensurate with the Allegro and Andante. The cadenza was not written to make the Rondo *per se* more interesting or more suitable for publication. The appearance at virtually the same time of editions of the Rondo in both of its forms substantiates the independent validity of the two versions.

In its expanded form, the Rondo becomes an excellent finale to the sonata; for this purpose Mozart's remarkable cadenza is a *conditio sine qua non*.[25] The cadenza is certainly not a mechanical extension of the original version; no mere "Einschiebsel," as Abert has put it. It changes the Rondo fundamentally. Instead of the brief concluding section of the first version, we experience a sudden interruption of the motion toward the expected

---

[25] Despite the disappearance of the cadenza's autograph, no writer seems to have seriously entertained the idea that it is not by Mozart. And indeed, to whom else would one attribute it? In a recent article, Eva Badura-Skoda qualifies a statement that Mozart wrote the cadenza by adding that it is at least highly probable that he did so. Eva Badura-Skoda, "Textual Problems in Masterpieces of the 18th and 19th Centuries," Piero Weiss, trans., *The Musical Quarterly*, LI (1965), 313.

conclusion; this interruption is effected by means of a deceptive progression almost the same as that which had occurred three times in the Allegro. This progression ushers in twenty-seven measures of some of Mozart's boldest writing for piano, culminating in a stretto and dominant pedal of extraordinary power and scope. This cadenza completely changes the architectonic concept of the first version. Through the introduction of a dramatic climax, not present in the tranquilly flowing Rondo Andante of 1786, a new center of gravity is created. The coda in low register now takes on a new meaning and effect through its marked contrast with the cadenza. The Rondo in its second version, played as an independent piece, might well sound unbalanced by the giant cadenza; the listener is not prepared for such a sudden outburst of demonic energy. Within the context of the sonata, however, the process of listening is different. After the eventful and dramatic Allegro and Andante, the very beginning of the Rondo comes as a surprise. The juxtaposition of deep and high registers between the end of the Andante and the beginning of the Rondo produces a fascinating contrast. The rarified atmosphere of the high register, the continuation of the Rondo in a light texture of mysterious simplicity, and the very gradual unfolding of its design hold the listener in a state of suspense; he expects some climactic event commensurate with the dramatic intensity of the first two movements. The cadenza provides this very climax and rounds off the sonata in a masterly fashion.

Failure to understand the distinction between the two versions has led some editors to publish the Rondo as an independent piece *with* cadenza. Not only nineteenth-century editions (e.g., the Breitkopf *Gesamtausgabe*) but also more recent publications (such as Kurt Soldan's edition of Mozart piano pieces brought out by Peters in 1936) are guilty of this error. And the inclusion of the cadenza in the numbering of measures in the Köchel listenings of 494 has obscured the issue even further. It is no hairsplitting but merely a question of accuracy to state that the number 494 can apply only to the first version of the work—namely, the Rondo Andante of June 10, 1786. Therefore the designation of the sonata—found in several editions—as 533/494 is inaccurate, and at best is acceptable only as an expediency. The "correct" K. number is impossible to determine because of our ignorance of the chronological evolution of the sonata scheme and of the composition date of the cadenza. The simplest and best solution would be to give the number 533 to the entire sonata, which, of course, includes the second version of the Rondo.

Let us now turn to the question of differences in tempo, articulation, dynamics, etc., between the autograph and the Hoffmeister print. The first and most striking divergence is that of tempo indication. The autograph and Mozart's thematic catalogue give andante; the Hoffmeister edition indicates allegretto. We are convinced that each marking is correct within its proper setting. As an independent composition, the Rondo is in andante tempo; the correspondence of autograph and catalogue leaves no doubt of Mozart's intention. As a sonata finale, the Rondo demands a slightly quicker pace for contrast with the second movement; two consecutive andante movements are a virtual impossibility. The allegretto designation in Hoffmeister's edition, therefore, is undoubtedly correct; we cannot agree with editors of the sonata (e.g., Martienssen-Weismann, published by Peters, 1951) who adhere to the autograph in prescribing andante for the sonata finale.

To what extent can we credit the other divergences found in Hoffmeister? A printed edition takes precedence over the autograph only in so far as it incorporates alterations by the composer. How certain can we be that the deviations found in Hoffmeister represent Mozart's intentions? At least one of Hoffmeister's changes is undoubtedly authentic. The first bar of the sonata finale contains a slur lacking in the autograph but present in Mozart's thematic catalogue (see above, p. 12). This correspondence between first edition and catalogue does not necessarily invalidate the un-slurred version of the autograph, but it does suggest that Mozart's revision of the Rondo may have extended beyond the addition of the cadenza and the change of tempo. It is certainly possible that Mozart prepared a second autograph of the Rondo, incorporating these revisions, for the Hoffmeister publications. However, it is also possible that Mozart merely wrote out the cadenza, left instructions about the altered tempo and one or two other changes (such as the slur in the first bar), and let a copyist prepare the manuscript.

Even if we assume the authenticity of a now lost second autograph, we cannot be sure that Hoffmeister's edition is faithful to it in all respects.

On the other hand, we can be certain of every indication found in the auto-graph. On purely objective grounds, therefore, the superior reliability of the autograph seems incontestable. As we have noted, the Badura-Skodas assert the primacy of the Hoffmeister text because of the Mozartian charac-ter of its deviations from the autograph in articulation marks (see above, p. 20). Yet even the Badura-Skodas doubt the authenticity of the turns found in bars 178 and 184 of Hoffmeister (bars 151 and 157 of the shorter auto-graph version). Close comparison of the autograph and the Hoffmeister print leads us to question the genuineness of some of Hoffmeister's other indications, including those governing articulation. Some of the divergences seem appropriate and plausible, especially those that supplement rather than change the autograph (e.g., the dynamic markings in the coda). In other instances, however, the Hoffmeister version seems less refined and coherent than the autograph.

In the first place, Hoffmeister eliminates the distinction between staccato dots and dashes; he uses only the latter. In this autograph, Mozart's use of the two symbols is consistent and highly suggestive for the per-former. To be sure, not all authorities agree about the significance of the various staccato signs in Mozart; even those who find the differences im-portant grant the difficulty of incorporating them satisfactorily in a printed edition.[26] We believe that an editor should attempt to follow Mozart's distinctions between dashes and dots—including his inconsistencies—unless intermediate shapes are so numerous and ambiguous that the pro-cedure becomes impossible. The performer should be given the oppor-tunity to decide for himself whether or not the differences are significant. Our present autograph offers no ambiguities; unfortunately even Lampe (in the edition of the sonatas published by Henle in 1955), who combines elements from the autograph and Hoffmeister, eliminates this distinction.

In addition to making uniform Mozart's staccato signs, Hoffmeister's printing contains some obvious engraver's errors. In this respect, the edi-tion is no worse than many others of its time; as a matter of fact, it is con-siderably less error-ridden than Storace or Bossler. Nevertheless, those

---

[26] The interested reader will find much pertinent information in the five essays of Hans Albrecht, ed., *Die Bedeutung der Zeichen Keil, Strich, und Punkt bei Mozart* (Kassel, Bärenreiter, 1957), *passim.*

mistakes that do exist should be eliminated, even by editors who choose to base their reading primarily upon Hoffmeister. Comparison with the autograph would seem to be an indispensable aid to such correction. Let us examine a single instance. Example 4 shows bars 79–81 of the autograph. Example 5 shows the obviously incorrect Hoffmeister reading.

Nathan Broder, who bases his excellent edition on Hoffmeister, has attempted to correct the error. Comparison with his edition (published by Presser in 1956) is instructive; Broder's version is less logical and beautiful than that of the autograph.

Finally, there are instances where both sources seem plausible in themselves but where the autograph version underscores and clarifies motivic relationships obscured in Hoffmeister. In bar 43, for instance, the autograph contains a slur over the entire right-hand part. Hoffmeister, on the other hand, places a staccato dash over the first note. The resulting articulation points up a resemblance to the similar figures of bars 17 and 38, but at the cost of clouding slightly the more important relationship to bar 5,

EXAMPLE 4

EXAMPLE 5

of which bar 43 is a variation (Example 6). Furthermore, the Hoffmeister version is inconsistent; the corresponding figures in bars 49 and 124 omit the staccato signs.

EXAMPLE 6

In bar 121 the autograph retains the articulation of bar 2, of which 121 is a variant. Hoffmeister places a staccato dash over the last eighth note; the simpler version of the autograph is to be preferred (Example 7).

EXAMPLE 7

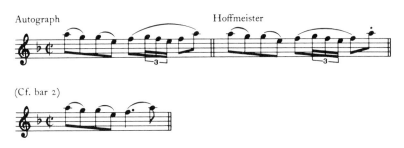

Our next example is somewhat problematic; here the autograph itself is not completely clear or consistent. We have mentioned the difficulty of determining the exact length of some legato slurs. This problem confronts us in connection with a figure that occurs four times in the composition (bars 31, 33, 144, and 146). All four bars begin with a duplet of eighth notes, the second of which bears a staccato dash. A long upbeat passage of sixteenths precedes the two eighth notes; a legato slur begins with the first sixteenth of the upbeat passage and continues over the bar line; the slur's termination, however, is not easy to ascertain. In bars 31 and 33, the slur goes beyond the first eighth, but stops short of the second. The same holds true of bar 144; in bar 146, however, the slur reaches the second note.

Hoffmeister includes only the first eighth under the legato slur; most

modern editions (the Breitkopf *Gesamtausgabe* is an exception) agree with
him. Although Mozart does not often place a staccato sign over the last
note of a slur, we are convinced that here the slur must cover both eighths.
The first eighth note functions as an appoggiatura to the second; this fact
alone suggests connecting the two tones. In addition, separating the tones
impairs the coherence of the composition's motivic design. The eighth-note
duplets preceded by upbeats of sixteenths recur in bars 35 and 36; here
the slurs must cover both notes to make musical sense. A rest follows the
second note; to end the slur with the first note would leave the
second isolated. (In bar 36 the slur also stops short of the second tone in
the autograph. Hoffmeister inconsistently omits the slur in 35 but presents
it correctly in 36.) The duplets of bars 35 and 36 must relate to those of 31
and 33; this relationship becomes obscured if they are slurred differently
(see Example 8). All these duplet figures originate in the first two tones of
bar 2, which are slurred. The projection of this significant relationship
requires the longer slurs in bars 31, 33, 35, 36, 144, and 146. (In his 1955
edition of the sonatas, W. Lampe adopts the longer slurs in bars 144 and
146, but not in 31 and 33. He probably does so because the autograph
presents somewhat longer slurs in the later section. There is no valid
musical reason for articulating these corresponding measures in two
different ways.) A suggested articulation is shown in Example 8.

EXAMPLE 8

Suggested Articulation (bars 30–36)

We have mentioned that some of Hoffmeister's more plausible emendations supplement rather than change the version of the autograph. Among these we can mention the row of staccato signs covered by a slur in bars 37 and 99. Even in bar 37, however, we prefer to end the upbeat slur *before* the bar line, in accordance with the autograph, rather than after the first eighth as Hoffmeister does. For bar 37 is only outwardly similar to 36 and 35. Bar 37 begins with a beautiful and surprising E♭, which serves to prevent a melodic peak on the leading tone and at the same time motivates the subsequent chromatic descent. The performer can better project the agreeable shock of this E♮ by not slurring it to the preceding sixteenths. Other plausible variants in Hoffmeister include the staccato indications in bar 11 and those over the paired eighth notes in the second, third and fourth bars before the end. None of these represents a change of fundamental importance.

In very few instances does the Hoffmeister print alter the actual notes of the autograph version (except, of course, for the addition of the cadenza). In bar 79, Hoffmeister's version adds a fifth, G, to the octave C of the original. The addition makes explicit the implied voice leading of the autograph version; the G represents the normal continuation of the third of the tenor voice of the preceding chord. Both versions are possible; in this instance the Hoffmeister reading may well reflect Mozart's intention at the time he revised the Rondo. We agree with the Badura-Skodas, however, in questioning the turns inserted in bars 178 and 184 of Hoffmeister (151 and 157 of the original). (See above, p. 28)

We have mentioned that Hoffmeister agrees with Mozart's thematic catalogue in slurring the first two tones of the right-hand part of the Rondo (see above, p. 27). In the autograph, these two half notes are unslurred. Here both versions are undoubtedly authentic; that is, each represents Mozart's intention at a different time. In the autograph, the slur is missing not only in bar 1 but also in its analogues, bars 7 and 149. The omission in all three bars can hardly result from an oversight. On the other hand, the agreement between Mozart's catalogue and Hoffmeister speaks for the authenticity of the slur in bars 1, 7, and 176 (in the expanded version 176 is the equivalent of 149 in the original). The editor can easily inform his readers about the two versions by means of a footnote. For the performer, however, the choice between the two versions is by no means easy. His decision involves considerations extending beyond bar 1 and its parallels to the many other melodic ideas beginning with a pair of half notes (for example in bars 13, 19, 95, and 103). Should the slurs be applied there as well? In the autograph, all the paired half notes occur without slur; in Hoffmeister, all are slurred except those in the cadenza.

The performer who decides upon the slurred version of bar 1 might perhaps wish to omit the slurs in playing some of the other pairs of half notes. For example, at the beginning of the F-minor section (bar 95), the second half is tied to the first eighth of the following measure. The tie suggests a slight emphasis on the second note that is more easily achieved in an unslurred performance. Soon after, however, the paired halves appear without the tie (bars 103 and 105). Coherent performance demands that bars 103 and 105 be articulated in the same manner as 95; at the same time, the absence of the tie removes the justification for separating the tones in the context of a performance in which paired half notes have generally been slurred.

We believe, therefore, that the articulation adopted in bar 1 should apply to all pairs of half notes throughout the Rondo; in other words, either the autograph or Hoffmeister should be followed consistently. Only the stretto passage of the cadenza presents us with an exceptional case. Here the paired half notes traverse wider intervals (ascending fourths and one ascending fifth) than earlier in the Rondo finale; as in bar 95, the second half is tied to the first eighth of the subsequent measure (bars 152–159 of the expanded version). In this passage, Hoffmeister does not slur the two half notes as he does elsewhere; close examination of the music shows that his seeming inconsistency is justified and indeed necessary. In the first four entrances (bars 152–155), the paired half notes occur in normal fashion; both tones belong to a single voice part. (As mentioned above, the half notes mostly span an ascending fourth. The second entrance presents a fifth rather than a fourth in order to provide a viable suspension in the bass.) At bar 155, the technique of voice leading changes. Entrances of the motive continue in breathtaking ascent. The listener hears the ascending fourth in half notes from B♭ to E♭ (bars 155–156), F to B♭ (bars 156–157), and C to F (bars 157–158). This impression results from an ingenious deception, a sublime musical pun. For the two half notes no longer occur in the same voice part. Each new high note results from the shift of an inner voice above the previously highest part. Through this technique of overlapping parts, Mozart can continue to build his ascent without increasing the number of voice parts above five. Since the two half notes no longer belong to the same voice, they cannot receive a slur without visually obscuring the already very complex voice leading. To include the slurs in bars 152–155, only to omit them in 155–158, would be misleading, as it might suggest that the ascending fourths are no longer of motivic significance in the latter measures.

The existence of this Rondo in two versions presents special problems to the editor. Where the autograph and Hoffmeister differ in detail, he must make clear which source he employs and indicate the variant reading in a footnote or extra staff. To our knowledge, no edition completely satisfies this basic requirement. Furthermore, the editor must clarify for his reader the distinction between the Rondo Andante of 1786 without cadenza, and the expanded Rondo finale of 1788. Because of the work of Einstein and his successors, we can assume that all forthcoming editions of the piano sonatas of Mozart will include K.533, with the second version of the Rondo as finale. For reasons of economy, publishers of the sonata version will probably no longer include the first version of the Rondo in their editions of Mozart's other piano works. The disappearance of this version of the Rondo from printed editions (and consequently from our concert programs) would be a loss and would diminish our knowledge of Mozart's art.

Tonality in Early Medieval Polyphony

TOWARDS A HISTORY OF TONALITY

FELIX SALZER

ITHIN the vast amount of literature dealing with the music of the past, two distinct approaches are discernible. The distinction applies, regardless of whether books or articles are concerned with an entire period of music history, with the output of a specific composer, or with a particular work. Although the pitfalls of oversimplification inherent in all generalizing statements are obvious, it is nevertheless important that the existence of such a dichotomy is recognized in musicological approaches and methods.

This dichotomy can best be labeled *description versus analysis*. Both approaches are legitimate in themselves, since both have a definite role to play within what is broadly termed theoretical and historical musicology. There seems to be, therefore, no need for any explanation as to the *de facto* existence of methods based on either description or on analysis. What should be of deep concern, however, is their unequal poorly proportioned application. For it appears that the overwhelming majority of musicological publications use a descriptive approach, and that only a small minority attempt to present results of analytical investigation and penetration. The majority are bolstered by a not inconsiderable amount of literature that passes as analysis, but in reality amounts to description behind a thinly constructed analytical façade.

Although the following may shed some light on the rightful and necessary place of both types of investigation, it should be stated here that descriptive methods fulfill their true function only if they are employed in the opening stages of what one might call the total analysis of a work or a group of works.

Judging from much valuable work done in the field of description, it is evident that certain aspects of a musical era or of a specific musical work can be explained and defined by description and categorization. Here enter problems of style, most of which can be solved by descriptive and even statistical methods. The mere fact—to mention only one area—that it is today possible to place a newly discovered work by an unknown composer within a narrowly defined era of the total historical development of Western music is an unmistakable and positive result of the painstaking application of descriptive as well as comparative methods.

Although there can be no doubt that such methods lead to general knowledge about music, even the most thorough stylistic investigation results in knowledge of only the external characteristics of the actual music. It is a peripheral type of knowledge and does not, by itself alone, penetrate the musical surface. This penetration must be acquired by analytical investigations, which should be preceded, however, by stylistic description and characterization.

The study of style will always remain a means to an end. As such it is indispensable. Yet its very nature of dealing with the problems of musical surface explains also its limited function. This is borne out by the current attitudes and goals of musicology, which are in many ways synonymous with those of stylistic research. At its very best, stylistic research can form a basis, but only a basis, from which the still outstanding solution of the musical problems must be found. It should be understood, therefore, that musicological research, as it is usually practised today, can in itself not achieve musical understanding of the music it has so excellently described and so splendidly edited. As a result, only one segment of a complex picture has been explained.

For, with the exception of a few isolated instances, the fundamental problems of the music itself have, as of today, not been considered seriously within the framework of musicological studies. We have not yet solved the cardinal problem the music presents: the function of its tones, melodic lines, and sonorities within the totality or total form the composer has created.

The almost exclusive preoccupation with all aspects of description and categorization has led musicological research into an impasse. Since ability for stylistic description is not too difficult to acquire, it today represents the most popular branch of research. It has therefore far outrun its introductory and preparatory function. The literature is flooded with descriptive works of all kinds with the result that what should be considered as the beginning of musical insight is widely mistaken for insight itself. We are therefore presented more often than not with investigations on a but thinly veiled program-note level on the one hand and a nearly complete vacuum in musical penetration on the other. We sometimes even cannot help but believe that we soon will come to the point where we shall know everything about music, save the music itself.

The consequences of this neglect are only too familiar to those of us who have attempted to penetrate the music of the more distant past, for instance, the works of early Medieval polyphony. For we have gradually been forced to realize that although we may know a good deal about a work of Leoninus and Perotinus, the school and period from which it emanated, and the type of notation it demonstrates; although we may be familiar with the style of a specific work which we may be able to describe down to the smallest detail; although we may be familiar with the entire source material—still, after all this knowledge has been acquired, we have not come to grips with the music itself.

The situation seems confounded by additional considerations and problems facing us. Many of us have undergone training in various disciplines such as harmony, counterpoint, form, and analysis. What do they contribute to the understanding of Medieval music, to the understanding, for example, of the compositions of Leoninus and Perotinus and the motet of the thirteenth century?

Anyone seriously attempting the direct application of present-day theory to Medieval and Renaissance music will soon be overcome by a feeling of frustration. In this repertory, we encounter no harmonic progressions such as found in the music of the eighteenth and nineteenth centuries or in harmony books, nearly all of which are descendants of Rameau's *Traité de l'harmonie*. Furthermore, there appear to be no motivic and thematic designs comparable to those of later music. Contrapuntal studies will not help much either. Textbooks on sixteenth-century counterpoint are not relevant to the problems encountered in twelfth- and thirteenth-century polyphony. For, in many ways, this voice leading is different in outlook and practice from the sixteenth-century conceptions and differs even more from the textbook counterpoint of later periods.

And so, we are led to the theorists of the Medieval era hoping that they may be of some help in our analytical aspirations. Their main contribution lies in the fields of rhythm and notation, where they offer most valuable information. Furthermore, they deal with the problems of consonance and dissonance, with the various intervals, the ecclesiastical modes, and with specific problems of voice leading and setting. They also discuss the ethos of the modes, and some offer speculations on the relation of music to mathematics. Others again make important reference to contemporary musical practices.

The more familiar we become with the trends of Medieval musical thought, however, the less we can expect that the theorists could present anything resembling a theory of composition or analysis.[1] This would have been foreign to their way of thinking and could not have entered the range of their immediate interests.

Does this, however, mean that we must resign ourselves to the description of visible facts, just because the theorists of the time divulge so little about the meaning of their contemporaries' compositions? Are the writings of Medieval theorists the only legitimate avenue through which analytical access to the music can be gained? I do not think so. For, if such opinions had any validity at all, our chances of understanding Medieval music would be next to hopeless. Contrary to a still widely held view, there is no reason why meaningful analysis necessarily depends upon temporal proximity between composer and analyst or the absolute correspondence between a composer's theoretical outlook (or the writings of contemporary theory) on the one hand, and the type of analysis presented on the other.

Since neither Medieval treatises nor conventional theories open the way to analytical penetration of early polyphony, a major readjustment and a new outlook in theoretical approaches will be needed to solve the problems the music presents. It will furthermore become apparent that if a keen

---

1 Even the most helpful, such as the Anonymous IV, reveal only the most rudimentary aspects of compositional technique. See Coussemaker, *Scriptorum I*, 327–64.

awareness of musical organization, continuity, and coherence in Medieval music is to be achieved, we cannot remain content with completely impersonal or objective methods of registration and categorization. We will have to go beyond the limits of purely descriptive procedures, which, very often, present little more than an enumeration of facts. By and large, we have become so afraid of being accused of "interpretation" that the last vestiges of the bold adventurousness of early musicology seem to have all but vanished. "Historical objectivity" has become not only a slogan but an obsession that all too frequently has resulted in a completely neutral, unimaginative, musicological reportage. There still exists, one would hope, the difference between meaningful interpretation and meaningless or arbitrary interpretation.

Nevertheless, any approach to the musical contents of Medieval polyphony must have a broad and general validity allowing the music, as it were, to tell its own story. Although we can never separate or dissociate ourselves completely from our twentieth-century outlook and mentality, with its specific kind of analytical questioning and curiosity, we must prevent esthetic considerations of later centuries from influencing our evaluation and appreciation of Medieval music. Above all, we must not shy away from revising and reorienting our present concepts of counterpoint, harmony, form, and tonality. These are, as far as counterpoint is concerned, sixteenth-century or late Baroque concepts, and as far as tonality is concerned, those of the late eighteenth and nineteenth centuries.

It seems, therefore, that the problem has to be attacked from the one elemental factor which has been common—until fairly recently—to all Western music regardless of style and period: the factor of motion. Whenever we hear a succession of tones, we are entitled to investigate whether the succession has an inner necessity or logic. What makes coherent motion? What distinguishes it from unorganized, vague, and arbitrary motion? Has it direction?

If the succession of tones has direction, then it will show a definite beginning and a definite motion-impulse to the goal. Consequently, the single tones will receive their functional meaning from their role within this motion. The musical utterance of the West is largely characterized by the constantly recurring phenomenon of directed motion.

On the other hand, if the music is not directional, which is conceivable, then what is its *raison d'être*? What kind or organization and purposefulness does it reveal? I believe that any investigation of the actual music of Medieval polyphony will have to come to terms with these basic problems of motion and direction. Out of the solution of these basic problems, an analytical approach will evolve that, far from merely describing and enumerating facts, may open the door to hearing the details as parts of a larger whole; this kind of hearing, in my opinion, characterizes the essence of musical understanding.

The organum, as the earliest type of polyphonic music, has been described and illustrated in all standard works of the history of music. It therefore would be pointless to offer here any illustrations of its early stages of development; this subject will be touched on only in the form of a brief summary.

The parallel organum of the ninth century constitutes the nominal beginning of polyphony. Since, however, the added voice, the *vox organalis*, is a replica of the *vox principalis*, the plainsong, at the distance of a fourth or fifth below, no true polyphony has as yet been established. Nevertheless, the employment of parallel motion together with the establishment of normative vertical sonorities such as the fourth, fifth, and the octave, as well as of the chords $\frac{8}{5}$ and $\frac{8}{4}$ in the so-called composite organum, must be considered significant.

A freer, i.e., not strictly parallel, organum with its beginning in oblique motion hints at future possibilities. Basically, however, the dependency of the added voice on the course of the plainsong remains the same.

It was not until the eleventh century that a most important development took place: the introduction of contrary motion. Although illustrations for this type of organum are readily accessible, only one such example is cited here for purposes of later comparison. It is the organum *Cunctipotens genitor*, contained in the anonymous treatise *Ad organum faciendum*, dating from the late eleventh century.[2] It gives a clear indication of the development of

2 Transcription in Davison and Apel, *Historical Anthology of Music* (Cambridge, Harvard University Press, 1957), I, 26a; hereafter cited as *HAM*. Reprinted by permission of the publishers.

contrary motion, only occasionally permitting the presence of parallel and oblique motion (Example 1).

EXAMPLE I

Cun- cti- po-tens ge- ni- tor de- us,   om- ni cre- a- tor,   e-   ley - son.

Chri - ste De - i splen- dor,   vir- tus pa - tris - que so - phi - a,   e -   ley- son.

Am- bo- rum sa- crum spi - ra- men, ne- xus a - mor-que, e-   ley - son.

The *vox principalis* is now the lower voice, indicating that this voice is considered the fundament on which a countermelody is to be erected. By now, it had become obvious to the anonymous composer, craftsman, or improviser, that two melodic lines could move in parallel, oblique, and contrary motions. Since contrary motion constituted the latest discovery, it is understandable that the main emphasis was now on this type of motion.

The style of this and similar passages is determined by a note-against-note setting, *punctus-contra-punctum*. It thus can be assumed that this principle of counterpoint as the basic procedure of polyphonic motion was established by the eleventh century. From a musical as well as a historical point of view, there are two aspects under which the meaning of such note-against-note examples should be interpreted.

Under the first aspect, we must try to recapture—as much as this is at all possible—the novel and exciting experience of the period, of two voices moving simultaneously in opposite directions and only occasionally in similar motion. For the first time, a complexity of texture must have been felt through the succession of constantly changing sonorities. We must try to imagine the turmoil into which the listener must have been thrown by this invention of counterpoint and the clash of the conflicting interests of the vertical and horizontal orientation caused by the determined use of contrary motion. All this must have impressed those who sang this music and those who listened to it as a sign that a new era had started.

A second aspect, however, provides very contrasting vistas. It results from a question. What is the significance of this early polyphonic music as such and in view of later developments?

Compositions such as the one cited in Example 1 appear as the initial stages of counterpoint, as the first attempts at voice leading. It seems that the mere fact of two voices moving simultaneously, together with the resulting problems of spacing, choice of intervals, and position of the voices at the phrase endings, completely absorbed the composer's creative mind. In spite of the establishment of contrary motion, a dependency on and subordination to the Gregorian voice continues to be very strong. The selection of tones for the countermelody still completely depends on the course the melody of the chant takes. This course decides whether contrary motion, occasionally parallel motion, and—for short moments only— oblique motion are to be used. Although there are indications of melodic organization such as climax, the tones are mainly chosen for the sake of employing the possibilities of motion rather than for any other conceivable function. There are melodic motions, but no architectonic principle to provide goals.

Around 1100 Johannes Affligemensis, in the treatise *De musica*,[3] says about the organum that "different people treat it in different ways; but the easiest method is to pay careful attention to the variety of movement, so that when the plainsong goes up, the counterpoint goes down, and vice versa." These words tend to confirm the impression that counterpoint began as a craft and skill rather than being in the service of any higher artistic concept. In this connection, a further well-known aspect must always be kept in mind: two-part singing of this kind was often improvised, and thus required an agreement on rhythmic interpretation between the singers. It is therefore probable that whatever rhythmic variety might have

---

[3] In Gerbert, *Scriptores II*; new edition by Joseph Smits van Waesberghe in CSM I (1950). This treatise was formerly ascribed to John Cotton. Translation of quotation by Dom Anselm Hughes in *New Oxford History of Music* (London, Oxford University Press, 1954), II, 285. Reprinted by permission of the publishers.

existed in the interpretation of the Gregorian repertory before the eleventh century was increasingly neglected and evened out by the overriding need to sing together and thus literally to sing note against note. The result was an interpretation in uniform values at a probably slow, even, and strict pace.

Thus, a strange situation developed. A really new and revolutionary form of musical expression had been born, but for two or three hundred years after its inception, it remained completely dependent on the chant. This situation seems to dominate the eleventh century; it is difficult to see how polyphony could have developed had it not undergone a fundamental change.

This change occurred in the first half of the twelfth century, and led to a polyphony freed from complete dependency on the Gregorian chant. The deeper meaning of this development, however, is the definite emergence of a new structural principle, instinctively created by anonymous composers, and—as the musical development during the following centuries shows—peculiar to Western polyphony. The elaboration of this principle is a most significant aspect of the entire history of Western music.

It is the polyphonic works of the schools of St. Martial at Limoges and of Santiago de Compostela in northern Spain that give a vivid impression of the transformed stylistic picture. It will be our task to define the musical significance of these new developments, first concentrating on those specimens of organum that present the startling new style of sustained tenor tones underlying florid, melismatic passages of the upper voice or duplum.

Two examples (Examples 2 and 3) will be discussed presently. They constitute the beginning and the ending of two polyphonic settings of the *Benedicamus Domino*.[4]

The florid upper voices express an entirely new creative impulse in the horizontal, melodic dimension which in the eleventh century appeared somehow frustrated by a tone-for-tone dependency of the *vox organalis* on the motion of the *vox principalis*.

In comparison with the example from the eleventh century, it would

4 In *Liber Sancti Jacobi: Codex Calixtinus* (Santiago de Compostela, 1944). In volume II of this complete edition in three volumes, the authors, Dom G. Prado and Walter M. Whitehill, have transcribed the diastematic (Acquitanian) neumes of the original manuscripts into modern plainsong notation. To facilitate the reading, I have used modern clefs and quarter-note heads without stems.

seem that the greatest possible independence between the two voices had now been achieved. This independence, however, in no way indicates that the voices, so to speak, go their own way. On the basis of extensive experience in improvisation, musicians had apparently discovered that something significant could be achieved through a much elaborated setting in oblique motion, that is, through a modification of the point-against-point concept into a concept of one point against several points. The motion of the duplum produces a succession of different intervals with respect to the sustained tenor tone. Here too—as in the note-against-note style—the contrapuntal texture consists of a series of intervals. Unlike the earlier settings, however, the lower voice now seems to have acquired a specific meaning in relation to the melismatic duplum—it represents a stabilizing element. The melismas of the duplum are by no means as arbitrary and vague as a cursory hearing might lead one to believe. It will therefore be advisable to add, in form of voice-leading graphs, a detailed analysis to each of the two excerpts. (Example 2).[5]

The initial phrase ranges from the opening unison to the concluding unison on F over the syllable "di." Its contents are an upward motion from F to C, a motion around C, using neighbor notes, which constitutes what may be called a prolongation of C, and finally a descent from C to F (see graph 2a).

The meaning of these events can be defined as follows: whereas an interval in the eleventh-century organum was immediately succeeded by another one, now a single interval, the fifth F–C, appears not only in vertical position but horizontalized as well. Thus the existence of the interval F–C is not momentary; it is extended and prolonged. It unfolds, it moves in time, or as we may say, it has been activated in time.

The prolongation of an interval or chord constitutes a form of tonal organization. Consequently, such prolongations give rise to motion which is directed: from F up to C, then around C, and finally from C down to F. Within this directed motion, one should listen to three different motion

---

5 *Ibid.*, II, 83. Two problems confront the analyst of Medieval polyphony. In the earlier sources, the vertical alignment of the parts is often rather ambiguous; in the later repertory, certain works have survived in a number of versions, some of which vary considerably. It goes without saying that a difference in reading or transcription may lead to a different analysis. The broad structural principles, however, underlying much of this music would not be fundamentally altered.

EXAMPLE 2   School of Compostela

impulses: the rapid ascent from F to C, the lingering around C, and the gradual descent from C to F.

In graph 2a, stems have been given to the main tones F and C, thus indicating their relative prominence. The motions from F to C and from C to F—from one tone to another—are indicated by slurs, while the circling around one tone—its prolongation—is shown by a dotted beam connecting the repeated statements of the tone C.

In analyzing Example 2 as a whole, a motion from F to G is evident. Whereas, however, the tenor moves directly to G, the way the duplum leads to G is indirect and fascinating. A kind of overlapping between duplum and tenor is created inasmuch as the duplum horizontalizes a G-sonority as an anticipation, while the tenor is still on F. Only when the duplum reaches G does the tenor also sing G. Thus we hear a transition from F to G over the syllable "ca."

This is followed by a confirmation and prolongation of G over the syllable "mus," which concludes with a motion of the duplum from D upward to G. Attention should be given to the significance of repetition as an important principle of melodic organization. Note that the ascent from F to C over "Be" is repeated over the syllable "ca," that the descending fifth from C to F is repeated by the fifth D–G, finally that the prolonging motion around C is repeated with a similar use of neighbor notes in the prolonging motion around D.

Graphs 2b and 2c represent a progressive reduction of the contents to the basic structure of the entire excerpt; they do not require any further comment.

In summary, it should be realized that two new factors of musical composition are at work in Example 2: first, the linear realization or prolongation of a basic underlying interval or sonority; second, the creation of directed motion, directed either within a prolonged and horizontalized interval, or from one interval to the other.

Turning now to Example 3,[6] we must try to grasp the meaning of the whole phrase. From the whole we shall arrive at an understanding of the detail. The tenor should not be heard just as a succession of five single tones, but rather as a motion circling around the tone D by using an embellishing tone, F, and a neighbor note, C, resulting in a figuration or prolongation of tone D. As a counterpoint to this tenor, the duplum hovers around A as a pivotal point, and then moves down to D. Basically, therefore, both voices show a prolongation of an underlying interval D–A (see graph 3b). The detailed melodic events shown in graph 3a constitute an elaboration of the basic melodic line as given in graph 3b. Branching off from A are two motions of a third from A to C. The second is an expansion and a variation of the first. A–C becomes A–B–C, with each note embellished. Here can be seen the significance of varied repetition for musical continuity. From the first embellishing C, which is supported by an embellishing F, a descending fifth branches off which acts as a preparation for the main line of a fifth, A–G–F–E–D.

6 *HAM*, I, 28b.

EXAMPLE 3   School of Compostela

(Domi)-no -

Graph 3a

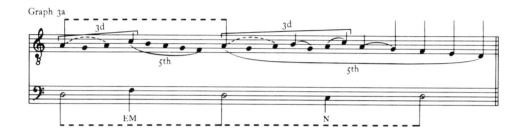

Graph 3b

After the first third, A–C, a return to A takes place. Although the tone A also reappears after the second third, its function is now different. It is now an appoggiatura to G (one should keep in mind that the sixth was regarded as a dissonance in the twelfth and thirteenth centuries). Thus the structural motion proceeds from the A (at the beginning of the second third) on to G and thence to the final D.

From the phrase as a whole we learn that the concept of directed motion within a horizontalized interval is by no means contingent upon a single sustained tenor tone. The structural continuity of that interval persists as long as the intervening sonorities have a definite function to fulfill within the course of the developing prolongation. This means that the fifth F–C,

EXAMPLE 4   School of St. Martial

Vi- de- runt   He- ma- nu-   - el

Graph 4a

Graph 4b

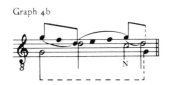

the octave C–C, and the sixth C–A, whose functions have been explained, do not offset the continuing structural role of the dominating fifth D–A which—only at the end of the excerpt—moves to the unison D through the descent of the duplum.

We now turn to a two-voice example from a St. Martial manuscript, based on a trope of the Christmas Gradual *Viderunt omnes* (Example 4).[7]

7 Transcription in *HAM*, I, 27a. From a St. Martial manuscript (Paris, Bibl. Nat. lat. 3549).

It is partly in sustained-tone, partly in note-against-note style. In Example 2, the tenor was restricted to sustaining the main tones F and G; in Example 3, the circling around one tone—D—was obvious. In this excerpt, we confront a more complex and involved tenor itself consisting of a highly embellished line from G to D. Together with a very active duplum, this makes for increased contrapuntal intensity.

I believe that the clue to musical understanding lies in the recognition of a number of motions in the duplum, indicated in graph 4a: (1) after the neighbor-note F, a descending fourth G–D; (2) regaining of G by an ascending fourth; (3) additional descending fourths; thereafter, through the ascent of the tenor, both voices reach D.

For the setting of the name "Hemanuel," the following motions can be heard: (1) a varied repetition of the descending fourth followed by a varied repetition of the ascending fourth, both motions showing greater contrapuntal activity; (2) finally, from G (after the neighbor-note A), a rapid descent first to C, then more deliberately to the final tone G an octave lower. However, the tone D has been brought in through voice crossing. Thus, one more descending fourth is introduced, although G and D are not sung by the same voice part. The meaning of voice crossing is the exchange of top voice and bass roles between duplum and tenor. The tenor, as the lower voice, brings the top voice D. The duplum, as upper voice, brings the bass tone G. It is important to understand that the tenor does not always represent the fundament or bass of a passage, a fact which will be increasingly evident in the discussion of Example 5.

Comparing now the three examples so far analyzed with the one from the eleventh century (Example 1), some tentative conclusions can be drawn. In the polyphony of the eleventh century, each interval stands for itself; it appears in a row with others. Each has been arrived at because the composer has written a counterpoint in contrary, parallel, or oblique motion to the plainsong. Beyond these factors, there is no principle of musical organization at work that would cause the motion of the two voices and the resulting intervals to function as parts of an organic whole. Indeed, there is no organic whole. The motion is not directed.

With the first half of the twelfth century, however, the effects and implications of a new creative outlook and concept became increasingly

apparent. Composers, in using a chant fragment for polyphonic purposes—
for instance D–F–D–C–D as in Example 3—no longer seem to think only
of single intervals above each tenor tone achieved through the application of
the three known types of motion. Instead, they must have instinctively felt
that those five tones could be conceived as the prolonged and elaborated
expression of a single tone, D, or of a sonority based on D. Thus the tenor,
together with the motion impulses of the duplum, horizontalizing the
interval or sonority D–A, expresses a principle of direction, coherence, and
unity. It had become possible to imbue the two voices with a common purpose which lets the single tones and intervals function as parts of a larger
whole.

The increased contrapuntal activity, as found in Example 4, leads one
directly to those sections that are in a strictly note-against-note style. From
the stylistic point of view, one appears justified in considering note-against-
note sections to be essentially a conservative style carried over from the
eleventh century, in contrast to the more up-to-date sustained tone style
In fact, it would seem quite probable that the new structural ideas discussed
above could be found only within passages in the new style that lend themselves
so readily to its expression. Consequently, one might expect that whenever the
old note-against-note style is used, the pragmatic contrapuntal concept of
the eleventh century would continue to prevail. Careful examination of the
repertory of Santiago and St. Martial does not bear out such conclusions.
For in many instances, the new ideas of tonal direction and organization
pervade even the note-against-note sections. Example 4 has already given
a hint of this.

In order now to present an example which is entirely in a note-against-
note texture, we turn to the amazing little composition in conductus style,
Congaudet hodie (Example 5).[8] A one-staff version (Example 5a) is added to
make the technique of voice crossing clearer. Here, to visually distinguish

[8] From a St. Martial manuscript in the British
Museum (Brit. Mus. Add. 36881). This piece has
been transcribed into modern notation by Dom
Anselm Hughes in the *New Oxford History of
Music*, II, 296. A transcription in quarter notes
seems preferable. I have, therefore, omitted the
bar lines, which created upbeats, and also the half
notes and the following rests, which caused too
much of a caesura.

EXAMPLE 5   School of St. Martial

Con-gau-det ho- di- e coe- les- tis cu - ri - a, Quod ho-mo per-di- tus e - rit in glo- ri - a,

Na- to de vir- gi- ne qui re - git om - ni - a.

Graph 5a

Con-gau-det ho- di- e coe- les- tis cu - ri - a, Quod ho-mo per- di- tus e - rit in glo- ri - a,

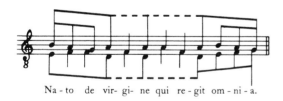

Na - to de vir- gi- ne qui re - git om - ni - a.

Graph 5b

Graph 5c

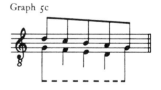

EXAMPLE 5a

the course of both voices, the tenor tones have been written as whole notes, whereas the duplum shows quarter-note heads with connecting beams.

Before approaching the voice leading as presented in graph 5a, we should like to clarify the use of the terms "setting" and "voice leading." By setting is meant the specific distribution of tones among the individual parts—in this example, between tenor and duplum—which creates the impression of wavelike lines in both voices, repeatedly crossing each other in their course. The setting, in other words, represents the surface appearance of the composition and is significant for an understanding of its style.

By restricting our attention to the setting, however, we lose sight of the whole—in other words, of the result of the two components. For the combination of duplum and tenor results in a contrapuntal progression—the voice leading—which gives direction to the whole. The voice leading, like the setting, has an upper or top voice, and a lower voice or bass. The question is whether the voice-leading top voice is always identical with the duplum, and whether the voice-leading bass is always identical with the tenor. The answer is: by no means always.

Let us compare the one-staff version (Example 5a) with graph 5a. If we look at the second phrase, for instance, we realize that duplum and tenor are identical with the top voice and the bass of the voice leading. The tones with upward stems are identical with the tones of the duplum; the tones with downward stems are identical with those of the tenor.

The technique of voice crossing, however, causes the duplum only partly to represent the top voice of the voice leading. This is particularly evident in the last phrase. Similarly, we find that the tenor does not function as bass throughout its course. Instead, each, duplum or tenor, may act in both capacities. According to the voice leading, the top voice in the last phrase is an elaboration of B–A–G (see the notes with the longest stems connected by beams in Example 5b).

EXAMPLE 5b

The actual duplum, however, is a far more interesting line, showing top voice *and* bass tones (Example 5c). It makes a great deal of difference in

EXAMPLE 5c

the total sound whether the top voice and bass of the voice leading are identical with the duplum and tenor of the setting, or whether the voice leading results from voice crossing. The problem for the active listener, therefore, is to hear and understand both, the individual setting of the single voices, and the direction of the whole resulting from the voice leading.

Now to the analysis of the whole. The degree of tonal coherence achieved through directed motion and combined with a definite correlation between text and music are truly astonishing. The one long sentence from "Congaudet hodie" to "Qui regit omnia" is set to a single musical sentence giving horizontal expression to the interval G–D.

In its essence, the one musical sentence can be indicated as in graph 5c. The prolongation of this progression shows that it is subdivided into three phrases which correspond to the three verses of the text: for "Congaudet hodie coelestis curia," we hear a prolongation of the tonic sonority (Example 5d); for "Quod homo perditus erit in gloria," a forward driving

EXAMPLE 5d   EXAMPLE 5e   EXAMPLE 5f

impulse (Example 5e); for "Nato de virgini qui regit omnia," a quick
motion from E–B to D–A, which is prolonged as the step next to the last
(Example 5f). Notice also the diminution of B–A–G in the top voice at the
beginning and end of this final phrase. We furthermore recognize the continuing stress on the third as a kind of middle voice between the fifths
creating an impression strongly suggestive of triads.

A summary of the most significant tonal developments demonstrated in
Examples 3, 4, and 5 leads to the conclusion that, by the middle of the
twelfth century, the basic principle of tonality had been created. This
principle can be defined as *directed motion within the framework of a single
prolonged sonority*. All the different styles and expressions of tonality that
follow in the succeeding centuries have this one principle in common.
Furthermore, a comparison of these three examples shows that Example 5
presents even more definitely than the preceding ones the concept of
counterpoint, not as an end in itself, but as the architectonic and directional
force that unfolds sonorities in time.

LEONINUS

THE INNOVATIONS of St. Martial and Santiago find their climactic development in the works of the two great masters of the school of Notre
Dame: Leoninus and Perotinus.

Several examples from Leoninus' *Magnus Liber Organi* will be presented.
They are taken from William G. Waite's transcription.[9] The achievements
of Waite's book lie not only in the fact that it represents the first edition of
the *Magnus Liber* in modern notation, but that it appears to solve, for many
at least, a much debated problem. It is still a matter of controversy whether

9 William G. Waite, *The Rhythm of Twelfth-Century Polyphony: Its Theory and Practice* (New Haven,
Yale University Press, 1954). Reprinted by permission of the publishers.

the long melismas in the organal sections are conceived already in modal rhythm or are, like the St. Martial music, in so-called free rhythm, leaving only the note-against-note discantus sections to be sung in modal rhythm.

Waite has, I believe, convincingly stated the case for modal rhythm in both styles. And a thorough study of the music in his transcription leaves one convinced that, in addition to all the supporting evidence he has presented, the music itself, its kinetic forces, its direction, and its coherence, strongly supports his view. For there is a remarkable correlation between the melodic direction and organization on the one hand, and the modal rhythm, as indicated by Waite, on the other. It appears, furthermore, that the transcription into modal rhythm in no way hampers the strong aural impression of freely flowing expressive melodic lines devised, occasionally, in bold contours. Waite says that "in organum style a certain liberty in the performance of the modes is admitted, for the individual notes of the modal pattern may be lengthened and shortened, while at the same time the essential outline of the pattern is preserved."[10] This view too is corroborated by the music's directional functions.

In listening to the repertory of the *Magnus Liber*, we are attracted first to the long melismatic passages over sustained tenor tones, i.e., the sections in organum style. Frequently, they are much more extended than similar settings of the St. Martial period. It is this length, combined with a greater melodic range, that presents definite problems to the listener. In our attempts to orient ourselves in these chains of tones, we realize that the concept of directed counterpoint and tonal coherence created by the anonymous monks of St. Martial and Santiago have undoubtedly received a significant impetus through the introduction of a rhythmic system. It is one of the great and everlasting merits of Leoninus to have achieved definiteness in melodic direction by imparting a precise rhythmic profile to the duplum melodies. His mastery in achieving a fusion of rhythmic profile with melodic synthesis, and at the same time a freedom of expression, seems inexhaustible. And it is this phase of his art that will be emphasized in the following.

The first example consists of the first twenty-four bars of the opening organum, *Judea et Jerusalem* (Example 6). The quotation is a two-voice

10 *Ibid.*, p. 120.

EXAMPLE 6   Leoninus

Graph 6a

Graph 6b

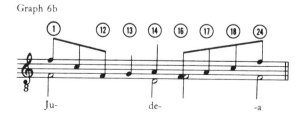

Graph 6c

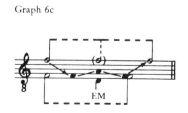

setting of the word "Judea." It shows a conception of melodic continuity at once intense and subtle. For the purpose of orientation, the reader is advised to concentrate on graph 6a while, so to speak, keeping in touch with graph 6b.

In its broad outline the entire melody appears to be organized into three phrases:

I. Bars 1–12: beginning on F, followed by a descending octave, and ending in bar 12 on the unison F. This descending octave is subdivided into motions of a fourth and fifth.

II. Bars 13–16: transition to embellishing interval D–A, which is briefly prolonged, followed by a return to the unison F.

III. Bars 16–24: ascending octave ending in bar 24 on octave F.

Now that we are aware of the broad implications of the melody as a whole, we can profitably turn our attention to significant detail. The musical events of the first phrase consist of the interwoven succession of subsidiary melodic particles: (1) bars 1–5: a descending fourth from F to C and motion around C; (2) bars 6–9: variation of the descending fourth F–C, followed by an anticipation of the descending fifth, while C is prolonged and thus structurally sustained; (3) bars 10–12: a descending fifth from C to F, ending on unison F.

The short second phrase requires no further written comment. It is interesting to note, however, that the third phrase, like the first, consists of three subsidiary events: (1) bars 16–18: an ascending motion from the unison F via A and B♭ to C; (2) bars 19–22: prolongation of C with upward motion impulses in preparation for the regaining of F: C–E–C; C–F–C; (3) bars 23–24: another impulse upwards and by skip to the final F. Note also the parallelism between phrases I and III in spite of their different direction. Furthermore, the significant points in melodic structure and prolongation coincide very often with the strong beats of the modal rhythm as indicated by Waite.

In conclusion, we can only marvel at the striking development of melodic ingenuity, direction, and prolongation. Probably not more than four or five decades can lie between the St. Martial and Santiago manuscripts and the time around 1160 when Leoninus created his masterwork.[11]

11 *Ibid.,* p. 2.

EXAMPLE 7

Leoninus

Hec

EXAMPLE 7 (*continued*)

We are now prepared to deal with an even longer and more complex work. It is the entire organum *Hec dies* (Example 7) consisting, in the transcription, of fifty-eight measures. To be able to hear this composition as a tonal organism of which all details are organic offshoots (prolongations), we are in need of large dimensional hearing. At first, the reader should concentrate on the fragment from the Gradual *Hec dies* that served Leoninus as the tenor for this particular organum (Example 7a).[12]

EXAMPLE 7a

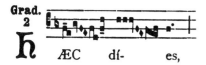

EXAMPLE 7b

Example 7b is a rendition of the chant fragment in even whole notes. The tonal organization of this fragment as used by Leoninus is presented in Example 7c, which may provide some orientation for the reader in the succession of tonal developments.

The underlying tonal organization can be recognized only through a study of the most ingenious upper voice. It is the top voice which gives the tenor its particular meaning and function. In conjunction, tenor and duplum first prolong an A-chord using G- and B♭-sonorities as neighbor chords and the F-chord as embellishing chord, all subordinate to the governing A-chord of which they are prolongations. These events are

---

[12] *Liber usualis* (Tournai, Desclee & Cie S.A., 1956), p. 778. Reprinted by permission of the publisher.

EXAMPLE 7C

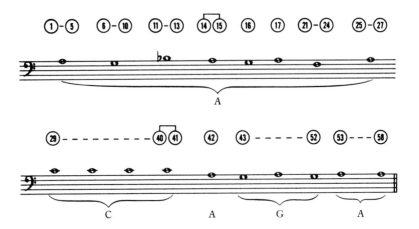

followed by prolongations of a C-, then a G-sonority, and finally a return
to the starting point A, bars 54–58 (first see graph 7b).

In studying the detail, we realize that the two voices in combination
express a three-voice sonority; if we listen to bars 1–10 the successive
change from the $\frac{8}{4}$ to the $\frac{8}{3}$ sonority (bars 1–5 and 6–10) is apparent. The
reader should now compare graph 7a with the reduction of graph 7b.

The process by which a single voice expresses an underlying polyphonic
structure has been called *polyphonic melody*.[13] This polyphonic effect is
achieved by the composer through various techniques of melodic elaboration or prolongation, such as the unfolding of intervals. The unfolded
fifth, A–D, and the unfolded fourth, D–G, in the first group of bars, followed
by G–C and C–F in the other groups, create, together with the tenor, a
quasi–three-voice texture which has been indicated by the tones with
upward stems versus those with downward stems. All tones of the duplum
are tones of the melody, but they express not only a voice-leading top voice
but a voice-leading middle voice as well. In graph 7b[1] is indicated that
the tones D and C are prolonged incomplete neighbors (IN) of E and D. The
top-voice tones A and G are *retained* tones of which the descending fourths
are prolonging offshoots.[14]

13 Felix Salzer, *Structural Hearing: Tonal Coherence in Music* (2d ed.; New York, Dover Publications, 1962), I, 121.   14 For the retained tone, see *ibid.*, p. 43.

Graph 7a

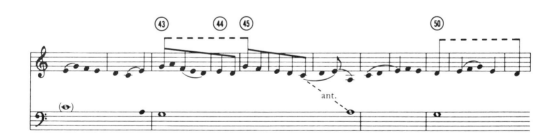

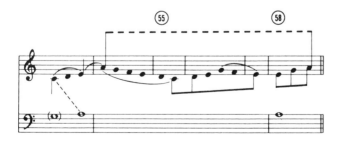

Graph 7b

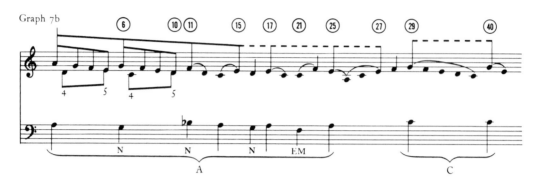

Graph 7b₁

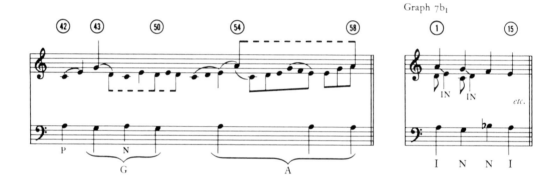

Graph 7c

Graph 7d

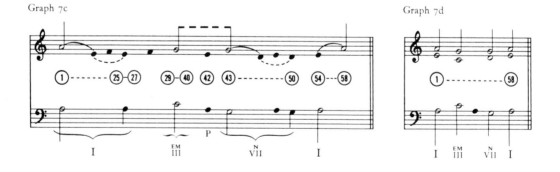

For the analysis of the entire piece, graph 7a should not only be compared with graph 7b, but also with graphs 7c and 7d, which represent further reductions to the essential events of the whole. Additional written comment is unnecessary since the graphs present a detailed analysis. The concept of Medieval tonality or, as it will later be called, modal-contrapuntal tonality, finds its basic expression in graphs 7c and 7d. The reader's attention is drawn to the labels $^{EM}_{III}$ and $^{N}_{VII}$ for contrapuntal chords of higher structural order; EM or N pointing to the specific contrapuntal function, the Roman numeral indicating the scale degree. We are confronted here by a typical structural progression of this particular style of tonality; more about this subject will be said later.[15]

Although the preceding organum shows the prolonged and elaborated expression of a single, overall governing tonality, it is important to realize that this concept of tonality did not all of a sudden become the prevailing one. For it appears that after the momentous innovations of St. Martial and Santiago, three possibilities were open to the composer of the twelfth and thirteenth centuries: (1) All details, all prolongations become parts of a larger whole. A single, all embracing tonal framework spans the entire work; (2) A composition may present a clearly directed motion from one tonal area to another, or, in other words, a transition between two sonorities; (3) Continuation of the old, nondirected, counterpoint.

From a point of view that tries to survey the entire development of the tonal language over approximately one thousand years, it appears that after St. Martial and Santiago some doubt as to the course to pursue prevailed for some time. Although it is too early to make any definite statements in a field of musicological investigation that is still in its early stages, it can be safely stated that nondirected counterpoint gradually but no less surely loses whatever appeal it may have had in the first centuries of polyphonic texture. It eventually disappears.

Of the first and second possibilities (only these two can be called concepts of tonality), the second seems for some time to have lived in coexistence

---

[15] The more general label CS (contrapuntal-structural) used in *Structural Hearing* is still preferred for the not very frequent occurrences of such chords in later music, especially within the predominantly harmonic structures characteristic of the era of harmonic-contrapuntal tonality (see p. 97f.).

EXAMPLE 8

Leoninus

with the first. Thus, we find compositions showing movement from one sonority to another alongside those which are conceived in one tonality. During the fifteenth century, the first concept becomes the overwhelmingly dominant one in Western music. This means that organized motion from one sonority to another becomes a subordinated part of an overall governing structural progression expressing one single tonality. The second concept thus becomes an organic part of the first; it is more and more used as prolongation of the structural tonal framework.

Here two notes of caution are called for. They are valid in relation to music from the twelfth to the twentieth century. A composition which opens and concludes with the same sonority is not necessarily an expression of the first concept. It could conceivably be an exponent of the third concept, by merely beginning and ending in the same key without any direction and coherence in between. And a work which begins with a non-tonic sonority should not automatically be understood as expressing the second concept. We are thinking here of several works of Machaut.[16] Also the three-voice *Alleluya Nativitas* by Perotinus comes to mind. Already in the Middle Ages, composers had discovered the possibility of starting a work expressing the first concept with a non-tonic sonority, without in the least affecting the governing function of the single tonality. Only thorough analysis provides the answer to such problems.

We will now turn to an organum from the *Magnus Liber* which uses a chant fragment starting and ending on different tones. The short organum "Gaude Maria" (Example 8) offers a striking example of what has been termed the second concept of tonality. (A flat has been added to B of bar 23 in the graphs in the belief that the B♮ in the transcription is incorrect.)

It is amazing to see how Leoninus organized this chant fragment— in itself, a rather amorphous row of tones—into the basis of a polyphonic and organically developed motion from D via F to G. The main emphasis is given to the last sonority.

A comparison of Examples 8a and 8b indicates that there are two interdependent phrases or sections which cause a subdivision within an essentially through-composed form. The first section consists of eight bars and

---

16 One of these works is analyzed in Salzer, Example 533.

EXAMPLE 8a

Gau -   de   Ma -   ri -   a

EXAMPLE 8b

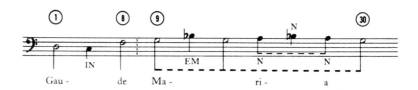

Gau -   de   Ma -   ri -   a

represents the music for the word "Gaude." The larger second section contains twenty-two bars for the word "Maria." In the first section, the main motion is from D to F. The second section is entirely in G. In view of the total progression, D–F–G, the F-sonority appears as a passing chord of structural significance.

In concentrating first on the motion of bars 1–8, it is essential to understand that both voices, although in different note values and utterly divergent in motivic and rhythmic appearance, express the same motion: D–C–F. It is as if the melismatic top voice were the elaborated and figurated variation of those three tenor tones. Therefore—and this is the essential characteristic—the variation does not follow the "theme" but constitutes its counterpoint; in other words, we have simultaneous rather than successive variation (Example 8c). The tenor tone, C, is an incomplete neighbor note of D. Instead of Example 8d, we hear Example 8e, the arrow pointing to the main motion of a third, D–F, while the fourth, C–F, forms a secondary interval.[17]

In the duplum's elaborated variation of the progression from D to F, the tone C has additional functions of appoggiatura and complete neighbor note. From the C in bar 6, which, as far as the fourth is concerned, corres-

[17] It is noteworthy that the chant in at least one source opens with a cephalicus, indicating the grace note character of the second tone, C. Thus, the type of notation suggests the tone's function. See Peter Wagner, *Einführung in die gregorianischen Melodien II* (Leipzig, Breitkopf and Härtel, 1912). See facsimile, p. 187.

EXAMPLE 8c

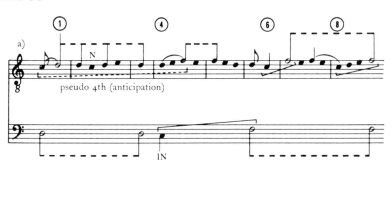

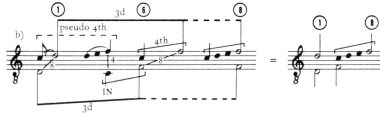

EXAMPLE 8d   EXAMPLE 8e

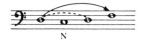   

ponds to the tenor's C in bar 4, there occurs a skip to F, followed at the
end by a stepwise motion of the fourth from C to F. These final fourths are
anticipated by what has been called a pseudo-fourth in the graph because
of the appoggiatura function of the tone C at the beginning. This first
motion up to F is counterpointed by the tenor tone C. The resulting vertical
interval of a fourth is—in the counterpoint of the twelfth century—a consonance. The preceding tones D and E are like an expanded appoggiatura
to F. The parallelism to bar 1 is obvious. It should be added that the tone
C in the duplum (bars 6 and 8) cannot be labeled an incomplete neighbor

note of D as was the C of the tenor. The duplum C rather is the inner voice tone of an F-sonority. This is another indication of polyphonic melody hinting at an underlying three-voice chord.

We come now to the elaborated prolongation of the G-sonority; a graph of the entire piece is presented, followed by two reductions (Example 8f). The signs ▭ and ◡ point to parallelism in melodic construction achieving motivic significance. Note also that the vertical B♭–F appears first as an embellishing sonority and then as a neighbor-note chord of the prolonging A, all this occurring with the prolonged G-sonority.

EXAMPLE 8f

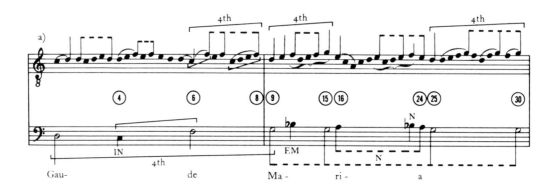

One hardly knows whether to admire more the gradually developing but clearly directed drive of the top voice taken as a whole—from D to G—or the anticipated ending in bar 15. The latter is followed by the contrasting entrance of the A-sonority which creates artistic doubt as to what to expect.

The doubt is finally dispelled by the regaining of the G followed by the jubilant confirmation of the two ascents of the fourth D–G.

The momentous accomplishments of Leoninus should not, however, obscure the fact that the structural idea of directed motion was born at St. Martial and Santiago. In many instances, the earlier dupla show a definite degree of melodic profile. It is herewith implied that, even without a system of rhythmic notation, the voice leading and, specifically, the voice direction strongly hint at some measure of rhythmic organization. Once one has analyzed the organa of that early period according to their directional functions, one hears indications of lingering effects, straightforward motion, delays and detours, occasionally even of accelerandos or retards, all of which contribute to the impression of an underlying rhythmic concept. It is, however, probable that such an impression will always remain in the realm of conjecture.

THE COUNTERPOINT OF PEROTINUS

WE NOW TURN to three- and four-part counterpoint as it appears in the works of Perotinus. To penetrate to the essential traits and characteristics of his concept of counterpoint, it is necessary to understand not only the function of the single voices but also the function of each tone within the framework of the basic voice leading giving expression to an underlying sonority.

To acquire this understanding a specific didactic procedure is suggested in Examples 9 to 13. And it is hoped that out of the procedure to be outlined, a teaching approach to the counterpoint of the twelfth and thirteenth centuries may evolve. Such an approach does not exist today. So-called sixteenth-century counterpoint is taught extensively, but for the truly contrapuntal periods of the twelfth, thirteenth, and fourteenth centuries, the periods of contrapuntal writing without harmonic interference or influence, there are no methods of teaching. This constitutes a serious lack in the education provided for young musicologists. What follows, therefore, is an attempt to attack this problem.

Three of the contrapuntal exercises, (Examples 9, 10, and 11) are based

on passages from the three-voice conductus *Salvatoris hodie*, ascribed to
Perotinus.[18] It is suggested that the instructor select a specific passage as a
model for the contrapuntal exercises, for instance, Example 9 (bars 27–30
from the second part of the conductus).

EXAMPLE 9   Perotinus

It will be the instructor's task to lead the student by means of a stage-by-
stage approach from the general to the specific, i.e., from the fundamental
chord or interval to the individually shaped voices of this passage. Therefore, the teacher should start by indicating the fundamental chord, as given
in stage 9a.

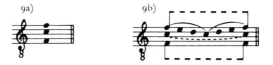

At stage 9b, as the basic prolongation of the sonority, the following progression could be suggested: a motion to the inner-voice C and back again
to F. For the time being, the other voices can hold their tones C and F.
No decision as yet can be taken as to their individual course.

At stage 9c, to create more voice motion, the typical device of voice

18 After H. E. Wooldridge's transcriptions in *Oxford History of Music* (1st and 2d eds.; London,
Oxford University Press, 1901 and 1929); note values reduced by four.

9c)

crossing could be applied. This would show the basic prolonging idea of stage 9b but distributed between two voices. The tone C could be still sustained as a possible middle voice to be developed later.

In the course of assigning specific functions to the three voices, and, above all, to make the voices more individual, we shall proceed to two further stages, 9d and 9e. In this and the following examples, the tones of the three voices will be indicated in the following way: the triplum by quarter notes stemmed upwards, the duplum by stemless quarter notes connected by beams, and the tenor by quarter notes stemmed downwards.

At stage 9d, a duplum may be chosen to execute the downward octave motion. What about the other octave moving upward? This does not have to be performed by a single voice, that is, not by the tenor alone. Therefore, the following could be suggested: the tenor moves up until it reaches C. From here on it may become an inner voice by hovering around C, using the upper neighbor-note D.

In stage 9e, the moment the tenor is prevented from becoming a top voice (from C to F), the assignment for the triplum becomes evident. It will start on C and then will take on the role of the top voice by going up to F.

9d)

9e)

The sustained C still has to be replaced by a melodic motion. At stage 9f, the sustained C will be replaced by an elaborate motion around C: C–Bb–A–Bb–C; or, if D is substituted for the second Bb : C–Bb–A–D–C.

Thus the function of the three individual voices has been clarified. In view of the coming examples, it might be added that the specific rhythm of the "model" can most naturally be expressed in the final stages by inserting bar lines and indicating the note values of the modern transcription in at least one of the voices.

This new approach, of course, in no way means to indicate steps in the creative process of the period. It would, in fact, be a quite mistaken belief that such a method could enable one to compose in the twelfth- and thirteenth-century manner. We are concerned here solely with trying to understand what we hear in the counterpoint of Perotinus; it is for this purpose alone that this particular approach is adopted. We want to determine the function of three individually shaped voices in creating tonal organisms. We now continue with an excerpt, bars 1–4, from the first part of *Salvatoris hodie* (Example 10).

EXAMPLE 10   Perotinus

Stages 10a and 10b show an underlying chord and a possible basic prolongation. At stage 10c, a prolongation of the final interval of a fifth could be suggested; also a support of the top-voice C with the bass C, true to the Medieval concept of *not* avoiding parallel fifths or octaves.

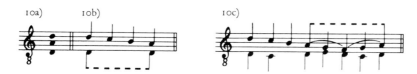

At stage 10d, a duplum part is introduced as a middle voice, while the tenor and the triplum perform the voices as indicated in stage 10c. In itself, the melodic line is not bad, but it is not idiomatic, since in this period a voice, such as the duplum, relatively seldom acts as the middle voice for its entire course. The tenor, furthermore, is still rather dull and unimaginative.

As shown in stage 10e, voice crossing might be resorted to by shifting the tenor up into the inner voice region, i.e., to A, which then will move on to G. This means that the duplum will proceed downwards and provide the bass with neighbor-note C and then move on to D. In order to be still within D, after the tenor has moved up to A, the opening D-chord is extended by the neighbor-note C (D–C–D).

Stages 10f and 10g carry out what had been planned in stage 10e. In stage 10f, a stepwise motion of the duplum downward to C and on to D is suggested. From there it is possible to continue just as indicated in stage

10d. Stage 10g shows a continuation of the tenor, which becomes bass again towards the end.

Example 11 constitutes bars 54–58 of the second part of the *Salvatoris hodie*. Stages 11a and 11b show an underlying interval and a basic idea of prolongation.

EXAMPLE 11 Perotinus

As shown in stage 11c, an ascending octave in the tenor may prove a suitable counterpoint to the descending fifth of the top voice. Since the omission of a few tones in the upward moving octave is desirable—note the contrapuntal task of setting five against eight tones—it appears natural in this style to leave out the tones B and E in order to avoid half-tone steps. The result is a pentatonic motion quite characteristic for the period. A possible middle voice should start on A; thereafter voice crossing becomes imperative. At present it is necessary to preserve the basic top-voice idea.

As stage 11d shows, the duplum could now be allowed to move downward from E to A as the basic melodic line. The triplum could start from A and be shifted by voice crossing via D up to F. Through this procedure, we get an embellished descending fifth as a voice-leading top voice and simultaneously an inversion of the tenor (if B is left out). Thus, an ascending sixth is answered by a descending one.

At stage 11e, to give the voices more individuality, the duplum can be prolonged or elaborated by leading it down to A—a motion that intensifies the effect of voice crossing and that individuates the line by substituting A for D.

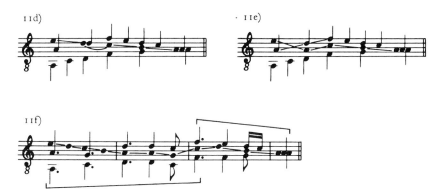

Stage 11f carries out this plan in detail, thus leading to a further elaboration of duplum and triplum. The skip of a descending fifth in the duplum is filled in by scalewise motion. This, combined with the use of a lower neighbor-note G in the triplum, creates a C-sonority in bar 1. The idea of the lower neighbor note is continued in the next bar by both voices creating another C-chord as a quasi-upbeat; and in bar 3, the neighbor-note D in the duplum heightens the dissonant effect of the sonority attained.

Two short excerpts dealing with four-part counterpoint will now be presented. Before demonstrating the various contrapuntal stages, I should like to explain the indications adopted in the graphs for the different voices of the four-part setting: for the quadruplum, upward stemmed quarter notes; for the triplum, quarter notes without stems; for the duplum, downward stemmed quarter notes; and finally a whole note for the sustained tone or tenor of the chant. This sustained tone, as a most characteristic tool in much twelfth- and thirteenth-century counterpoint, plays a major role in the intricate web of voice leading and the succession of sonorities.

The first of the excerpts (Example 12) is a very short but highly instructive example for dissonant chords created by a clearly directed voice leading of the upper three parts moving against the contrasting sustained tenor tone.[19]

EXAMPLE 12   Perotinus

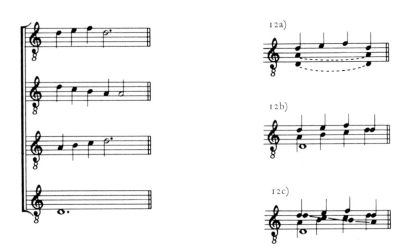

Stage 12a shows a prolongation of an underlying chord through an embellishing top voice. At stage 12b, the duplum, as inner voice, starts on A and leads up to D. As stage 12c shows, it is natural for the triplum to go in contrary motion by descending to A (voice-crossing). The dissonant effect is clearly enhanced through the pedal point on D.

Now to the second four-voice excerpt from the same work by Perotinus (Example 13). Stage 13a presents a possible melodic prolongation of the underlying D-chord, which could be counterpointed by D–F–E–D. Stage 13b suggests prolongations of the opening sonority and the tone A through a circling motion and a lower neighbor-note G.

At stage 13c, voice crossing could be applied in an interesting way. While the quadruplum goes stepwise down an octave, the triplum, instead

19 Examples 12 and 13 are taken from Perotinus' organum *Sederunt*, after Husmann's transcription in *Die drei und vierstimmigen Notre Dame Organa* (Leipzig, Publikationen älterer Musik XI, 1940).

EXAMPLE 13 Perotinus

13a)

13b)

13c)

13d)

13e)

of moving an octave upwards, may divide this upward motion, through a skip, into two distinct little phrases. The first circles around D, thus providing the bass. Then the skip occurs, and the second phrase moves from A to D, thus taking over the role of the top voice. In this process the second tone D is eliminated.

Stage 13d shows the elaboration of the second triplum phrase and of the quadruplum (see the use of neighbor notes). What course is open for the duplum? The duplum will most probably start from A and should present the top-voice tone D which had disappeared in the voice crossing of quadruplum and triplum (stage 13e). The line of the duplum will move from A to D; here could be used the same succession of tones as later are used in the triplum ("Stimmtausch"). Thus, the final ascending fourth of the whole, expressed in the triplum, is prepared for by the ascending fourth of the duplum which, however, is still partly covered by the descending line of the quadruplum.

The characteristics of twelfth- and thirteenth-century counterpoint will now be summarized. One might, incidentally, question the inclusion of the thirteenth century in this summary, since Perotinus, having died around 1235, seems only to a limited degree to be representative of this century. Except, however, for the omission of the long, sustained tenor tones, the counterpoint of the thirteenth-century motet is based on the same principles as those found in the works of Perotinus.

The close spacing of the voices, that is, the narrow frame of voice motion, will be mentioned first. It was evidently felt that the counterpoint of two, three, or four voices should not trespass the range of the underlying sonority which, in most cases, is a 5, 8, or $\frac{8}{5}$, occasionally an $\frac{8}{4}$.

To give the voices some freedom for individual development, voice crossing was used with remarkable skill and imagination. Nevertheless the closeness of texture leads frequently and quite naturally to the use of unisons and doublings.

Because of the large-scale adoption of voice crossing, the actual setting of a three-voice composition does not show a specific register for each voice. One is confronted rather with a setting of closely interwoven and overlapping lines all moving within one and the same register.

Each melodic line, however, contributes to the basic two- or three-part voice leading. This means that any tone of any voice of the setting (tenor, duplum, or triplum) may function as a top voice, middle voice, or bass tone of the voice leading.

If, for instance, the tenor rises into the middle-voice region, one can be sure that one of the other voices will take over the function of the tenor. This alone should serve to prove that the much-used term "linear" tends to obscure the fact that these linear voices may have a common purpose, an ultimate goal. This goal is either to move from one sonority to another, or to express a single sonority in time.

All intervals and chords, consonant or dissonant, result from the purposeful and directed motion of the voices and their crossings. The dissonances function mostly as passing, neighboring, or embellishing intervals or chords.

Finally, one may point to the characteristic and very frequent use of parallel octaves and fifths in the actual setting, as well as in the basic voice leading.

Most of these principles contrast with those of the sixteenth century. It would, however, be a great mistake, just because of these differences, to label this type of counterpoint unreal, or even inferior. At different times, there exist different conceptions of what constitutes good or bad voice leading in terms of the prevailing esthetic of composition.

As for the compositional function of Medieval counterpoint, it will be realized that the single voices, in spite of their individual shaping, subordinate themselves to the higher goal of achieving coherence and unity. Both are attained through directed voice leading which, in many examples, moves within single horizontalized sonorities. These underlying intervals or chords present the tonal basis, whereas their prolongations or contrapuntal realizations bring about the first tonal organisms in Western polyphony.

This brings us to the two final examples. The first is a three-voice organum (Example 14), which, if not by Perotinus himself, shows most clearly the musical architecture of the period.[20] Since the organum *Hec dies* by Leoninus (Example 7) is a two-voice organum on the same chant fragment, a comparison of both works should prove to be instructive. How each composer used the chant is shown in Example 14a.

[20] Example 14 is from W1: fol. 81; transcription in *HAM*, I, 31.

EXAMPLE 14

School of Perotinus

EXAMPLE 14 (*continued*)

EXAMPLE 14a

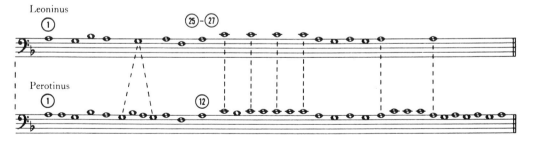

Graph 14a

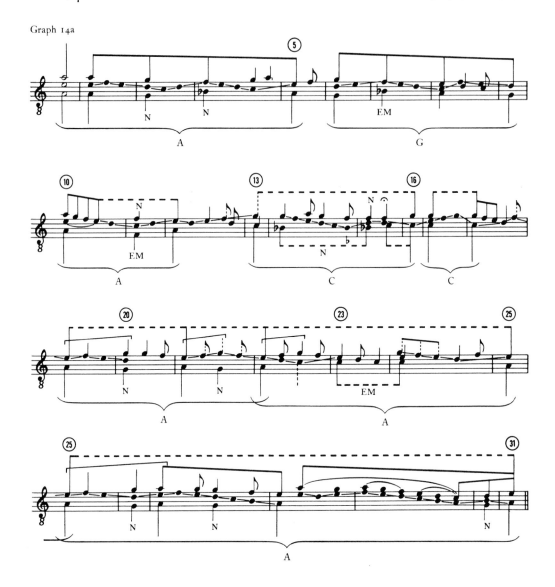

It will become apparent that Perotinus (or the anonymous composer), although expanding the chant, actually creates a shorter and more tightly knit polyphonic work.[21] Thus, for instance, the two-voice setting of the first eight chant tones brings Leoninus with his characteristically wide melodic arches to bars 25–27. This progression of eight chant tones is

Graph 14b

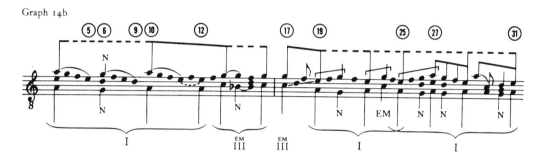

Graph 14c

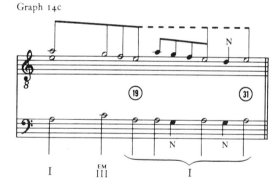

expanded by Perotinus through repetition of the first A and the three tones B♭–A–G. In spite of this expansion the corresponding point of the chant is reached in bar 12 of the three-voice version. In graph 14a, tones of the triplum have upward stems; the tenor is stemmed downward. Duplum tones are connected by beams. In this composition, the duplum seldom assumes the role of the top voice without doubling the triplum. In such

[21] See the Anonymous IV (Coussemaker, *Scriptorum I*, 342) on Perotinus' shortening of the *Magnus Liber* (abbreviavit eundem . . .).

instances upward dotted stems are provided. If the duplum furnishes the bass, a downward dotted stem is added.

Both compositions conceive the first eight tones of the chant and their polyphonic elaborations as a large-scale prolongation of the A-sonority. While Leoninus has achieved his first intermediate goal, the fifth A–E, in bars 15–17, which he then prolongs up to bar 27, Perotinus reaches his first similar goal at the end of the entire prolongation (bars 10–12). It also seems significant to observe the melodic expansiveness of Leoninus, which contrasts with the melodically terse, though contrapuntally logical, setting of Perotinus. (Compare graph a of Example 7 with graph a of Example 14).

On the highest structural level, the contrasts are also substantial. Apart from the fact that Leoninus returns at the end to A of the top voice, while Perotinus remains on the melodic structural tone E, this retaining of E is not an aimless circling around or lingering on. There ensue dramatic attempts to reach A again by the repeated motion impulses from E to G, until finally the impluse succeeds in once again reaching A before the final return to E. This return is expressed in two prolonging lines from A to E, the second being a variation of the first. They repeat what has been expressed on a structural level up to bar 19.

We now turn to our last and longest example, taken from Perotinus' *Alleluya Posui* (Example 15). After the polyphonic setting of the "Alleluya," sung by the soloists, the choir concludes the first phrase of the chant by singing the remaining two tones; it then continues with the second and third phrases. Thereafter begins the polyphonic version of the verse "Posui." The excerpt includes all the foregoing up to bar 69.[22]

Because of the difficulty in grasping the tonal unity of this large fragment we begin with reductions (graphs 15a, 15b, and 15c). Only later, after the reader has been introduced to the overall musical meaning and the large-scale progressions, will a study of the detail, graph 15d, be of value. Especially in graph 15a, the tenor tones have been repeated several times to impress the fact that they are sustained and thus always present. The music should be carefully compared with the graphs.

---

[22] Source: Montpellier, Faculté de Médecine, H196. fol. 16v. Facsimile in Y. Rokseth, *Polyphonies du XIIIᵉ Siècle* (Paris, Editions de l'Oiseau Lyre, 1935), vol. I. For a slightly different transcription, see Rokseth, II, 31–33. The reader should also consult Husmann, pp. 104–5.

EXAMPLE 15

Perotinus

EXAMPLE 15 (*continued*)

EXAMPLE 15 (*continued*)

EXAMPLE 15 (*continued*)

EXAMPLE 15 (*continued*)

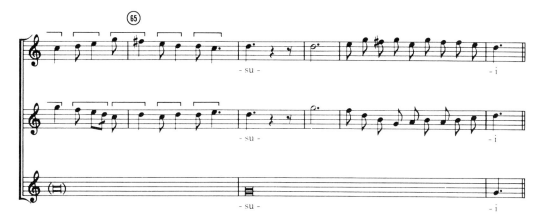

In listening to the polyphonic "Alleluya," one might at first believe that it represents—like Leoninus' *Gaude Maria*—a composition moving from one prolonged sonority or tonal area to another. Although the A-sonority in bars 44–46 concludes the polyphonic "Alleluya," in terms of the complete work it is not a final goal. For the monophonic rendering of the "Alleluya," which follows the shortly prolonged A-sonority, clearly reestablishes G. Any possible doubt about G constituting the tonal basis is finally dispelled when the polyphonic "Posui" begins on the G-chord in bar 47. Thus the A-chord which ends the polyphonic setting of the "Alleluya" is a neighbor chord, and is part of a structural framework $1-\frac{N}{II}-1$ in the G-tonality.

The musical contents of the polyphonic "Alleluya" consists thus of the detailed prolongations of the G-sonority (bars 1–8, 9–16), followed by the movement to prolonged neighbor notes. The tonic sonority returns fleetingly in bar 33, then more definitely in bars 38–43. The "Alleluya" concludes with the A-sonority mentioned above. As far as the total form is concerned, we are confronted with a single large, intricately organized prolongation of the G-sonority from bars 1–43 before the composition reaches the A-chord, the sonority of the upper neighbor note. Here again is tonal planning in large dimensions, and once again the need for orientation within this wide frame of tonal architecture through comparison of

Graph 15a

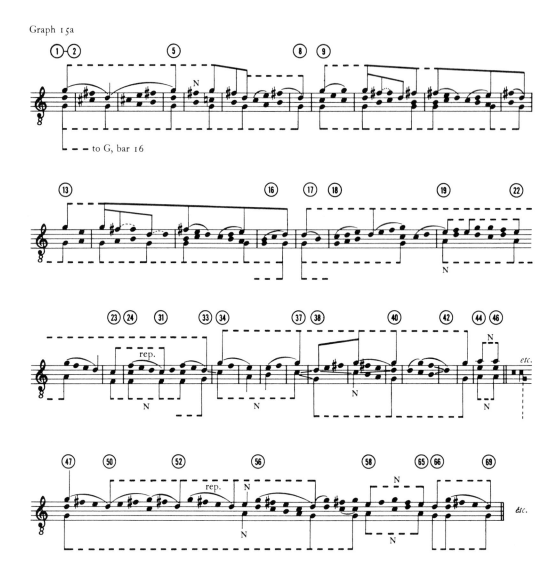

Graph 15b

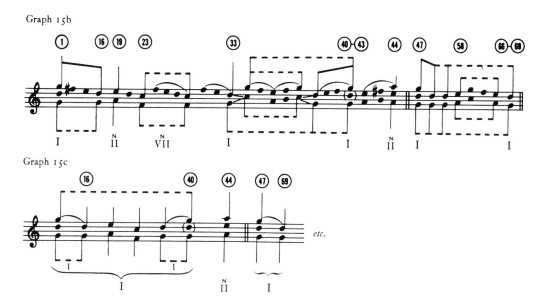

Graph 15c

etc.

graph 15a with graphs 15b and 15c is stressed. Only this type of orientation will give the needed frame of reference to understand the details of
graph 15d.

In concentrating now on the chant as it is used within the polyphonic
texture up to bar 40, we realize that, toward the end of this section (bars
38–40), the chant does not present the voice-leading bass. At this vital
point, which concludes the first huge G prolongation, the chant tones
D–C–D become inner-voice tones, while the crucial G is furnished by the
duplum. Similarly, in the following A-chord (bars 44–46), the chant tone
E becomes the middle voice and the bass tone A is sung by the duplum.

Since this happens repeatedly in Perotinus' works, the conclusion that
the chant should be considered the basis of polyphonic texture proves to
be only partly correct. Instead, it should be stated that the chant is interwoven into the three-voice texture and may form the bass or middle voice
of the contrapuntally prolonged sonorities. Occasionally the chant even
becomes part of the top voice (see Perotinus' *Alleluya Nativitas*, bars
218–227).

In conclusion, a detailed analysis (graph 15d) is presented. An attempt

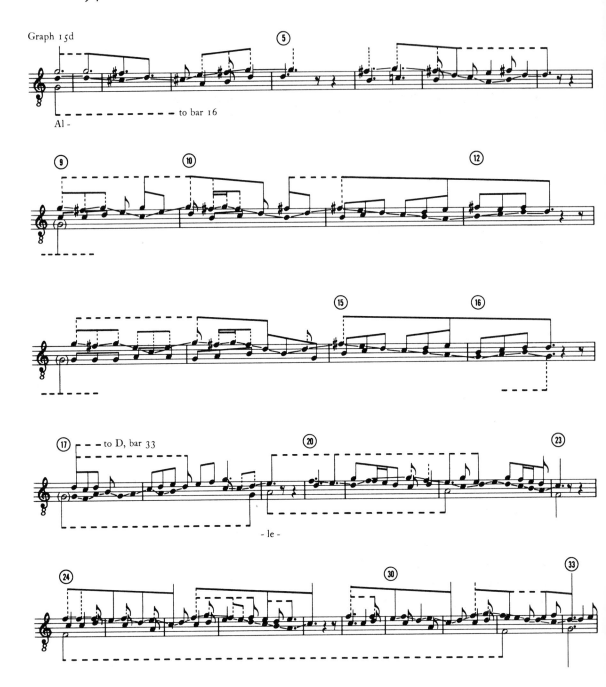

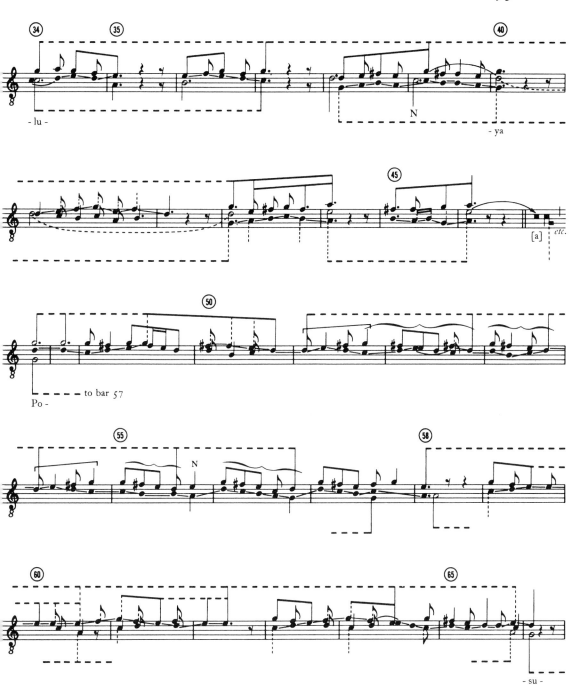

has been made to indicate the function of even the smallest tonal relationships and elaborations of the musical foreground. These, however, reveal
their meaning only if the reader compares the graph 15d with graphs 15a,
b, and c. To understand the detail in its relation to the larger whole becomes the main issue.

In graph 15d, the single-voice parts are indicated by the same kind of
stemming as was used in the analysis of Example 14. Here, however, the
duplum more often functions as the top voice, and the triplum thus acts
in those cases as the middle voice. The sustained tenor tones which add a
highly significant voice-leading factor to each measure of triplum and duplum must also be constantly kept in mind. The flow and succession of
consonance and dissonance are greatly determined by those sustained
tones.

It must be realized that these sixty-nine measures are only a part of
a large work of 198 measures in modern notation. For a long time
after Perotinus, Western music shows no comparable examples of tonal
planning on so vast a scale. It is nothing short of miraculous that—
hardly a century after St. Martial and Santiago—music could be conceived
showing such wide architectural arches and spans. At the same time, the
detail is convincingly brought into relief, but always as elaboration of the
total direction. Concerning such music in particular, one cannot really see
how performers can afford not to be intimately acquainted with the voice
leading. Only the knowledge of its direction, its detours, and its prolongations can help one decide which voices or which tones, at a given time,
should receive more emphasis or profile than others. Without this knowledge,
performances can only result in a rhythmically monotonous and mechanical
note-after-note rendering. What can still be grasped instinctively in much

music of later periods must here be arrived at through analytical understanding. We are only at the beginning of such penetration and understanding.

MODAL-CONTRAPUNTAL TONALITY

A SUMMARY of the results of our analytical investigations makes us realize that all examples by Leoninus and Perotinus are expressions of a definite type of tonality that is only partly characterized if the use of modes for the single voices of the polyphonic texture is stressed. The real difference between the type of tonality illustrated throughout this article and the tonality of later periods lies in the absence of any harmonic conception in the works of Medieval polyphony. The concept of a harmonic relationship existing between certain chords was still unknown. The direction of the voices is not influenced by harmonic progressions such as I–V–I or I–IV–V–I. In this music there are no secondary or applied dominants, no deceptive cadences, no progressions of descending or ascending fifths in the bass, all of which are characteristics of "harmonic" thinking.

All chords and sonorities of the examples arise out of the directed voice leading of two, three, or four simultaneously moving parts. It is therefore a contrapuntal tonality which is encountered in Medieval polyphony. The term contrapuntal, of course, does not imply that no awareness of chords existed in this period. The anonymous composers of the twelfth century, as well as Leoninus and Perotinus, must have been conscious of the vertical dimension, for their voice leading results in definite, repeatedly occurring, idiomatic, consonant and dissonant sonorities. These sonorities, however, are not deployed on the basis of any functional relationship. Therefore, they should not be termed harmonies.

Since linear movement in Medieval polyphony is more or less based on the modes, with only fleeting appearances of major-minor elements, the term for this type of tonality should be *modal-contrapuntal* tonality.

What only gradually develops during the fourteenth and fifteenth centuries is a new usage of the tonal language made possible through the probably completely unconscious discovery of associations and relationships existing between triadic chord-tones and thus between certain triadic chords. The birth of the harmonic concept and the resulting harmonic progressions, all based on I–V–I, however, in no way diminished the role of counterpoint. The new developments rather gave the contrapuntal voice leading a different orientation and a new perspective. They also influenced the contrapuntal voice leading as such in a radical fashion. This new type of tonality can be termed *harmonic-contrapuntal* tonality, based on the major-minor duality. Chromatic tonality, of course, is closely associated with this new type of tonality.

All these developments can be classified as developments of tonality because their very essence is the same. Tonality *is* chord prolongation. This means that the horizontalization of a sonority or the motion around a sonority is the unifying element of the contrapuntal voice-leading texture. This is the common denominator within the totality of a single language expressing itself in a rich variety of styles.

Correction slip for cards   (blue)

Call
no.

Author

Title

Call no. _____ Notes _____
Author entry _____ Tracings _____
Title _____ Shelf list _____
Imprint _____ Main entry _____
Collation _____ Other _____

Check all cards; ___ Check only this card; ___ Checkbook also ___

Date/sig _____ Date/sig _____ Date/sig _____
       Checker   Typist   Cataloger

Mode and Polyphony around 1500

THEORY AND PRACTICE

PETER BERGQUIST

U s i c of the period around 1500 presents some of the most interesting problems the analyst is called upon to solve; the music of Josquin, Agricola, Isaac, Obrecht, and the numerous other masters who worked at this time is of the greatest beauty, expressiveness, and elegance, and is justly fascinating to sensitive musicians for these reasons. The decades immediately before and after 1500 saw a great flourishing in music theory as well as in composition; such figures as Johannes Tinctoris, Bartolomé Ramos de Pareja, Franchino Gafori, Giovanni Spataro, and Pietro Aaron wrote a number of significant treatises that broke new paths for theory and outlined the major areas which the discipline would explore during the sixteenth century. One would assume that the work of these men would be of some assistance in analyzing the music of their contemporaries, and this assumption seems to be more or less tacitly made by many musicologists. The aim of this study is to subject this assumption to critical examination and to consider how, if at all, it should be modified or abandoned in order to achieve a better analytical comprehension of the music.[1]

It may be noted first that not every aspect of music theory around 1500 bears on the analysis of tonal structure. Theoretical discussions of esthetic, ethical, and philosophical aspects of music, for instance, though of great importance in their own right, do not contribute to an understanding of structure, although once such an understanding is reached, important cor-

[1] The author wishes to acknowledge the support of a Faculty Summer Research Award from the Office of Scientific and Scholarly Research, University of Oregon, in the preparation of this article.

relations might be made between structure and these other aspects. Theorists of this period typically explained the intricacies of mensural notation at considerable length. The analyst must, of course, know notational practice thoroughly in order to do justice to rhythm in relation to tonal structure, and the theoretical accounts are often helpful in illuminating practice, but the entire area of notation is largely tangential to the purposes of analysis. The same may be said of the new systems of tuning and temperament with which several theorists around 1500 were concerned. A specific system of intonation may contribute to a more or less forceful expression of various elements in the tonal structure, but it is not likely that considerations of tuning would change one's notion of structure completely.

The practice of *musica ficta* unquestionably can have vital bearing on tonal structure; it surely matters to the analyst whether a note should be G♯ or G♮. Such alteration may in a sense be preanalytical, since such decisions must be made by editor or analyst before analysis even begins. As it happens, theory at the period under consideration had little to say on this subject, and what little was said was too generalized to be of help in ambiguous situations, which are, of course, precisely those in which help is most needed. Accordingly, the traditional rules handed down by earlier writers must be applied as well as possible, without extensive help from writers of the Renaissance.

The two aspects of Renaissance theory that are most directly concerned with tonal structure are discussions of the modes and of counterpoint, and it is these which will be considered in some detail in their relation to musical practice and the needs of the analyst.

For the purposes of this study, it has seemed convenient to examine the work of one theorist, Pietro Aaron, as a specimen of theoretical attitudes rather than to attempt a composite account of several writers.[2] Corrections or modifications of his statements can be supplied when Aaron strays from the consensus on theory or practice. This happens relatively seldom, since

[2] Ed Peter Bergquist, Jr., "The Theoretical Writings of Pietro Aaron," unpublished Ph.D. dissertation, Columbia University, 1964, 578 pp., contains a comprehensive account of all aspects of Aaron's work. The exact source of statements attributed to Aaron and other theorists without specific reference in this article may be found in this dissertation. The discussion below of mode as it appears in practice in Gregorian chant is indebted to Willi Apel, *Gregorian Chant* (Bloomington, Indiana University Press, 1958), pp. 133 ff.

Aaron was not a radical innovator. His closeness to the practice of his day has long been recognized, and his observations are solidly based on what eminent composers and theorists before him had done and said. Such an attitude also commends him as a sample for this study. A further advantage is his chronological position, which is slightly later than that of the other writers mentioned, and which thus allows him to speak of a later generation of composers—the Josquin generation—in which Renaissance style, the intended subject of this essay, reached maturity.

With respect to the two areas of theory (modes and counterpoint) mentioned above as of principal interest to analysis, Aaron is particularly noted for his discussions of modality in contrapuntal music, a subject he was the first to explore intensively. His discussions of counterpoint are based largely on Tinctoris and Gafori and expand on them only slightly. Nonetheless, Hugo Riemann has characterized Aaron's work as the best introduction to counterpoint available from that time.[3] Accordingly, a summary of Aaron's statements in these two areas will be presented, followed by commentary on their possible application to analytical problems. Thereafter some suggestions will be made as to the most effective procedures now available for analysis of Renaissance music, with illustrations from selected compositions from Aaron's period.

The limitations of this approach are obvious and acknowledged. This essay is not intended as an exhaustive survey of every possible insight that may be gained from Renaissance theory, but rather a sampling, both of the theory and the music, as an indication of some of the possibilities and probable limitations. Other theorists may present insights which escape Aaron, and other compositions than those examined may present different problems of analysis. A geographic limitation is implicit in the choice of theorists and composers, since the treatises and compositions to be cited all appeared in Italy, whatever the origin of their authors. Italy was unquestionably the leading nation in music theory at this period, but other nations have just claims to eminence in composition, and differences of national style might conceivably emerge in analysis of tonal structure. Such differences, if they exist, would be of great interest as differentiations of style

---

[3] Hugo Riemann, *Geschichte der Musiktheorie im IX.–XIX. Jahrhundert* (2d ed., 1919; reprinted, Hildesheim, Olms, 1961), p. 357.

beyond those already known, but their establishment is beyond the scope of the present study.

MODES

AS INDICATED above, Pietro Aaron was perhaps the first theorist to consider explicitly and in detail the modality of contrapuntal music. His *Trattato della natura et cognitione di tutti gli tuoni di canto figurato* (Venice, 1525; supplement, 1531), the relevant portions of which appear in translation in Strunk's *Source Readings in Music History*,[4] was probably the first treatise to examine the question at all thoroughly, and its unique value in this respect is enhanced by citation of examples of each mode, taken from contemporary compositions. Aaron held to the traditional system of eight church modes which had governed music theory through the Middle Ages and early Renaissance. Thus he had some difficulty with compositions using the diatonic scales on C and A which Glareanus some twenty years later accepted as modes in their own right.

Aaron's method of determining mode in polyphony was essentially to consider the mode of the tenor part to be the mode of the whole complex of voices. Here obviously is a crucial problem. The concept of mode was developed to explain the behavior of the unaccompanied chant, and its application to polyphonic complexes necessarily, it would seem, leaves unaccounted for the relationship between or among voices, the chordal element. In any case, this aspect of polyphony in its relation to modality did not attract the attention of Aaron or any other theorist of his period.

The mode of the tenor was determined by more or less traditional concepts of modal theory. The final (the tone, analogous to a tonic, on which the melody ended) and the range encompassed above or below the final were the two principal such concepts. The normal finals were D, E, F, and G, with two of the eight modes sharing each final. Medieval and Renaissance theory customarily referred to the modes by number: the first and second modes shared the final on D and were authentic and plagal respectively, third and fourth similarly on E, fifth and sixth on F, and seventh and eighth on G. The terms Dorian, Phrygian, Lydian, and Mixolydian were

---

4 Oliver Strunk, *Source Readings in Music History* (New York, Norton, 1950), pp. 205–18.

not often used in Medieval or early Renaissance theory, but are convenient
when no distinction is made between authentic and plagal on the same
final, so that Dorian refers to both modes ending on D, Phrygian on E,
etc., and they will be used in the latter sense hereafter.

The range was stated in terms of a combination of the perfect fifth and
the perfect fourth into an octave. The final was the lowest note of the fifth,
and the fourth was located conjunctly either above or below the fifth; the
range thus lay entirely above or centered around the final. In the former case,
the mode was called *authentic*; in the latter, *plagal*. The three tones and one
semitone which the diatonic perfect fifth contains may appear in four
different orders: TSTT, STTT, TTTS, and TTST, from the lowest to highest
tone. These are the four species of fifths described in modal theory, which
are characteristic respectively of Dorian, Phrygian, Lydian, and Mixolydian modes. Three species of perfect fourths were similarly described:
TST, STT, TTS. The first species is found in both Dorian and Mixolydian, the
second in Phrygian, and the third in Lydian. Each mode thus had a specific
ordering of tones and semitones, and the transposed modes, to be discussed below, depend on this fact.

In practice, melodies might occupy more or less than a full octave, and
Aaron's method of dealing with this situation was essentially that which
had been followed by other theorists in Italy for more than two hundred
years. The inclusion in a melody of only one tone or semitone above or
below the modal octave was not usually considered abnormal. Melodies
which filled the range of both the authentic and plagal modes and had the
same final were assigned on the basis of predominance of one or the other
range in the *tessitura*. The term *modus mixtus* was often applied to such
melodies. Melodies of limited range caused difficulty when they lay within
the area common to both authentic and plagal; these also were determined
by the predominance of high or of low range within their compass.

Italian modal theory formulated one concept of interest to the modern
analyst, *modus commixtus*, in which a melody during its course emphasizes
or outlines intervals, mainly fourths and fifths, which are characteristic of
modes other than the melody's own complementary plagal or authentic.
For example, a melody in the first mode (final d, range d–d¹, fifth d–a,
fourth a–d¹) stresses in its course the fifths f–c¹ and g–d¹, as leaps or as

prominent tones in a stepwise succession. These belong respectively to the fifth and seventh modes, and such a melody would be called "first mode *commixtus* with fifth and seventh." The theorists thus were not unaware of the fact that a melody may have structural features which are not taken into account in a simple classification scheme of range and final. Such an observation would be all the more true in polyphony, where the emphasis on and expansion of intervals other than those formed in a triad above the final can be structural factors of considerable importance.

Aaron and his predecessors seemingly accounted for all possible contingencies by their categorizations of melodies of exceptional range, but he himself was finally moved to state that some melodies cannot be judged by all this apparatus. These he called *euphoniaci*, "of good sonority," indicating that they do not show the octave, fifth, or fourth characteristic of one or another mode. Edward E. Lowinsky has suggested that Aaron here referred to melodies in what Glareanus later called Ionian or Aeolian modes,[5] but a pupil of Aaron's, Illuminato Aiguino, says Aaron was speaking of melodies which occupy a range no larger than a third.[6] Aaron may have had in mind the Gregorian tones for lessons and prayers, which have never been assigned to a mode. Such a melody, though, would seldom if ever be used as the tenor of a polyphonic composition.

Although Gregorian chant and modal theory are fundamentally diatonic, both always provided for at least one chromatic tone, B♭, which in the chant most often alternates with B♮, seldom occurring alone throughout a melody. In modal theory, B♭ was considered to be an inflection introduced to avoid a tritone in the melody, assuming that the mode still ended on its customary final; the mode was then considered to have undergone no essential change. This notion was adequate for the chant, but polyphonic compositions from earliest times had used a signature of one flat throughout a composition, especially with final on F, which could produce scales not found among the eight church modes. Aaron retained the traditional view on this point, which was first challenged only by Glareanus, whose system of twelve modes took account of the untraditional scales.

5 Edward E. Lowinsky, *Tonality and Atonality in Sixteenth-Century Music* (Berkeley and Los Angeles, University of California Press, 1961), p. 34.

6 Illuminato Aiguino, *Il Tesoro Illuminato di tutti i tuoni di canto figurato* (Venice, Giovanni Varisco, 1581), f. 11v.

Modal theory had always admitted the possibility of transposed modes, with the final a fifth or fourth higher than normal. A set of cofinals or irregular finals, on which the modes could end in the event of transposition, was thus postulated. Such transpositions had evidently been performed on a number of chant melodies to make them conform to the diatonic scale (including B♭) which Medieval theory gradually evolved. Transposition in polyphony was of a somewhat different order, basically a matter of adding one or, more rarely, two flats to the signature and forming the traditional modal patterns at a new tonal level, e.g., Dorian with one flat and final on G. Thus modal theory in polyphony had a different sort of transposition to explain, but the concept itself could be retained from monophony. Theorists from Tinctoris on tended to refer to polyphony in discussing modes, and transposition and its concomitant cofinals were accordingly spoken of in the newer sense.

Aaron gave some attention to the notes on which a melody in each mode might begin, but the possibilities are so numerous that the initial tone is of little use as a modal determinant. With only a few exceptions, any mode may begin with any note. The fact is of some interest to the analyst of polyphony, since one is thus cautioned against assuming that a mode is necessarily determined by the first tone or first chord in a composition. One other concept derived from the chant enters into Aaron's theory of mode in polyphony, the difference (*differentia*). This is the note or formula of notes which concludes the chanting of a psalm tone; most of the tones have several possible differences. That used is chosen so that a smooth connection may be made to the first phrase of the antiphon which follows as well as precedes a chanted psalm in the Roman liturgy. Aaron uses the difference to explain irregular closes in polyphonic music which do not coincide with what has gone before according to conventional modal theory.

Aaron puts all of the above concepts at the service of polyphony by applying them to the tenor of the composition (or to any other part which contains a preexisting melody). The final, range, and species of fourth and fifth remain the principal means of determining the mode. Any one of the four regular finals unequivocally determines the mode, with the further distinction of range between authentic and plagal, unless there is a key signature.

If the tenor closes on a note other than a regular final, this note may be a cofinal or a difference. The latter term was invoked for compositions ending on A or C with no signature, which later were considered Aeolian or Ionian.

Such a use of the difference does not seem entirely adequate, even on Aaron's own terms, since every note may be a difference in several different modes. In dealing with transposed modes, the concept of species is of prime importance, since even if a regular final were used, the tones and semitones above it would be changed in order, and the species of fourth or fifth would thus be different. Thus with the final on G but with one flat in the signature, the species of fifth would not be that of the seventh and eighth modes but of the first and second; Dorian would be the correct designation.

A significant exception to this principle is that group of compositions with a final on D or F and one flat in the signature. Here Aaron ignores the difference in species and maintains that such compositions are Dorian or Lydian respectively. Even though B♭ appears throughout, he insists that it is only an inflection of the diatonic mode. *Musica ficta* would presumably be related to mode as a more temporary inflection, which would nonetheless effect significant changes on the tonal structure at times, but Renaissance theory never spoke directly of this relationship.

After describing these basic principles in the first three chapters of *Trattato*, Aaron examines each of the four pairs of authentic and plagal modes in the next four chapters, giving examples of each possible note on which the tenor may end in a given mode, and citing compositions as examples of each. The majority of his examples can be classified according to his criteria with no essential injustice to the nature of the music, as long as the tenor alone is considered. It does not seem necessary to comment on them in detail here.

The major exceptions to this regularity are those compositions which are better considered Aeolian or Ionian. Some examples having D as final and one flat in the signature fall into this category, as do every one of his examples with F as final, since all have a signature of one flat. The pure Lydian mode was almost nonexistent in polyphonic music because of the tritone with the final, F–B.

Aaron assigns compositions ending on A with no signature to either

Dorian or Phrygian, which he distinguishes by the internal cadences and species of interval used in each composition. Those assigned to Dorian tend to cadence often on D, and the fifth and fourth of the Dorian mode, D–A and A–D, are thus emphasized. The A at the close is then considered a cofinal or difference.

The Phrygian pieces cadence often on E. Their designation seems to derive from the fact that C and A are the reciting tones of the third and fourth modes respectively. Chants and polyphony in either mode emphasize both notes strongly, so a composition stressing A and E would undoubtedly have sounded Phrygian to Aaron, even though A rather than E was the final. The fifth A–E is usually prominent in polyphony in the Phrygian modes, both melodically and harmonically, sometimes so prominent that the close on E sounds surprising and inconclusive. The close relationship of the modes ending on E and A was well known in the sixteenth century, as is shown in statements made by Glareanus and Zarlino.[7]

Several compositions endings on C are assigned to the Mixolydian mode, but would be more adequately described by the later term "Ionian," since they lack a signature. One composition has its final on B♭, with a signature of one flat—Josquin's motet *O admirabile commercium*.[8] Aaron considers it to be in transposed Lydian, but E♭ appears so frequently, either indicated or required by the most basic rules of *musica ficta*, that Ionian is the more accurate designation.

Valuable as Aaron's pioneering effort was, it was superseded by the system of twelve modes advanced by Glareanus and Zarlino. Aaron's chief problems were the Aeolian and Ionian melodies that only with difficulty fit into the eight-mode system, and he was not so radical (or original) as to propose fundamental changes in the traditional system. But whether eight or twelve modes are used, only one part at a time is analyzed; how adequately the whole composition can be analyzed by categorizing each part separately is a more fundamental question. Before considering it, let us complete our examination of Aaron's theory.

[7] Strunk, pp. 224, 253–54.

[8] Josquin des Prés, *Werken: Motetten*, A. Smijers, ed. (Amsterdam, Vereeniging voor Nederlandsche Muziekgeschiedenis, 1922), I, 24. Examples reprinted by permission of the publisher.

COUNTERPOINT

AARON's writings about counterpoint are based more directly on the work of previous theorists than are his descriptions of the modes in polyphony. Tinctoris inaugurated a new manner of treating counterpoint in theoretical writing, which later writers followed for a century or more. This new manner stemmed from the new style of composition established during the fifteenth century by Dunstable, Dufay, and their successors, of which a leading characteristic was a richer, more sonorous chordal texture. Tinctoris and his successors concerned themselves in turn primarily with this element, with the vertical rather than the horizontal aspect of melodic combination. Paradoxically, the modes, the principal construct which defined tonality in Renaissance theory, were defined in linear terms, while counterpoint, the relation between two or more musical lines, was discussed in vertical terms. In each area the opposite view prevails today.

Aaron's treatment of counterpoint follows the pattern set by Tinctoris and continued by Gafori and others, but Aaron adds his own observations and modifications of his predecessors' work. The principal sources for his writing on counterpoint are *Libri Tres de Institutione Harmonica* (Bologna, 1516) and *Toscanello in Musica* (Venice; 1523; revised with supplement 1529, 1539, 1562); a few amplifications and emendations are found in *Lucidario in Musica* (Venice, 1545). He offered few examples from the literature to support his statements, since his purpose was avowedly didactic, and he often described techniques in a simple form that would be more elaborated in most actual compositions. Accordingly, some comparison with practice will be supplied as a commentary. For this purpose, four more or less representative compositions will be used: two three-voice pieces from the *Odhecaton*, Brumel's motet *Mater Patris* and Agricola's chanson *Ales mon cor*;[9] Josquin's four-voice motet *O admirabile commercium*; and a frottola attributed to "Aron" which is possibly by Pietro Aaron himself, *Io non posso piu durare*, from Petrucci's *Frottole Libro Quinto*.[10] All four will be analyzed below.

[9] *Harmonice Musices Odhecaton A*, Helen Hewitt, ed.; literary texts, Isabel Pope, ed. (Cambridge, The Mediaeval Academy of America, 1942), pp. 351, 357. Examples reprinted by permission of the editor.

[10] Ottaviano Petrucci, *Frottole Libro Quinto* (Venice, 1505); my transcription appears below as Example 18. The question of Pietro Aaron's authorship of the piece is discussed in my dissertation, pp. 19–21.

The first step for the theorist of counterpoint in Aaron's time was to classify intervals into consonances and dissonances. Aaron's division is entirely conventional; perfect octaves, fifths, and unisons and their compounds are perfect consonances; thirds and sixths are imperfect consonances; and seconds, sevenths, augmented fourths, and diminished fifths are dissonant. The perfect fourth he considered a dissonance in two-part writing, but consonant when supported by a third voice sounding a third or fifth below, thus following Tinctoris' lead in rejecting Medieval tradition and favoring current practice. This division of consonance and dissonance would still be accepted today, and it hardly needs rigorous confirmation from the literature of the period. Renaissance music consistently treated thirds and sixths as consonances coordinate with the fourths, fifths, and octaves which had been the basis of Medieval music; frequent use of the complete triad is one feature which distinguishes Renaissance music from that which precedes it.

Aaron was one of the first theorists to state a preference for four voice parts, although practice had established such a preference some fifty years earlier. Compositions around 1500 amply confirm his preference, since four voices are used more often than any other number. *Toscanello* and *De Institutione Harmonica* both include the famous description of the new manner of composition in which composers carried forward all the parts simultaneously instead of writing them successively. Both of these considerations, like *musica ficta*, will seldom be central to analytical investigation, though they may bear on it in certain instances. The situation might equally well be reversed, though, when detailed analysis confirms or denies a preliminary hypothesis on any of these points that had been formed before analysis is undertaken.

The necessity to begin and end only with consonances was mentioned by Aaron as by his predecessors. Aaron went so far as to allow the initial sonority to be an imperfect consonance, which the generation of Tinctoris had not condoned, insisting on a perfect consonance only. In this license, Aaron appears to have been advanced, judging from a limited sampling of music. In the first volume of the *Historical Anthology of Music*,[11] in numbers

[11] Archibald T. Davison and Willi Apel, *Historical Anthology of Music* (Cambridge, Harvard University Press, 1957), vol. I.

73 to 86, dating from late fifteenth century, those compositions were tabulated which begin with a simultaneous chord or interval, or which begin as transcribed with a point of imitation in which the *comes* enters less than a measure after the *dux*. The preference is overwhelmingly in favor of beginning only with perfect consonances, on the order of eighteen to one. In the next section of the same anthology, numbers 87 to 139, dating from the first half of the sixteenth century, the proportion is less lopsided, four to one, but the preference is still clear. Some difference according to genre would seem likely; secular vocal music and the lighter types of instrumental music might well employ the less formal beginning of an imperfect consonance more frequently. But the nature of the opening sonority is of less moment for analysis than its function in the composition's tonal structure.

Aaron dutifully repeats the rule against parallel perfect consonances, which had been increasingly observed by composers from the fifteenth century on. The most extensive exceptions to the rule are the seemingly intentional, parodistic crudities found in some villanescas and related genres.[12] Rare examples may be found in other, more serious, types of music also, such as the one from Josquin's Vergilian motet, *Dulces exuviae* (Example 1).[13]

EXAMPLE 1   *Dulces exuviae*   Josquin

Aaron and most other theorists, past and present, would take exception to this example. The analyst's chief interest in such progressions will be to

12 Gustave Reese, *Music in the Renaissance* (New York, Norton, 1954), p. 333.

13 *Fünf Vergil-Motetten*, Helmuth Osthoff, ed., in *Das Chorwerk, No. 54* (Wolfenbüttel, Moseler, 1956), p. 6, has a similar transcription. Reduced note values and bar lines are those of the modern edition in this and all other musical examples.

EXAMPLE 2

determine how they arise. What is the background of the progression? Are the parallels essential chordal intervals, or are they figuration? Their role in the larger context is always foremost. In Josquin's motet both fifths are chordal; both tones of the first are suspended, resulting in simultaneous 7–6 and 4–3 suspensions over the B♭ of the bassus. Both suspensions attain conclusive resolution only on the metrically strong third quarter of bar 42. D is preceded by an unaccented anticipation, while the resolution of A to G appears to have been ornamented in two stages, first by a leap to F preceding the resolution, then by the eighth-note G as a passing tone between A and F, as shown in Example 2.

Decoration of the resolution could have eliminated the parallel fifths, but in the final stage of the evolution as suggested above, the accumulated figuration ends with the same parallels from which the simple chord succession started. As a trait of style, either accepted or frowned on by theory, parallel fifths may be explained by analysis; but in examining tonal structure, forbidden parallels are seldom of primary importance.

The succession of a perfect fifth to a diminished fifth had been allowed by Ramos de Pareja some forty years before Aaron, so it is not surprising that Aaron allows it also, at least in his final statement on the subject. Aaron supplies his own examples, to which one may be added from the four specimen compositions, although the succession in the latter is reversed, the diminished fifth preceding the perfect. In *O admirabile commercium*, bar 38, an example may be found (Example 3).

Interestingly enough, both tones of the diminished fifth are consonant with the bassus, while both tones of the perfect fifth are figuration; the upper tone, A, is passing, the lower tone, D, a neighbor, following the resolution of the suspended F. Further consideration suggests that the chord beginning bar 38 is a G-minor triad in root position. The explanation of the superius would be the same as above, but the altus would be con-

EXAMPLE 3   *O admirabile commercium*   Josquin

sidered to have undergone rhythmic manipulation so that the E, which would be a passing tone between F and D in the simplest version of the succession, is delayed by the suspended F, so that it appears over the G in the bassus, not the F with which it really belongs (Example 4).

EXAMPLE 4

Although a consonant sonority is formed when the E sounds, and then only during the G of the bassus, the sense of the passage still seems to be I–II–V–I rather than I–VII⁶–V–I, to express it in modern terminology. Aaron, of course, only indicated the possibility of a similar succession of intervals without explaining why they might be used or what their meaning would be. The same may be said of his acceptance of the diminished fifth in ⁶₃ chords, although his examples in *Lucidario* seem to indicate what may be the fact in practice, that such chords tend to appear most regularly in the approach to a cadence.

Aaron has remarkably little to say about dissonance treatment, compared to the detail with which Tinctoris and Gafori discussed the subject. These two predecessors were somewhat more restrictive than practice would indicate, and Aaron was perhaps in general agreement with them. In any case, he says little more than that dissonance should appear quickly and unobtrusively in the middle of a progression, not at the beginning or end, and in the shortest note values. (Spataro pointed out to him in a letter that this description does not take account of the suspension.)[14] These principles were observed for the most part by contemporary composers, but in combining simultaneous dissonances in several voices, they sometimes may have broken the spirit if not the letter of the rule. The four specimen compositions present few examples of dissonance treatment worthy of extended comment. Passing tones and neighbor tones, accented or not, are introduced largely on weak beats and in small values, most often semiminims, while suspensions are properly prepared and resolved, often in longer values. One exceptional handling of a suspension is found in the Agricola chanson, bar 34, in which the dissonance is quitted by leap without resolution (Example 5). Another exception to the stepwise resolution

EXAMPLE 5   *Ales mon cor*   Agricola

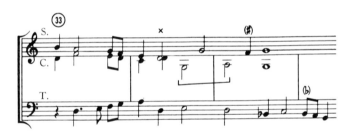

of dissonance (a principle nowhere stated by Aaron) is the figure which fills in a descending fourth incompletely with only the upper of the two passing tones between (Example 6). Josquin's motet uses this figure especially frequently, notably over the words "dignatus est" around bar 65; Jeppesen observes that the figure was common in Josquin's period.[15]

14 Rome, Biblioteca Apostolica Vaticana, Ms. Vat. Lat. 5318, f. 210r–v. The passage is quoted in my dissertation, p. 344. Knud Jeppesen, "Eine musiktheoretische Korrespondenz des früheren Cinquecento," *Acta Musicologica*, XIII (1941), 27, called attention to this passage.

15 Knud Jeppesen, *The Style of Palestrina and the Dissonance* (London, Oxford University Press, 1927), pp. 191 ff. It can also be found in Medieval music as early as the works of Leoninus.

EXAMPLE 6

In conjunction with two simple passing tones of differing time values, a pungent combination is formed in bar 90 of the same motet, but the direction of the voices is clear, moving from an E♭- to a B♭- triad (Example 7). Other simultaneous passing motions form strong successions of dissonances

EXAMPLE 7   *O admirabile commercium*   Josquin

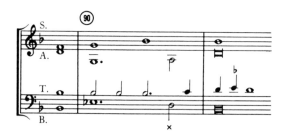

in the midst of a clearly directed succession, as in bar 15 of the same motet (Example 8; see also Example 5, bar 33). Such progressions, especially when clarified by a sustained tone in another voice, were not foreign even to Palestrina.[16]

EXAMPLE 8   *O admirabile commercium*   Josquin

16 *Ibid.*, p. 144.

CHORDS

PIETRO AARON is one of the most prominent figures in the early history of chordal awareness in music theory. In *Toscanello*, he devotes ten chapters and a large table to describing possible ways to construct a chord in four parts. The chord in Aaron's description is generated by the interval between cantus and tenor; this interval gives rise to one or more possible positions of the bassus, each of which in turn generates one or more possible positions of the altus. The modern method of computing chords from the bass had not yet come into use at this time, and did not do so until closer to the seventeenth century. Though Aaron's method suggests that the composer write one voice part at a time and then fill in the others, the contradiction with his preference for simultaneous composition is probably not so strong as it may appear. Hugo Riemann observed that the tables of chords could very well be used in simultaneous composition of the voices, since the composer would probably situate the cantus or tenor first, then fit in the other voices one by one, and proceed from chord to chord in this manner through the composition.[17]

It would be a thankless task to locate examples of every chord that Aaron describes; none of them seem implausible in the light of musical style at the time of *Toscanello*. Only a painstaking, extensive statistical survey would reveal how thoroughly Aaron covered the subject and how frequently his combinations were actually used or not used, and such information hardly seems useful even if it were available. His table was probably intended more as a guide than as a complete list of possibilities. Of more pertinence to the present study is the distaste for $^6_3$ chords which he expresses in one of the chapters on chord construction; he regards such chords as rough and to be used only in unavoidable necessity. In view of the frequency with which $^6_3$ chords occurred in approaching the cadence in fifteenth-century music, Aaron expresses indirectly a taste for the more modern cadences which use the cadence now termed authentic in the bass. In the four examples, however, several $^6_3$ chords may be found, several but not all at cadences. In Josquin's motet, for instance, several cadences are approached by a $^6_3$ chord, while other such chords, e.g., in bar 18, cannot be so explained. Some of

---

17 Riemann, p. 355.

them result from ornamentation of a $\frac{5}{3}$ chord by neighbor-note motion over a sustained bass, as in bars 49–50. In any case, Aaron seems somewhat restrictive in this statement, less in tune with practice than usual.

One of the more interesting features of *De Institutione Harmonica* is its discussion of chord progressions in which the soprano and tenor move in parallel thirds or sixths. The problem Aaron considers is how to distribute altus and bassus in such progressions so that parallel fifths and octaves may be avoided. His solutions have the bassus moving 8–10–8–10 or 10–8–10–8 with the cantus, while the altus fills in the chords so as to make complete $\frac{5}{3}$ or $\frac{6}{3}$ triads (Example 9).

EXAMPLE 9

Such progressions would be found most readily in compositions of a relatively chordal texture; of the examples chosen only the frottola is such, and it happens not to contain any such progression. One example may be found in Josquin's *Ave Maria . . . Virgo serena*, bars 40–44,[18] in which superius and tenor have parallel descending sixths (Example 10). The bass,

18 Des Prés, p. 1.

EXAMPLE 10 *Ave Maria*   Josquin

however, is not entirely like Aaron's examples. Other such examples surely exist, possibly more ornamented than Aaron's illustrations.

CADENCES

FOR HIS DESCRIPTIONS of cadences, Aaron relied but little on Tinctoris or Gafori, neither of whom said much on the subject. He is perhaps most dependent on the treatise of Guilelmus Monachus, *De preceptis artis musice*,[19] but is clearer and more systematic. The cadence, like the chord progressions described above, is determined principally by cantus and tenor; the altus and bassus fit in according to the motion of the other two voices. The basic cadential pattern is a sixth between tenor and cantus, which expands stepwise to an octave; the sixth must be major, its upper tone raised through *musica ficta* if necessary. The cantus ordinarily has the same tone for its antepenultimate as for its final, thus describing a lower neighbor-note motion in the final three notes, tonic–leading-tone–tonic. The tenor's antepenultimate may form an octave, fifth, or sixth with the cantus, and the cantus may suspend this tone to make a 7–6 suspension over the penultimate of the tenor (Example 11).

EXAMPLE 11

19 Edmond de Coussemaker, *Scriptorum de musica medii aevi nova series* (1864–76; reprinted, Hildesheim, Olms, 1963), III, 295b–297a especially.

In combination with these two voices, Aaron prefers that the bassus describe the cadence later designated as perfect or v–i, doubling the tenor's final note at the unison or octave. The bassus of the antepenultimate chord is dependent on the interval between cantus and tenor. The altus is a filling voice in the cadence, taking the tones not sounded by the other voices and usually ending on the fifth above the bassus (Example 12). In addition to these general descriptions, Aaron shows how to modify the cadence for a composition in which equal voices are used; the resulting narrow compass usually demands a cadence of cantus and tenor at the unison rather than the octave.

EXAMPLE 12

Aaron's descriptions of cadences are unquestionably in accord with practice, and there seems no need to adduce examples of the fact. He refers more to final than internal cadences perhaps, since the bass at internal cadences often moves stepwise, like the tenor in Aaron's examples. Aaron gives the simplest, most straightforward, possibilities; in practice the cadence could be prolonged, ornamented, or covered in some manner. In *Trattato*, Aaron himself mentions the possibility of a prolonged final cadence in which one or more voices continue some sort of embellishing motion while the cadential tone is sustained in at least one other voice; *O admirabile commercium* is one of many compositions by Josquin which end with such cadences. In the same motet, several cadences are covered in order to avoid a strong closure. The superius cadence in bar 17 is turned aside by the entry of tenor and bassus so that a chord on D is formed rather than the F-chord indicated by the superius. In bar 70, the cadence on C, an intermediate stepwise cadence, is further covered by the altus' motion to the sixth above the bass; when it resolves to the fifth, the superius enters with a new phrase. Such overlapping, of course, is characteristic of polyphonic textures at this period, and Aaron's descriptions would apply most literally to chordal textures or to final cadences.

IMITATION

AARON is one of the first theorists to describe techniques of imitation. He is concerned only with strict imitation or canon in the modern sense of the word. "Canon" in Aaron's time referred generally to an inscription, sometimes in the form of a riddle, placed at the head of a composition to indicate some particulars about its performance. The term for strict imitation was "*fuga*," which received its present meaning definitively only in the eighteenth century. One passage in Aaron's *Lucidario* suggests that the shift in meaning had begun as early as the sixteenth century. In it he discusses

EXAMPLE 13

a musical example containing two voices in free imitation, which he says is erroneously called by some *fuga* (Example 13). It cannot be *fuga* because that category must have absolute identity between the two voices, in quality as well as size of intervals. Since the example lacks such identity, Aaron says it may be called canon.[20] Aaron seems to use the terms in the opposite relation to each other from that now current, i.e., "*fuga*" for the stricter form of imitation than canon, but "canon" does refer to an imitative technique rather than a superscription, of which the example has no hint.

[20] Aaron, *Lucidario in Musica*, Book II, ch. 10, f. 9v.

EXAMPLE 14

Aaron defines *imitatio* or *fugatio* (the latter apparently Aaron's own variant of *fuga*) in *De Institutione Harmonica* as the repetition by one voice of the solmization syllables of a preceding or following (!) voice but at different pitches, resulting in the appearance of one voice following or imitating another. He designates as the interval of imitation the distance between the voices at the entrance of the *comes*, not, as is customary now as well as in Aaron's time, the interval between the first notes of *dux* and *comes*. The latter is the more essential relationship of pitch between the two voices. Aaron's examples have the *comes* follow the *dux* at a distance of only one or two notes and proceed in parallel intervals with it throughout. The subjects are ascending or descending scale fragments of five or six notes; the *comes* begins with or immediately after the *dux* (Example 14). From Aaron's description based on simultaneous intervals, these examples are called *fugatio* at the third, sixth, tenth; fifth and sixth; sixth and fifth; and third and sixth.

Such imitation is, of course, rudimentary at best. Examples probably exist of simple ascending hexachords in canon as Aaron described them, but most compositions have more elaborate musical subjects, whether for strict or free imitation. The close interval of time between voices is quite common at the period. It may be found often in a composition which exploits paired voices, such as *O admirabile commercium*. This motet even starts with the intervals 5–6–5 between the voices, employing the syncopated relationship described by Aaron. The small time interval may also be seen in *Mater Patris*, bars 33–35, 40 ff, and 59 ff. A very close approximation of Aaron's description of 5–6–5–6 progressions is found in Josquin's

Ave Maria, bars 94–101, between superius and tenor (Example 15).
It seems more accurate to say that Aaron described in its simplest terms
a principle that could be applied as well to more elaborate melodic lines.
He was certainly in touch with what composers were doing, but his descriptions fall short of the complexities of practice.

EXAMPLE 15   *Ave Maria*   Josquin

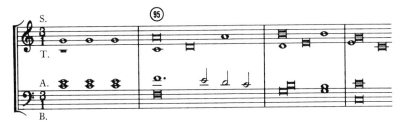

LIMITATIONS OF AARON'S THEORIES

THE PRECEDING sentence might serve as a description of Aaron's work as
a whole in relation to the goals of analysis. He was a perceptive and open-
minded theorist in his day, but his conceptual framework does not carry
us far toward the goal of comprehensive analysis of tonal structure, neither
with respect to the modes nor to counterpoint, and the same must be said
of other theorists of the fifteenth and sixteenth centuries, before and after
Aaron.

A basic problem in Aaron's treatment of the modes was mentioned
above: a linear concept is used to analyze music composed of several lines
that move simultaneously and that constantly enter into vertical relationships with one another. The problem remains whether one thinks in terms
of eight, twelve, or two modes. The system of eight modes is less satisfactory for polyphony in its own terms than that of twelve modes, but
neither considers the vital chordal factor. Despite all the apparatus Aaron
invokes to determine the mode, he still ends by talking about individual
lines only. It would be possible to do this for each line in the polyphonic
complex, but this still analyzes line only, not chord, and any thorough
study of tonal structure must include both.

An even more fundamental difficulty is that when a mode has been determined, it is still only a category, such as "major" or "minor." Naming the mode, in other words, is not analysis. In principle, a given mode may be expressed in as many different ways as, say, C major or G minor, and every composition deserves individual study to discover how it expresses its mode or key, and what it has in common with other compositions in the same mode or key. Some aspects of mode, such as cadence patterns and characteristic melodic figures, may be more or less conventional and thus predictable, but in polyphony they do not constitute an entire composition. A further question thus arises: how do these patterns and figures contribute to the expression of the mode by the complete composition? What is the role of everything other than the cadences and melodic figures? It is generally assumed that polyphonic music can be assigned to a mode; writers about Renaissance music frequently do just this, referring not to a single voice but to the entire complex of voices. The assumption perhaps deserves more thorough examination than it has been given, and the analyses offered below will do this as far as the pieces at hand allow. But as stated above, modal assignment only categorizes, it does not analyze. Determining the mode is only a preliminary step in analysis.

The situation is no more satisfactory with Aaron's discussion of counterpoint. He describes several details of motion or vertical relationship with no word about their relationship to a larger framework. His efforts are in roughly the same category as labeling chords by root and position; names are assigned, but function is only hinted at, and even this only in the smallest contexts.

Classifying consonance and dissonance is another preliminary step, but no more than that, in analysis of tonal structure. The number of parts, their order of composition, the interval with which one begins, the successions of intervals allowed or forbidden between two parts, all these, as suggested above, are matters for preparatory investigation; they are seldom the aspects of composition of central and vital importance for the analyst. Knowledge of the conventions of dissonance treatment at a given period may help decide obscure points in a composition, but only in questions of small details.

It is of some importance that theorists were becoming aware of chords as entities in Aaron's time, but composers were certainly far ahead of them.

Western music from the fifteenth century almost to the present has organized its vertical (and, for that matter, its horizontal) element around triads. It makes no sense to ignore this fact or any of its logical consequences simply because it had not made its way fully into consciousness in the early stages of its practical development.

Aaron's descriptions of chord progressions and cadences are likewise of interest in showing current awareness, but are not helpful in analyzing the music because of his failure to comprehend fully both the horizontal and vertical elements in his examples. His descriptions in terms of line fail to do justice to the vertical element, partly because the importance of bass function was not yet recognized at the time. Aaron still thinks of the tenor as the governing voice, which is true in some respects, but not with regard to the vertical complex of voices. One now hears chords with reference to the bass and top voice, and the likelihood is that this was equally true in 1500, despite Aaron's emphasis on the tenor. As evidence for this assertion, one may adduce the acceptance of the perfect fourth or tritone between two upper voices but not with the bass, as well as the common use of disjunct bass lines which seem to function as chordal support rather than as melodic lines of similar character to the other voices. Aaron does not do full justice to what we hear in his cadences and other chord progressions, which are in any case fragments. The latter is true also of his descriptions of imitation. The use of imitative technique is of highest significance in defining style and determining formal plan, but understanding of tonal structure depends at least as much on the composite result of an imitative texture: what do the voices sound like as a whole?

ANALYTIC PROCEDURES

THE RESULTS of our investigation thus far seem somewhat negative. Aaron and other theorists of his period offer us little that can be used in analyzing tonal structure, though their writings were surely useful on their own terms. Their analytical limitations appear to stem from the purpose of their treatises; most of their discussions of counterpoint and the modes were addressed to the student who was learning to compose. This is clearly brought out by Giovanni Spataro's comments on *Toscanello* in letters to

Aaron, in which he criticizes Aaron for relaxing some of the stricter requirements of the preceding generation. Spataro says that rules are for the
guidance of the beginner so that his imagination will not run away with
him, and so that he can learn his craft initially in a controlled situation that
presents only limited possibilities. The experienced master does not need
to follow rules, but proceeds according to the dictates of his well-trained
musical instinct.[21] Since the music of interest to the modern analyst is
usually that of the experienced master, contemporary theory will necessarily
bear somewhat indirectly on the problems encountered there.

Theory around 1500 was little interested in analysis as we now understand the term. Aaron, in explaining the modes, cites several examples, but
no detailed analysis of any composition is offered. The compositions are
classified only after he has described the phenomena he wishes to call to
attention, almost as a footnote; indeed, Strunk's translation in *Source
Readings* very logically transfers these references to footnotes extracted
from the main text.

The same situation is true for the most part elsewhere in Aaron's writings;
compositions are sometimes cited to justify a statement, but with no significant analysis. Other theorists, notably Glareanus, do examine individual
works more closely, but the result is still not detailed analysis, but rather
categorization and appreciation. This being the case, it would be unreason-
able to expect sixteenth-century theory to offer the concepts needed for the
most thorough possible analysis of tonal structure. Content and purpose
of the treatises make such an expectation unrealistic.

Since our aims and interests are different from those of the older theory,
we shall have to formulate different techniques more suitable to our goals.
When theory in any period is unable to supply concepts that can account
for the nature of contemporary artistic creation, it is entirely suitable to use
more recent concepts that may realize this goal more effectively. The
question always will arise when taking such an attitude: are we distorting
a work of art by imposing conceptions on it that are foreign to its essential
nature? That is, is it possible to analyze sixteenth-century music properly
with techniques developed in the twentieth century? This question arises

---

[21] Rome, Biblioteca Apostolica Vaticana, Ms. Vat. Lat. 5318, f. 209r. Jeppesen, "Musiktheoretische
Korrespondenz," p. 24, called attention to this passage.

in musicological pursuits other than analysis, it may be noted. Interpretation or classification after gathering raw facts may be in a sense "conjectural" or "unhistorical," but the insight yielded justifies the practice, as long as the historian avoids distortion or suppression of his material. Similarly, attempts to analyze tonal structure may legitimately go beyond sixteenth-century terminology to a valid result when the analytical method does not distort the nature of the music. Here the analyst needs good historical training and good musical sense.

What sort of tools does he need? The most penetrating theoretical concepts available should be used. They should yield valid results on both large and small frames of reference; they should explain details as well as larger aspects of tonal organization and lead finally to comprehension of the tonal plan of the complete work.

These requirements are not fulfilled by conventional methods of analysis. Identification of chords or lists of dissonances and their resolutions do not lead to a larger view; while observing successive points of imitation, changes of texture, and points of arrival at cadences does show major sectional components of the work, but does not explain the internal construction of the sections nor their relationship to one another. I believe that the concepts formulated by Heinrich Schenker offer the most adequate means yet developed for analyzing the music of the Renaissance, as of all other periods of Western history with the possible exception of some music of the last few decades. Schenker, of course, wrote almost exclusively about the music of the eighteenth and nineteenth centuries, but others have shown the relevance of Schenker's procedures to earlier and more recent music.[22]

This method of analysis fulfills the requirements set forth in every respect. It accounts for every note in a composition in relation to its immediate environment as well as in its role in the tonal plan of the whole. It gives full consideration to both linear and vertical aspects of the music, the interrelation of which is so crucial in all periods. It sets forth clearly the goals of musical motion and the means of reaching them. It relies on the ear as the

---

[22] Notably Felix Salzer in *Structural Hearing: Tonal Coherence in Music* (2nd ed.; New York, Dover Publications, 1962), also in his article in this publication. Terminology used in the discussions below follows that of *Structural Hearing*.

final judge and does not impose analytical solutions that cannot be verified by aural experience. Finally, it makes possible a coherent history of the development of tonal structure in Western music complementary to the detailed history of musical style which musicology has already built up. This historical coherence does much to recommend and justify the method.

In support of these assertions, analyses, partial or complete, will be offered of the four compositions mentioned above. The analyses will be in the form of graphs which indicate successive stages of reduction from full detail to the basic structure which underlies the work or passage in question. In the commentary on the graphs, the term "harmony" is reserved for the I–V–I progression, its elaboration through an intervening chord preceding the V (I–II–V–I, I–IV–V–I, etc.), its incomplete forms, I–V or V–I, and analogous progressions involving the fifth relationship with other scale degrees. In music around 1500, harmonic relationships tend to assert themselves most strongly and consistently at points of cadence. Such progressions had been used, it appears, infrequently and without consistency before the fifteenth century, so that solid experience in their use was hardly more than a century old when these pieces were written, and the harmonic element was by no means as pervasive as it became later. Chord progressions other than those mentioned above are, by and large, contrapuntal, arising out of voice leading, although instances exist where harmonic and contrapuntal functions overlap.

It should be observed before proceeding that the literary texts of the music under consideration are not a factor in the analyses to be presented. In Renaissance music, sectional divisions tend to be determined by the internal divisions of the text, and the mood of the text or specific words or ideas in it are often reflected in musical terms. These factors are vital elements in the expressive quality of the music, but they do not necessarily influence or depend on the tonal structure. The careful analyst will, of course, be alert to the possibility of any significant relationship between the two, but in the examples at hand no such relationship appears to exist.

ILLUSTRATIONS

1. The first example (Example 16) to be analyzed will be bars 1–22 of Antoine Brumel's motet *Mater Patris*, number 62 in the *Odhecaton*, which

EXAMPLE 16   *Mater Patris*   Brumel

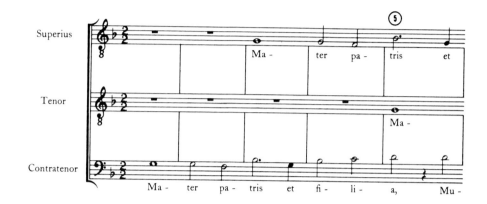

EXAMPLE 16 *(continued)*

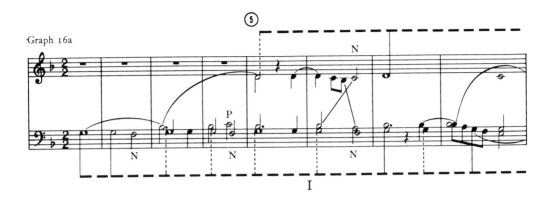

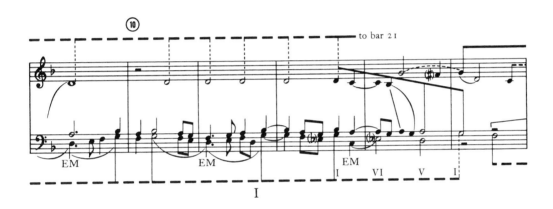

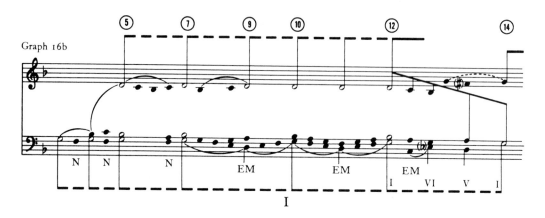

Graph 16b

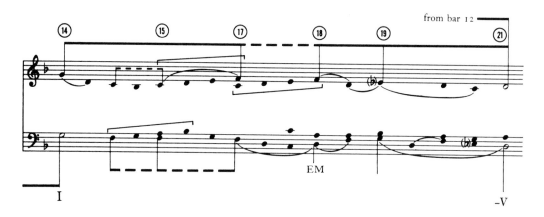

from bar 12

Graph 16c

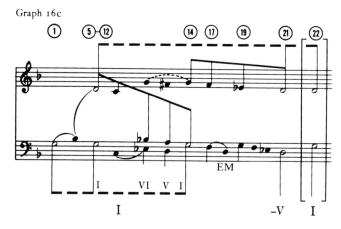

is reasonably straightforward from an analytical standpoint, but which presents some of the special problems encountered in music of this period. Helen Hewitt characterizes this work as a Latin vocal motet, for the three equal voices which were a favorite registration of Brumel, in a predominantly imitative texture. The text from a Marian sequence is set largely syllabically.[23] The piece may be designated as in the Dorian mode transposed to G, with the uniform signature of one flat in all three voices.

All three voice parts in this motet occupy much the same range, a feature more common in Medieval than Renaissance music. Together with similar ranges, another medieval technique is found—continual crossing of voices, so that the highest or lowest sounding part is taken now by one voice, now by another. In terms of the tonal structure, this means that neither the structural top voice nor the structural bass is presented exclusively by one part; rather, both functions pass frequently from one voice to another. Accordingly, the analysis indicates this interchange of function in graph 16a.

The analysis is best approached from graph 16c, which indicates the basic structure and the most essential features of its elaboration; graph 16b shows more of the elaboration, and graph 16a presents all details of the original. In these opening bars the most fundamental structural feature is the progression from a G-minor triad to an open fifth on D. The G-minor triad is prolonged in bars 1–15, with D the principal tone in the top voice. Bars 15–21 accomplish the progression from G minor to D; the top voice upon arrival at the latter chord in bar 21 is still D. It is noteworthy that the D-chord appears in three different forms in this passage: the major triad in bar 13 results from the necessary raising of F according to the rules of *musica ficta*; bars 7–12 and 18 contain several D-minor triads, while the goal of the passage in bar 21 is an open $\frac{8}{5}$ sonority over D, with no third. (The prevalent triadic texture seems to leave no doubt that the open fifth also represents a triad whose quality is undefined due to the absence of its third.) The question arises, to what extent do these chords function harmonically? All are built on D, the dominant of G, but their harmonic tendencies do not seem equal.

When the dominant is a major triad the progression I–V–I is unequivocally harmonic. The combination of root movement by a descending

[23] *Odhecaton* (Hewitt ed.), pp. 72–73.

fifth with the leading tone assures this with no possible doubt. But if v is a minor triad or an $\frac{8}{5}$, the harmonic quality is less explicit due to the lack of the leading tone. From the early Renaissance, the developing harmonic concept shows all three kinds of dominant function in harmonic progressions, but because of the less explicit harmonic quality of minor v or v^8_5, these two chords may at times assume an embellishing and thus contrapuntal function, so that chords which may be labelled I–v♭–I may be a contrapuntal progression similar to I–II–I, I–III–I, and the like. Only context can distinguish between the two possibilities, since a minor v or a v^8_5 in earlier music is ambiguous apart from its context.

The present example illustrates both types of function. The D-chord in bar 13 is unquestionably harmonic, a major triad serving as v in the progression I–VI–V–I, which concludes the prolongation of the G-minor triad. The minor dominants of bars 7–12 are embellishing chords, as indicated by the symbol EM in the graphs; the stepwise bass line and absence of cadential emphasis determine this. The D-minor triad in bar 18 is similarly embellishing; although it moves to a G-minor triad in the next bar, the 5–6 motion over D weakens any harmonic force the bass might tend to have, while the G-minor triad, as explained below, has a relatively dependent function itself. The v^8_5 in bar 21, on the other hand, must be considered harmonic because of its position as the goal of the entire section and the direct return to G minor in bar 22. The absence of any third at all perhaps aids the harmonic function to assert itself as compared to a complete minor triad, but even the latter at this point would have to be taken as harmonic. Such a harmonic function of the minor dominant is still to be found in later periods, where harmonic progressions are used more consistently, it may be noted, expressed either as a relationship between two chords or between two keys.

As the graphs indicate, D is the structural tone of greatest weight throughout the top voice. It is first reached through outlining the G-minor triad, G–B♭–D, in bars 1–5, then retained through bars 5–12 (see graph 16b). The bass for this tone is G throughout the first twelve measures. In bars 12–14, the tenor part takes the D of the structural top voice down to G again over the harmonic progression in the bass. In this harmonic progression, the upper voice contains two tones between D, the top voice of the initial tonic, and A, the top voice of the dominant. Alternate interpretations of the progression would be $\substack{\text{D-C-B}\flat\text{-A-G}\\ \text{I} \quad \text{II}_6 \quad \text{V} \, \text{I}}$, or that given in the graphs, $\substack{\text{D-C-B}\flat\text{-A-G}\\ \text{I} \quad \text{VI} \, \text{V} \, \text{I}}$. In either case, an embellishing bass tone is assumed to give consonant support to that tone in the top voice which is unaccompanied by a member of the harmonic progression. The choice made here between the two possible readings is based on the stronger metric position of the interval E♭–B♭, but even more on the superimposed G above this fifth which moves on to form a counterpoint against the two remaining members of the harmonic progression. These three tones, G–F♯–G, sounding above the conclusion of the tenor's descent, emphasize the three chords in which they respectively appear, and thus the E♭-chord, the VI, is given greater weight than the preceding C-chord.

This superimposed G initiates a melodic progression of higher structural order than the preceding descent from D to G, the main melodic prolongation of the first fourteen measures. The stepwise descent from G to D coincides with the motion of the bass from I to V, and is thus of a higher order than the previous descent, D to G, which occurred while the initial I was still being prolonged. The descent from G to D is prolonged by the motion into the inner-voice D in bar 14, then as the contra brings in the next bass tone, F, in the second half of that measure, the superius counterpoints it with C. The fact that a new point of imitation begins confirms the arrival of a new tone in the bass. These tones are retained through bar 15, but the bass F is presented in that measure by the superius, which continues its descent past C. The top-voice C appears in the tenor and ascends stepwise to F, imitating the motive of the contra and at the same time gaining the top voice of the F-chord, the F in bar 17. The superius in this measure also imitates the contra's subject, but when it attains the F, the bass has moved on to the embellishing chord, D.

The next tone in the top voice, E♭, is approached by way of its incomplete lower neighbor, D, in bar 19; both sound over G in the bass. One might be inclined to consider the G–D between bass and top voice as constituting a return to the tonic, but the preceding F in the top voice moves so strongly to E♭ and on to D in bar 21, that the D in bar 19 with the supporting F (D^6-chord) still appears as part of the embellishing D-sonority of bar 18. The G at the beginning of bar 19 does therefore not represent a return to the tonic, but acts as neighbor note of the following F. From the end of bar 19, the bass G descends stepwise to the cadential D, and the top voice moves in parallel sixths with it and thus approaches its cadential D from below. The D in the contra in bar 20 in a sense anticipates the cadential D in the following measure, but is an embellishment subordinate to the stepwise descent, G–F–(D)–E♭–D. Its subordinate role is further emphasized by the double suspension which sounds above it; these tones resolve only after the contra moves to F.

How might the modality of this example best be described? The categorization as Dorian on G conforms to the signature and final or tonic, but it is contradicted at crucial points within the excerpt. The harmonic progression at the cadence in bars 14–15 contains both E♭ and F♯, and the most important melodic prolongation has E♭, not E, in bar 19. It is true that elsewhere in the excerpt both E♮ and F♮ are used, so the situation is at least ambiguous, but it seems clear that the term "Dorian" can apply only with some reservation. The prominent harmonic elements, as well as the conflicting accidentals, make it possible to speak not only of G–Aeolian but also of G minor in something like the modern sense of the latter term, but no single such designation takes into account all facets of the tonal structure of this work. Most of the accidentals result from applying *musica ficta*, and some uncertainty about the argument may possibly be felt for that reason, but it would seem that those accidentals mentioned are the minimum necessary following the most widely accepted conventions of the period as we now understand them.

2. The next example, Josquin's motet *O admirabile commercium*, bars 1–31 (Example 17), is more typical of Renaissance style in several ways. A brief description of its style would note paired voices (typical of Josquin), imitative counterpoint, and smooth, careful treatment of dissonance which approaches the norms of Palestrina's style. The compass of the voices sets this composition apart from Brumel's work, since the full range of the human voice from soprano to bass is employed. Contrast between high and low voices is thus possible and is exploited in the voice pairing throughout the motet; only the first complete paired statement is examined here. In these opening measures one would undoubtedly remark on the antecedent-consequent relationship between the two phrases. The first statement by

EXAMPLE 17 *O admirabile commercium*

Josquin

EXAMPLE 17 (*continued*)

Graph 17a

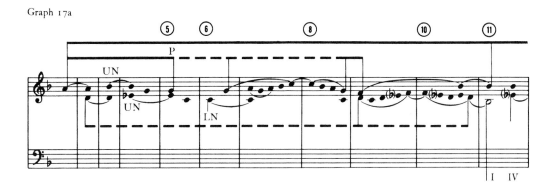

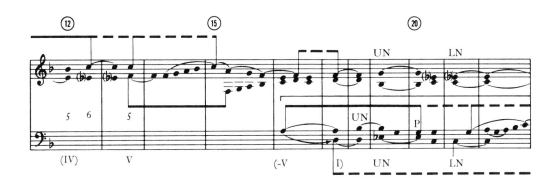

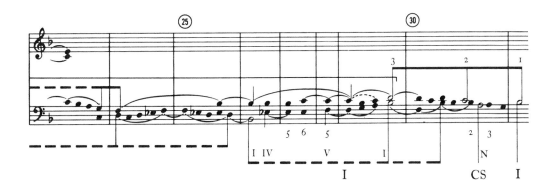

Graph 17b

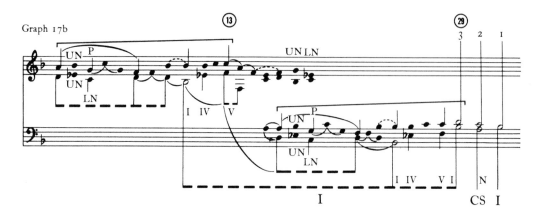

Graph 17c

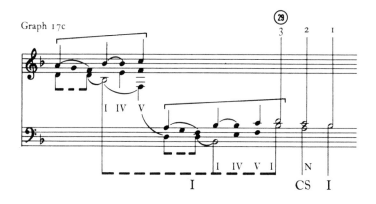

superius and altus reaches an inconclusive cadence in bar 17; the tenor and bassus enter at this point and begin their statement of the same idea, but carry it through to a complete cadence on B♮ in bar 31.

The passage is analyzed in detail in Example 17. The analysis is again best approached through graph 17c, which outlines the basic direction of the motion, while graphs 17b and 17a present successively more detail. Graph 17c shows the unfolding in the structural bass of the tones of the B♭-triad (the tonic), from the initial D in the altus, down a tenth to the B♭ in the bassus in bar 26, then up an octave to the B♭ in bar 31. The top voice does not allow these tones to express a B♭-triad throughout. The first D supports a D-minor triad (bars 1–9) with A and then F in the top voice. This triad constitutes a sort of introduction to the tonic, which appears only in bar 11. It is not unusual in any period for a composition to begin with a sonority other than the tonic, and this example shows what appears to be a typical application of that procedure in the Renaissance. In later periods, the tonic is more often approached directly or indirectly through the dominant, but here the introductory chord is contrapuntal rather than harmonic. It seems likely that a contrapuntal approach to the initial tonic may be more frequent in this period than later; here again the harmonic relationship does not assert itself so strongly as in succeeding centuries. (The Agricola chanson examined in Example 19, however, opens with a v–i progression.)

As the altus moves from D to B♭ (bars 9–11), the superius leaps from F to B♭. The altus moves briefly to E♭ before going on to F in bar 13, above which the superius reaches C. The fifth E♭–B♭ in bar 11 suggests a iv in the middle of the incomplete harmonic progression from i to v, because of the leap to E♭, in the altus. The connection of iv to v, though, because of the 5–6 above E♭, has a strongly contrapuntal character. After the altus reaches F in bar 13, the superius falls from C to F in bar 15 and makes a normal cadence on F, but the entrances of tenor on A and bassus on D (bars 16 and 17), together with the D in the altus, turn the cadence away from F and back to D again for the repetition of the initial phrase in tenor and bassus, one octave lower. This repetition proceeds exactly like the original statement until bar 29, where the top voice, instead of falling away from C over the F in the bass, pushes on up to D. The bass completes a harmonic progression under this ascent, rising from low B♭ to high B♭ through E♭ and F (ɪ–ɪᴠ–ᴠ–ɪ). From this high point of the phrase, a quick descent to the unison cadence ensues.

The goal of the entire passage is the top-voice D in bar 29; everything preceding it strives for this tone. The first attempt is preparatory, reaching only as far as C, but the repetition achieves the goal D (the brackets in graphs 17b and 17c indicate the melodic parallelism of the ascending melodic lines). The chordal support is basically a prolongation of the tonic chord, B♭ major, first through the introductory D-minor triad, then through the incomplete harmonic progression, bars 11–15 (ɪ–ɪᴠ–ᴠ). In the repetition the harmonic progression is complete (ɪ–ɪᴠ–ᴠ–ɪ), and the subsequent descent of the top voice in bars 29–31 is supported by a contrapuntal-structural, not a harmonic, progression, in the bass. This melodic descent supported by ɪ–cs–ɪ, a contrapuntal cadence, is the goal and fulfillment of all the motion preceding.

Some details of the prolongations deserve further comment. The initial D-chord, which appears at first as an open fifth, is prolonged by upper and lower neighbors to each tone of the fifth; parallel fifths are avoided by syncopation at the distance of a brevis. The fifth C–G in bars 5–8 is prolonged by the motion of the upper voice to C and back while C is retained by the lower voice. It is interesting to note that this C (bars 6–7) is held longer by the altus than the corresponding G in the superius (bar 5), in the latter's statement of the same subject. By this means, the time interval between the voices is lengthened so that the third D–F in bar 9 is reached simultaneously by both voices and thus established as a relatively significant interval. Therefore the corresponding tones in the figure of bars 6–9, superius, and 8–10, altus, have different structural values. The A in bar 7 (although prolonged by its own lower neighbor) is a passing tone between G and C, the fifth and octave above the C of the altus, whereas the corresponding D in the altus (bar 9) is a principal tone. The point of these observations is that melodic parallelism is no sure guide to structural value, since other factors can affect the situation decisively.

3. The next example is the frottola attributed to "Aron" (Example 18); this time the complete composition will be examined. Lowinsky has suggested that the frottola is one of the more progressive genres around 1500

in its use of tonality, and the analysis presented here bears this out, though in different terms than those employed by Lowinsky.[24] This piece conforms very well to Reese's general description of frottolas as dominated by treble and bass. The altus here is definitely a filler voice, leaping sometimes so much, as in bars 5–8 and 30–31, that vocal performance is highly un-likely. This fact has a direct bearing on the analysis offered. The superius is assumed to carry the structural top voice at all times, despite crossings that sometimes give the altus and tenor the highest tones sounding. These two parts are so distinctly subordinate to the superius and lacking by com-parison in melodic character and coherence that the mere fact of crossing the superius does not allow them to take over the function of structural top voice. The analysis is much clearer and more convincing this way, and it would also correspond to the probabilities of performance practice in that the superius would very likely be sung and the other voices played. Here stylistic analysis offers helpful confirmation of what analysis of tonal struc-ture alone would suggest only as a conjecture.

A few words are perhaps in order about the *musica ficta* supplied, which poses some touchy problems. The partial signature of one flat only in the bass has some bearing on these, as do other accidentals supplied in the original. In bar 9 the choice must be made between a false relation with C♯ in bar 8 or with C♮ in bar 10; since the chord in bar 9 is the same as in bar 8, separated only by a rest, the added C♯ in bar 9 seems the less harsh solution. In bars 19–22, a whole series of B♭'s and E♭'s result from the single B♭ in the bassus in bar 21. This note requires that all the other B's in the same measure be flatted, as well as the E in the altus. These additions make further alterations necessary in bars 19, 20, and 22, in order to avoid false relations and tritones. All other added accidentals result from the normal raising of leading tones at cadences and the avoidance of false intervals, and need no specific comment.

The analysis again appears in successive reductions in graphs 18a to 18c. The harmonic element is more prominent in this example than in the other three. The harmonic progression I–II⁶–v–I underlies the first section; harmonic progressions also form the highest level of structure in the second and third sections, and are used as prolongations within all three sections.

24 Lowinsky, pp. 3 ff.

EXAMPLE 18   *Io non posso piu durare*   "Aron"

EXAMPLE 18 (*continued*)

EXAMPLE 18 (*continued*)

pe - ria,   poi   che   son   fra   sco - gli in ma - re.

Non voler esser crudele
Un amante piu fidele
Io sero come el diamanto
Contra quel che tama tanto
Mai non fu ne piu constanto
Ch'io non vo dise mancare.
Io non posso, etc.

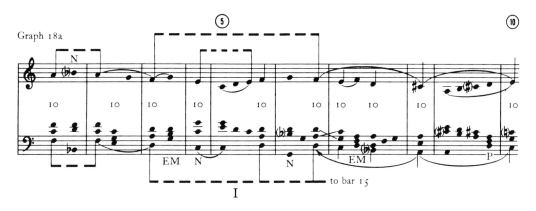

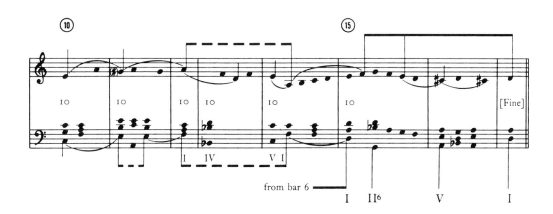

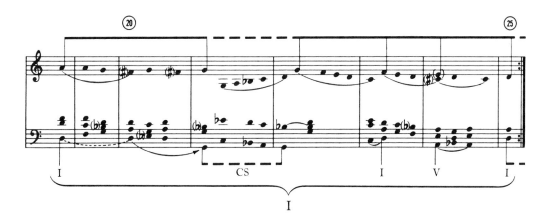

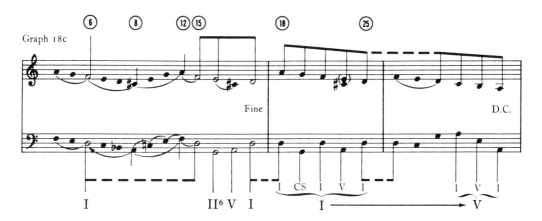

Graph 18c

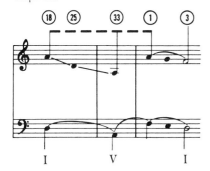

Graph 18d

Contrapuntal progressions are to be observed in prolongations, most notably in the long prolongation of the initial tonic (bars 1–15), which proceeds entirely in tenths, and in the I–cs–I progression of the second section, all indicated in graph 18a. An introductory chord preceding the tonic is found here, as in Josquin's motet, the same contrapuntal chord on the third degree of the scale, as a matter of fact. The balance between harmonic and contrapuntal elements in this composition seems much closer to what would be usual in later music than in any of the other examples.

The relationship between the three sections is perhaps worth close examination. In view of the piece in its entirety, the I–II⁶–V–I of the first section, since it is also heard last, must be considered to present the main structural progression. The second and third sections (which together form the second part of the A–B–A form of the whole piece) present an octave descent in the top voice, A–A, broken by the cadence in bar 25. This A connects very convincingly to the top-voice A at the beginning of the first part. The bass in the second section retains structurally D as its tonic, while the third section moves to v, again the minor v, this time prolonged by its own i–v–i progression. Here quite an ingenious connection is made to the *da capo*, in which the bass begins on F, leaping from the preceding A, and finally moving on to D. Thus the bass from the second section into the *da capo* outlines the tonic triad, D–A–F–D (see graph 18d). This bass progression in an interesting parallelism repeats the same outline of the prolonged tonic in the first section (bars 6–15; compare graph 18d with graph 18c).

The frottola thus exhibits a structure more harmonic and less intricate than the other pieces. Its interest as music per se is perhaps relatively slight; its simple, uncomplicated style, less intellectual than the other works, even allows the parallel octaves in bar 7. But it is of interest as an example of the trend towards greater use of harmonic progressions around 1500, and probably shows that trend in its most advanced state.

4. Our final example will be a complete work by Alexander Agricola, *Ales mon cor*, number 65 in the *Odhecaton* (Example 19). Again, this chanson is in only three voices; but each has its own range, and voice crossing is not so frequent as in the Brumel motet. The structural top voice is found almost always in the superius, and the structural bass in the contratenor. The style is imitative and predominantly triadic, with Agricola's typical rhythmic animation. The piece at first glance appears to be in Phrygian mode, but a strong affinity to A is evident on closer examination, even at the final cadence in bar 52, where superius and tenor have an octave E–E and contratenor the A below, which descends to E only in bar 54.[25] As graphs 19a to 19c show, A is the tonic of the piece, not E, and it is definitely in some combination of Aeolian and minor modes. The first four measures have an introductory function similar to that in the Josquin and "Aron"

25 Hewitt, p. 22, comments on the ambiguity of this cadence in discussing the modality of the compositions in the *Odhecaton*.

EXAMPLE 19 *Ales mon cor* Agricola

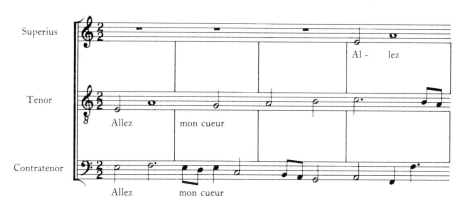

EXAMPLE 19 *(continued)*

EXAMPLE 19 *(continued)*

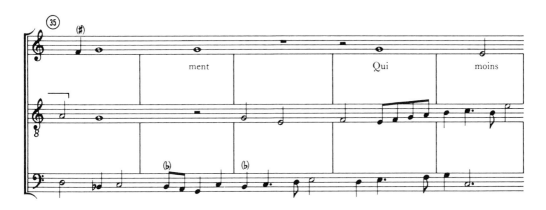

EXAMPLE 19 (*continued*)

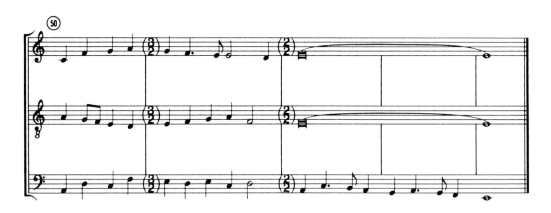

Et si je meurs par trop l'aymer,
Je vous charge en mon testament,
    Allez mon cueur, etc.

Elle vous peult sien réclamer
Car je vous laisse expressément
Pour la servir bien loyaulment,
Quant vous m'aurez mort veu paumer,
    Allez mon cueur, etc.

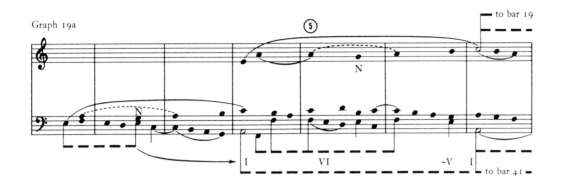

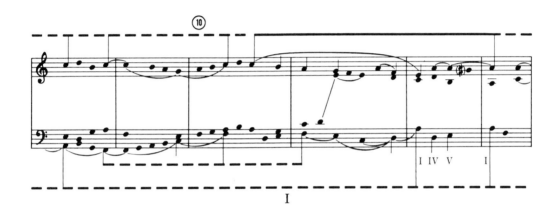

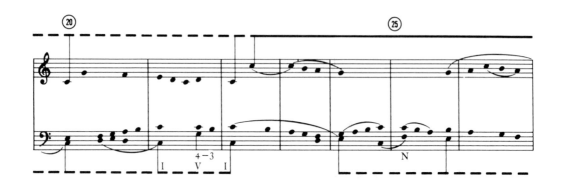

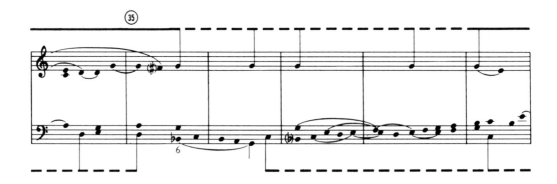

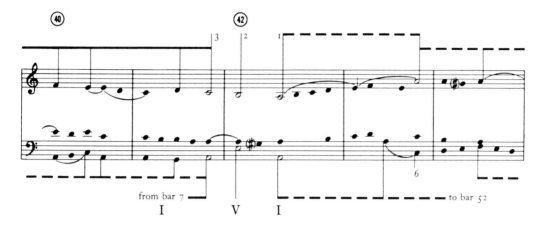

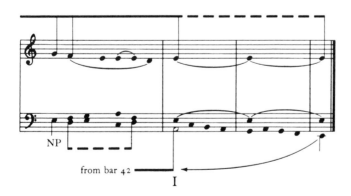

Graph 19b

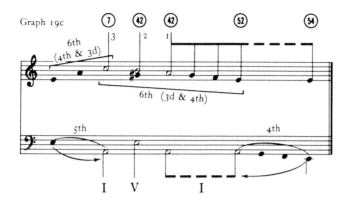

examples; in this case the minor dominant serves as a preface to the tonic, which is reached in bar 4. The ending on E is also not an indication of Phrygian, but part of a coda, that is, a section appended to the main harmonic movement of the piece. Here it has almost a retrograde character with respect to the opening measures, reversing the opening motion from E to A. In addition to the harmonic and contrapuntal elements which define A as tonic as shown in the graphs, the strong melodic relationships to A rather than E should be noted. The fourth, E–A, the sixths, E–C and C–E, and the third, A–C, are important features in the melodic design, as indicated by brackets and slurs in graphs 19a and 19b, and all, of course, tend to emphasize A and the A-triad rather than E. This point is one which sixteenth-century theory supports. Zarlino in particular argues that in such a situation the species of interval outlined should be at least equally important with the final in determining mode, and that if, in a presumably Phrygian piece, the octave E–E is more often divided E–A–E than E–B–E, the mode is not Phrygian but Hypoaeolian, regardless of the final cadence.[26] Agricola's chanson might well serve as a textbook example for Zarlino's observations, which afford a welcome confirmation of the present analysis by an observer close to the period in which the piece was written.

Bars 7–42 are governed by the foremost element in this work, the descending third C–B–A and the structural harmonic progression, I–V–I,

26 Strunk, p. 253.

of which it is the top voice; then follows, supported by the prolonged final 1, the melodic descent from A to E, which is completed in bar 52 (see graph 19c). It now becomes clear that the minor sixth with which the superius begins, E–ABC, is answered in a prolonged retrograde form in the superius between bars 7 and 52 (graphs 19c and 19b). A relationship of lesser structural weight, but nonetheless significant, is the direct, not retrograde, repetition after bar 42 of the melodic events of bars 4–13. The succession of ascending sixth, E–C, descending sixth, C–E, and ascending fourth, E–A, may also be found in bars 43–49 (see graph 19b). The structural function of the tones is different in the two passages. In the first, the goal of motion is the C in bar 7, the first structural tone of the top voice; while in bar 45, the comparable C is only an embellishing tone to the A in the top voice of the structural progression which was attained in bar 42.

The most prominent prolongation of the structural C–B–A supported by 1–v–1 is the beautifully managed stepwise transfer of register of the initial c^2 of the top voice to the lower octave c^1, the entire motion occupying well over half the composition, from bars 7–41. This descent is supported in the bass by an unfolding of the tonic triad, from A in bars 7–13 to C in bars 19–22, and on to E in bar 27, then back down, passing through D in bar 33 to C again in bars 37–39, and finally back to A in bar 40, just before the top voice regains c^1 in the lower octave (see graph 19b). The coincidence of motion between top voice and bass is such that the top voice's descent is supported in parallel fifths for much of its course, but this relationship is amply hidden by details of prolongation. The octave descent is anticipated on a lower structural level in bars 7–19; here the descent is less direct, going down a sixth, then up a fourth, and down again a sixth to reach c^1 in bar 19.

Agricola's composition is notable from the analytical point of view as much for its highly organized and extended technique of prolongation as for its bold tonal structure. The control and planning involved in the prolongation of the top-voice C in this composition are surpassed in later periods only in temporal dimensions, not in proportions or skill. The same may be observed in general with reference to all the examples considered here, and presumably, by extension, to all of the music of the period.

Examination of tonal structure from this point of view reveals new dimensions of craftsmanship on the part of composers around 1500. Not only were men such as Josquin and Agricola wonderfully skilled in those aspects of composition customarily examined in the course of stylistic analysis, but they also built tonal structures (however unconsciously) of the greatest elegance and subtlety. On this score, the music of the Renaissance need yield nothing to that of any other period.

CONCLUSION

ON THE BASIS of these analyses and others of music from the same period, it would seem that Renaissance music displays characteristics of tonal coherence and directed motion similar to those in the music of later periods. Such coherence and direction in the most meaningful sense of the word constitutes the tonality of this music. True, it is a different sort of tonality in some respects from that found in later and earlier periods. Harmonic progressions are used less than in later music, but much more than in Medieval music, which hardly knows them at all. Also unlike Medieval music, Renaissance music regularly uses a complete triad as a basic structural element. The wider compass of much Renaissance music offers different possibilities of prolongation than those used in the Middle Ages, but research in this area is so little advanced at present that it would be pointless to go beyond this statement. It seems possible that the kinds of progressions and techniques of prolongation used in different periods might characterize the periods in terms of structural procedures in the same sense that they are now characterized according to stylistic traits.

Theorists in the sixteenth century clearly made no close approach to defining tonal structure. Their theories of counterpoint, as we have seen, barely begin to deal with analysis in the sense in which we now know it. The theory of the modes cannot be dismissed so quickly, since they seem to have some validity at least in classification. The whole question of the relationship between modality and tonality comes into question here. The conventional view is that music was essentially modal throughout most of the sixteenth century and that it gradually became unequivocally tonal toward the end of the seventeenth. But the view advanced here is that most

Western music is tonal, and that the *character* of tonality, not the fact of tonality, is the element that fluctuates.

A commonly held assumption seems to be that a modal scale may generate diatonic triads in the same sense that a major or minor scale is conceived to do so. In this respect, one can talk of modal chord progressions centered around a tonic other than that which would be used in a major or minor key. In the context of the analytic method suggested here, such triads could be the principal structural elements in a polyphonic composition. If strict purity of mode were maintained, a contrapuntal tonal structure could be used, but even with modal purity, harmonic relationships can and do assert themselves through minor or $\frac{8}{3}$ dominants. Purity of mode is generally conceded not to exist in the polyphonic music of the Renaissance, and harmonic progressions are often strengthened in this music as a result of the modal impurities introduced by *musica ficta* and other chromaticism. In other words, music in the fifteenth and sixteenth centuries seems seldom to avoid harmonic progressions completely. Many theorists would probably consider harmonic progressions to indicate tonality, that tonality by definition is constituted of harmonic relationships. This would lead to a distinction of tonality and modality exactly comparable to the distinction here made between harmonic and contrapuntal progressions. But understanding tonality exclusively according to a chordal relationship is as unsatisfactory as understanding modality exclusively in linear terms. This is the chief failing, to my mind, of Lowinsky's *Tonality and Atonality in Sixteenth-Century Music*, which is in many ways an admirable study and a thoughtful attempt to get behind the conventionalities of the modal-tonal dichotomy. Lowinsky, in criticizing the conventional view of modality, accepts the conventional view of tonality and fails to achieve his purpose fully.

What then does modality mean in the expanded concept of tonality proposed here? The chords used in a Renaissance composition may often be the diatonic triads of a modal scale, and the piece may be modal in this sense. The melodic lines themselves can be classified as modal, though in relation to tonal structure this would define only the type of scale patterns used in prolongations. Specific melodic patterns or cadential patterns, such as Lowinsky has described,[27] may be attributed to certain modes, and a

27 Summarized in Reese, pp. 45–47.

piece may thus be categorized as belonging to a specific mode. This is only classification, however, not analysis. The structure of any composition is not to be understood by assigning it to a mode any more than the structure of an eighteenth-century composition is described by saying what key it is in. A further and more meaningful step would be to establish that certain structures are typically used in conjunction with certain modal patterns in melody or cadence. Such structures would almost certainly contain harmonic elements, and the concept of mode would need to be expanded beyond its present limits to include them. Such a correlation could be confirmed only by collation of a large number of analyses. Whatever results were obtained, modality would be seen to be at most a specific subspecies of tonality. The four compositions examined here all use harmonic and contrapuntal elements in such an intricate mixture that modality, in any historically strict sense of the term, can hardly be considered the only significant structural element that organizes them.

In the exploration of the tonal structure of Renaissance music, then, we must use the contemporary theorists with reservations. We should not tackle this music without a sound knowledge of how the musicians themselves thought about it, but having achieved this knowledge, we have only begun our investigation. To achieve a meaningful understanding of the music, of the forces that bind it together and make it move convincingly to a logical conclusion, we must go much further than the contemporary guidebooks take us. We can hardly say that the art itself has improved since 1500, but our understanding and knowledge of it certainly have, and it would be blind indeed to fail to make use of the best knowledge we have available in order to achieve a fuller understanding of whatever segment of the literature we wish to make our own.

The Tristan Prelude

TECHNIQUES AND STRUCTURE

WILLIAM J. MITCHELL

RICHARD WAGNER's Einleitung or Vorspiel to *Tristan and Isolde*, completed more than one hundred years ago, remains a challenge and an enigma. A simple count of the number of analyses that have been attempted since its publication, and a superficial comparison of them, would suffice to prove this.[1] Relatively few analysts, however, have reported on the entire Prelude, or in fact on much more than the first three bars, and then only to unravel the mystery of the sonority of bar 2, the so-called "Tristan chord."

It is not the intention of this article to review these countless analyses. Suffice it to say that many of them are resoundingly vacuous, others have moments of revealing insights, and the vast majority are committed to the point of view that if all chords are properly labeled and the modulations tabulated, the result will be one Prelude analyzed. To be sure, lip service is paid to the role of linear elements, but these seem to be confined to appoggiaturas and half-step progressions.

The aim here will be, rather, to approach the work in terms of its linear-harmonic elements, and to attempt to arrive at a view of the entire work as a unified, articulated structure. The assumptions behind such an undertaking are that: (1) there are discoverable morphological meanings in the lines and harmonies; (2) these can pave the way to the comprehension of an embracing structure reaching from the beginning to the end. The validity of

---

[1] Among the more recent analyses are those by Wolfgang Fortner in *Kontrapunkte, Band* 4, p. 101 f.; P. J. Tonger, *Musikverlage* (Rhoden- kirchen/Rhein); and Ernest Ansermet, *Les fondements de la musique dans la conscience humaine* (Neuchatel, Baconniere, 1961), pp. 303–8.

the assumptions must rest ultimately on the results achieved, the ways in which they are achieved, and the revitalizing view of the Prelude that they might provide.

The beginning of the Prelude is easy enough to locate; the end is another matter, since the work leads directly into Act I, Scene 1. Wagner provides us with valuable assistance in our search, for he composed a concert ending dated "Paris, December 15, 1859."[2] This ending of twenty-four bars, based on the closing pages of Act III, but clearly in A major, is dovetailed into the preceding Prelude in such a manner that bar 93 of the Prelude as usually performed is extended to two bars. In the new bar, bar 95, a plagally inflected A-chord replaces the accustomed F-chord of bar 94. There follows the remainder of the bars mentioned above. Wagner, in my view, heard the Prelude in A major-minor. The concert ending, placed by him in A, adds a substantial confirmation (see Example 1).

THE INCLUSIVE PLAN

IT WAS with reluctance that I decided to present a frame of reference for the entire Prelude before turning to the details. The decision was prompted by a desire to expedite as much as possible the analysis of an admittedly complex composition. The complications spring not only from the richness of detail, but also from the length of the work in terms of tempo as well as the actual number of bars. It is hoped that any seeming arbitrariness in the sketches of Example 2 will be removed by the analysis of detail to follow. Suffice it to say that in the analysis of the work, the inclusive plan was induced from the cumulative evidence of the detail, rather than the detail deduced from a preordained plan.

Example 2a presents the essential features of the outer parts in a linear-harmonic sketch. The upper part is notated in its proper register, but the bass has been assigned a register of convenience. Its proper octave registers will be indicated in the analysis of detail. Major-minor mixtures, so

---

2 It appears in a keyboard score as an insert after p. 272 in *Richard Wagner, Wesendonk Briefe* (Leipzig, Hesse and Becker Verlag). As an orchestral ending incorporated into the Prelude, it has been published as *Vorspiel zu Tristan und Isolde* von Richard Wagner (Leipzig, Breitkopf and Härtel).

EXAMPLE I

EXAMPLE I (*continued*)

EXAMPLE 2

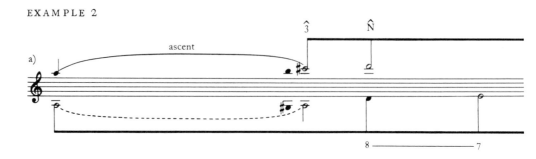

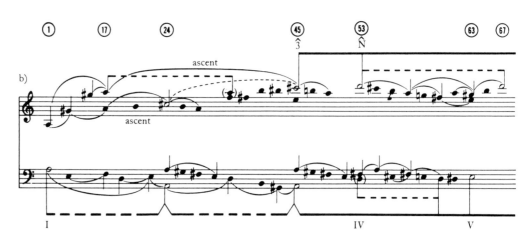

characteristic of the chromatic bent of the Prelude, intrude into the first sketches. Of interest in this respect is the predominance of the major mode, brought about by the long ascent to c♯³. Following the neighbor d³, c♮³ replaces the major third momentarily, but the concert ending clearly affirms A major, as do most of the details, despite the minor color of the opening bars. The bass also participates in mixed colors, asserting f¹ and b♭ (as a lowered or Phrygian second step) before the closing cadential bars.

Example 2b presents some of the detail of a higher order. Up to bar 45, the A-chord, with the help of two harmonically oriented prolongations in the bass (bars 1–24, 24–45), works toward the structurally significant c♯³. It is through a change of octave registers that this goal is achieved. Note that, after the opening a, a¹, a² have been established, an ascent to c♯² occurs (bars 1–24). Only after this (bars 24–45) is the dominating upper-

EXAMPLE 2 *(continued)*

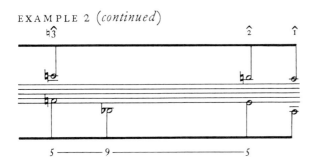

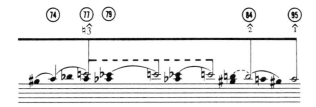

voice register attained. Bars 53–62 unroll an extended subdominant harmony as consonant support for the neighbor d^3. The entry and extension of the dominant harmony (bars 63–73) presents d^3 as a seventh which ultimately (bars 74–77) resolves to c^3 supported by f. It is here that the delirious abandon of the music makes the case for A major momentarily dubious (bars 79–83), until in bar 84 the dominant harmony is asserted. It rules until the arrival in bar 95 of the concluding A-major–chord, plagally suspended. As suggested by the total shape of the bass and the Roman numerals, the Prelude expresses the functions, nonmodulatory, of A, albeit with a high degree of chromaticism.

THE ANALYSIS OF SECTIONS

ALTHOUGH the Prelude is essentially a continuous structure, the layout of

Example 2b suggests a convenient subdivision into seven sections. These will be bars 1–17, 17–24, 24–45 (not 44), 45–63, 63–74, 74–84, 84–96, and further. As helpful as a keyboard reduction might seem, it is imperative that the orchestral score be the main, if not the sole, reference in the discussions that follow. Only one keyboard transcription[3] of the many that have been examined retains the all-important octave registrations of bars

EXAMPLE 3

3 *Tristan und Isolde von Richard Wagner*, Vollständiger Klavierauszug von Karl Klindworth ("Universal Edition"; B. Schott's Söhne in Mainz, 1906).

55–60 and 74–76. But even this otherwise commendable setting is occasionally slipshod with respect to Wagner's phrasing slurs.

To facilitate references to motives used by Wagner in the course of the Prelude, the principal ones and the "Tristan chord" have been quoted in Example 3 and identified by means of a letter or, in the case of the Tristan chord, by a convenient abbreviation. It is by these tags that they shall be cited in the detailed analysis. Note that motives A^2, B, C, E, F, and G have in common a terminating rhythm of an eighth note followed by a quarter note, a feature that adds to their interrelationship. Similarly, all but the first of these contain a dotted eighth note followed by a sixteenth.

Bars 1–17. Although the opening bars, particularly the sonority *Tr* of bar 2, present a continuing challenge, the inclusive structure of the bass is clear. Its broad context is formed by the initial a making its way to F in bar 17. Between these, a prolonged arpeggiation of the E-chord takes place, consisting of e (bar 3), g (bar 7), b (bar 11), and E (bar 16). Each of these is preceded by the half step above as indicated in Examples 4a and 4b. Above this bass, the upper voice moves from the opening a to a^2 of bar 17. The connection between these two points is formed by the $g\sharp^1$ of bar 3 making an ascent in a stepwise motion consisting of four groups of three notes each until the terminal a^2 is reached (Example 4b). Observe, in Examples 4a and 4b, how this complete motion opens up three octave registers and, in the octave exchanges of bars 12–15, suggests hesitantly a higher register before settling on a^2 in bar 17. The underlying sense of these seventeen bars is represented in Example 4c.

The details of the section are highly interesting. As Wagner arpeggiates the tones of the E-chord, he uses the minor third, g, with its major chord in bar 8, rather than g$\sharp$ and a thankless diminished chord. The basis of such a technique is the chordal mixture wherein the major third, g$\sharp$, replaced by the minor third, g, is reasserted in bar 16. The process of extending an overall a to F by means of an arpeggiated E-chord is unusual. A far more frequent breaking prolongation is that of Example 5 in which the basis of arpeggiation is the prevailing F$\sharp$-minor tonic harmony.[4]

Although the ultimate reading in Example 5c departs from that of

[4] F. Chopin, Mazurka, Op. 30, No. 2, bars 24–32.

EXAMPLE 4

a)   Bars 1–17

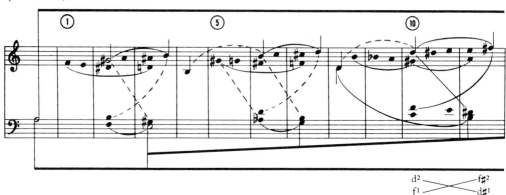

b)

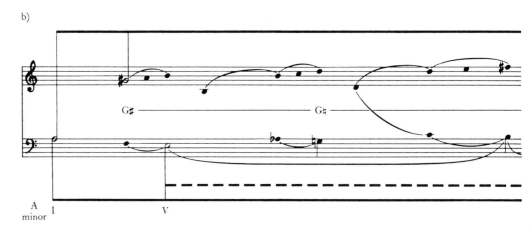

c)

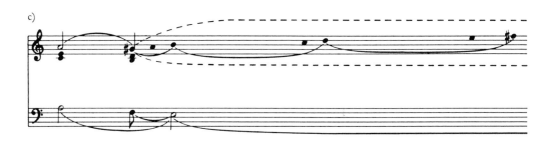

EXAMPLE 4 *(continued)*

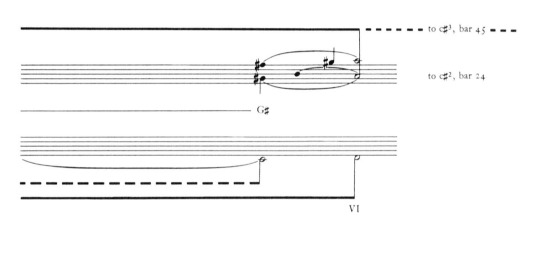

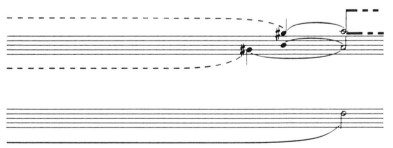

EXAMPLE 5

a)

b)

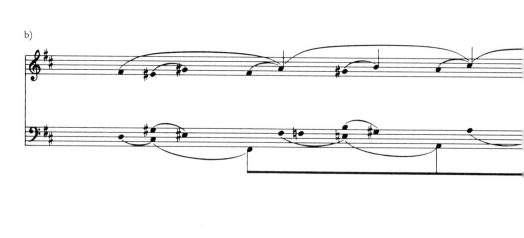

c)

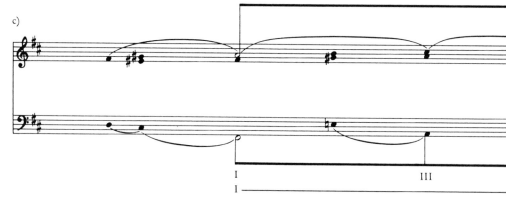

EXAMPLE 5 (*continued*)

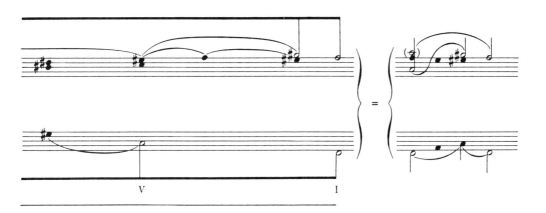

Example 4c, there are certain middle and foreground similarities that invite comparison and eventually help to arrive at an analysis of the first section of the Tristan Prelude. In both pieces, the interval of an augmented sixth appears frequently; in both pieces, likewise, the upper voice ascends in a quasi-sequential manner, the Prelude through a dominant chord arpeggiated, the Mazurka through a more usual tonic chord arpeggiated.

Let us examine the chord Tr in bar 2 of the Prelude. While Chopin's opening augmented sixth chord derives readily from a diatonic $^6_{4\ 3}$ (d, g$\sharp$, b, f$\sharp^1$), by simply sharping the sixth, b, Tr does not submit so readily, for its immediate derivation is $^6_{4\ 2}$ (f, b, d^1, g$\sharp^1$), a form of diminished seventh chord. This, in fact, is the historic derivation of the sonority.[5] In order to derive Tr from the source that provides Chopin with his chord (transposed to f, b, d^1, a^1), g$\sharp^1$ must be regarded as a long appoggiatura, moving on the sixth beat of the bar to a^1, the 3 of $^6_{4\ 3}$. This is the prevailing contemporary analysis, represented by the Roman numeral II, and standing in the so-called second inversion.

Such a reading must be reassessed. Nothing that Wagner does with the chord suggests such a harmonic "functional" analysis. Note that the phrasing slur for the oboe in bars 2–3 begins on the g$\sharp^1$ under examination and carries through to b^1 (Example 6a). But this is not characteristic of the usual two-tone slur (g$\sharp^1$ to a^1) for the indication and execution of an appoggiatura. It should also be observed that the oboe's g$\sharp^1$ to b^1 is accompanied by a very frequent kind of chordal interchange as the bassoon leaps from b to g$\sharp$ (Example 6b). Furthermore, the oboe's g$\sharp^1$, the alleged appoggiatura, rests in a much more comfortable sonority than the release, a^1, which forms part of the chord of the so-called double dissonance. Something is wrong here, for appoggiaturas, at least traditionally, move from relative stress to relative quiet (Example 6c). Closely related to the oboe's music in bars 2–3 is the initial passage of the cellos, which is transferred in bar 2 to the English horn in such a manner that, after the initial a, the cellos play

[5] A brief survey of the career of Tr in the hands of analysts appears in Alfred Lorenz, *Das Geheimnis der Form bei Richard Wagner* (Berlin, Max Hesses Verlag, 1926), II, 194 ff.

EXAMPLE 6

a)   The slur

b)   The interchange

c)   Tension-release?

d)   The motivic parallel

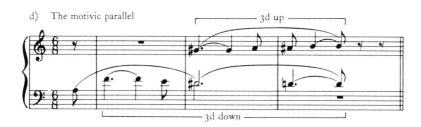

e)   The major seventh and the octaves

$f^1-e^1-d\sharp^1$, whereupon the English horn takes over to complete the motion from $d\sharp^1$ to d^1. Thus, a descending third, $f^1-e^1-d\sharp^1-d^1$, is answered by an ascending third, $g\sharp^1-a^1-a\sharp^1-d^1$ (Example 6d). Finally, the inclusive significance of $g\sharp^1$ is stressed by the fact that it stems from the opening a. This striking major seventh establishes a binding melodic connection which, considered with all of the preceding factors, must override any attempt to classify $g\sharp^1$ as an appoggiatura. Note that once the major seventh has been established, it is paralleled in bars 4–6 and 8–10 by the octaves b to b^1, d^1 to d^2 (Example 6e).

The reasons cited above seem persuasive, at least to this analyst, for regarding $g\sharp^1$ as a principal tone and a^1 as a dependent passing tone. Why is the prevailing analysis just the opposite? Probably, first, because the elevation of a^1 to the rank of a chord tone presents the analyst with a harmonic stereotype, a recurrent kind of augmented sixth chord. Probably, also because by a process of reverse harmonic expectancy, it would seem that the unmistakable dominant of bar 3 must have before it some recognizable kind of subdominant or supertonic chord. But such a mothering of the theory of harmonic functions seems excessive in the face of so many opposed textual and linear factors. Because $d\sharp^1$ of bar 2 is so clearly on the way to d^1 of bar 3, the underlying sonority of bar 2 has been represented in Example 4c as a form of diminished seventh chord, related generically to one of Beethoven's uses of it.[6]

The sonority of bar 6 has the same derivation as *Tr*, but bar 10 presents a different case. If Wagner had followed the line of least resistance and continued with the pattern established in bars 1–4 and 5–8, bar 11 would have produced a Bb-major–chord, as indicated in Example 7a. The basis of the manipulation employed to arrive at the B-major-chord, so essential an element in the broad arpeggiation of the E-chord (bars 3, 7, 11, 16), is shown in Example 7b. If additional justification of the present reading of an arpeggiated E-chord were needed, this particular summoning by Wagner of a B- rather than a Bb-chord would provide it.

A parting word must be addressed to the harmonic meaning of the opening upbeat and bar 1. The present tendency, with which I am in agreement,

---

[6] In Op. 13, 1st movement, *Grave*, bars 7–8, and in Op. 53, 2d movement, *Introduzione, Adagio molto*, bars 23–25. Attention is directed to the bass, Ab–G, in both instances.

EXAMPLE 7

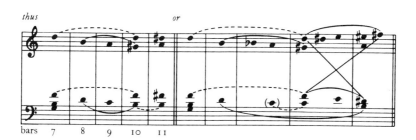

is to consider it I. In the past, the shape of the cellos' solo has been misin-
terpreted when the passage has been understood as an outlining of VI or IV.
The derivation is to be found less in the discipline of harmony than in that
of counterpoint. Example 8a illustrates a frequent kind of correction, in
the study of counterpoint, of the beginning of a fourth species exercise. Quite
correctly, a "license" is required, the addition of e^2 before f^2, in order to
clarify for the student the meaning of f^2 as a motion away from e^2, rather

than as a direct vertical offspring of the *cantus firmus* tone, a^1. In such didactic studies, literalness is required to derive techniques or explain meanings. In free composition, such literalness is certainly not required, nor to be expected. However, the study of counterpoint, if it has taught its lesson well, will take care of cases such as those of Example 8b, in which the fifth, though not literally present, remains nevertheless the implied linear source of the sixth.[7] In all of these cases, the harmonic meaning is uniformly I as indicated.

A highly interesting point arises when Wagner's sketches for the Prelude are consulted.[8] Originally the first note was b, and the corresponding note in bar 4 was d^1. Wagner's revisions are of critical importance. For one thing, the originally written diminished fifth $b-f^1$ creates a static environment, for both of these tones are contained in *Tr* which follows. Despite the tension of the diminished fifth, nothing happens. Compare this with the vital motion of a in the final version, as it moves to its successor, $g\sharp^1$, in *Tr*. Furthermore, the diminished fifth outlines an obvious supertonic chord, much less appropriate than the evasive minor sixth, $a-f^1$. As already observed, this latter interval has been variously analyzed as representing I, VI, or IV, by itself a telling indication of its suitableness to the groping, exploratory quality of the opening bars. Finally, from a broad structural point of view, a introduces the inclusive upper-voice tension of bars 1–17, consisting of $a-g\sharp^1-a^2$, while at the same time, as a partner in the motion, a–e–f, it contributes to the broad establishment of an enclosed A-chord in bars 1–17 and 17–24. The resultant structural balance is apparent in Example 2.

The case that follows from Wagner's decision to employ b rather than the originally sketched d^1 in bar 4 is similar to the earlier one. Aside from the superiority of b as a sequential consequent to the initial a, the resultant neutral sixth, $b-g\sharp^1$ (bars 4–5), maintains better than $d^1-g\sharp^1$ the tentative, searching quality of the early bars.

7 Examples 8b(1) and 8b(2): J. S. Bach, opening of Praeludium XX, Book II, and opening of Praeludium XIX, Book I, *Well-Tempered Clavier*; Example 8b(3): W. A. Mozart, opening of the "Dissonance" Quartet; Example 8b(4): opening of the Tristan Prelude.

8 Mr. Robert Bailey of Yale University who is studying the sketches has very generously in-formed me that "the first note is a *b* in the first sketch for the piece, which extends only to the seventeenth measure. Similarly, the first note of the second phrase is a *d*. The first note of the third phrase, however, is also a *d*, as in the final version." I am indebted to Mr. Bailey and look forward to the appearance of his study of the Prelude.

EXAMPLE 8

a)

b)

b1)

b2)

b3)

b4)

EXAMPLE 9

a)   Bars 17–24

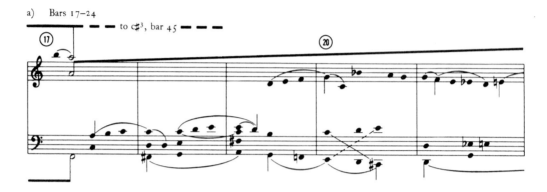

b)

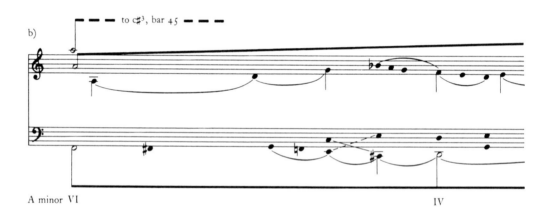

A minor VI   IV

c)

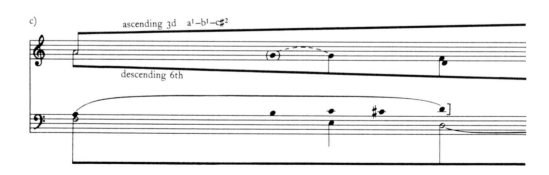

EXAMPLE 9 *(continued)*

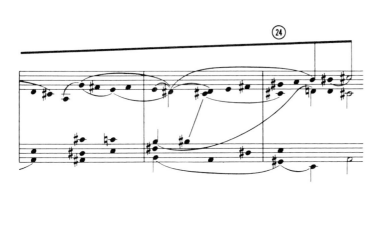

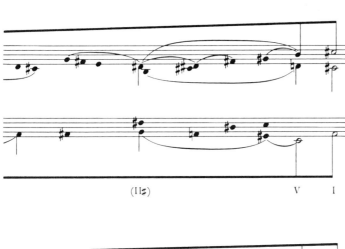

Bars 17–24. Bars 1–17 have, in the structural activity of the upper parts, opened up three octave registers, from a to $g\sharp^1$ and, in bar 17, a^1 and a^2. Bars 17–24 carry out a first ascent from a^1 to $c\sharp^2$ by way of b^1, as indicated in Examples 9a, 9b, and 9c. The bass of these bars brings to completion the first harmonic expression of A minor-major by picking up with F (bar 17), moving on to D (bar 21), and, after an intervening B (bar 23), concluding with E–A of bar 24. An important prolonging element is the middle-voice descent of a sixth from a^1 (bar 17) to $c\sharp^1$ (bar 24), as indicated in Example 9c. The tone a^2 and its register remain out of play until the following section.

The featured motive, motive *B*, is formed of concatenate thirds which carry out a broader connection between $a–g^1–f^1$ in bars 17–20–21 (Example 9a). The transitory nature of the supporting C-chord of bar 20 is explained in 9c. In bar 21, the apparent Neapolitan sixth is nothing more than a detail of the upper-voice motion from f^1 to d^1. Its accented position is characteristic of the prevailing texture of the Prelude, as has already been noted in discussing the rhythmic similarities of motives A^2, *B*, *C*, *E*, *F*, and *G* in connection with Example 3.

Bars 23–24 are complex. The descending sixth has, in bar 23, reached $d\sharp^1$, which stands over an inner voice b. This vertical third is inverted to become a sixth, $d^1–b^1$ (bar 24), in an arresting manner. The first violins, hitherto quiet, enter to span chromatically the distance from $d\sharp^1$ up to b^1, while the cellos initiate a motion from b up to d^1. After they have reached the intermediate $c\sharp^1$, the second violins intercept and complete the motion to d^1. The bass, meanwhile, breaks from B through G$\sharp$ to E before cadencing on A. These techniques and their relation to broad structure are shown in the illustrations of Example 9.

In summary, bars 1–24 form a unit, but for reasons of expository convenience they have been discussed as two subsections, 1–17 and 17–24. Over the bass, a, e, f, d, (b), e, a, three octave registers have been explored and, in the middle register, the first joining of a^1 to $c\sharp^2$ has occurred.

Bars 24–45. These bars are closely related to bars 1–24. Over the broad spread of supporting harmonies, the true register and upper voice, $c\sharp^3$, are reached, as indicated in the three graphs of Example 10.

As usual in structural analysis, the bass and harmonic frame require attention initially. Bars 24–31 are property of the A-chord. Its first expression is as a triad, but in bar 31 it acquires a minor seventh, g^1, which gives to it the color of an applied dominant to the approaching D-chord. The intervening activity is a matter of chromatic inflection rather than a modulation to E major. This becomes apparent as soon as analysis disengages itself from the chords of detail and focuses on inclusive activity, as illustrated in Examples 10a, 10b, and 10c, which should be compared with the equivalent bars in Example 2b. The D-chord prevails in bars 32–40. It is expressed first in the position of the sixth (bar 32), but eventually connects with the root (bar 37). From this point on, the minor third, f, is exchanged for the major third, f♯. The chord on B (bars 41–43) is passing by nature, for it takes its departure from the preceding D-chord and moves on to the cadential G♯- and A-chords of bars 43–44. The succession of A–D–B–G♯–A (Examples 10c and 2) offers conclusive evidence that the tonal properties of A alone are expressed in this section. Modulation plays no role.

In bars 24–31, motives C, D, and E are featured. In essence, motive C moves in parallel tenths with the bass as it courses from c♯^{2}, through b^1, to a^1. This three-tone succession is extended by suspending b^1 over F♯. As a fourth, its normal resolution should be to a third. However, before the appearance of a^1, the bass has moved on toward c♯ as shown in Example 10b, which should be compared with 10c, where the generic relationship is presented. Note in these bars, as represented in 10c, how each principal participating voice moves surely from one to another tone of the A-chord. Of particular interest is the fine parallelism to the upper voice of bars 24–28, provided by the top part as motive E in bars 29–32 moves from c^2 to a^1 and then from c♯^{2} to a^1. Intertwined in the manner of a cambiata are ascending secondary thirds, f♯^{1}–a^1, and e^1–g^1 (Example 10a).

From bars 32 to 40, over the support of the D-chord, an arresting change of register occurs that prepares the way for the arrival of c♯^{3} in bar 45. At first motive B is employed, much in the manner of its earlier use (bars 17–21), but an octave higher. By means of the third a^1–g^2–f^2 the upper register, last sounded in bar 17, is reopened. In bar 36 and further, motive F continues this play of registers by transferring f^1–g^1 and g^1–a^1 (bars

EXAMPLE 10

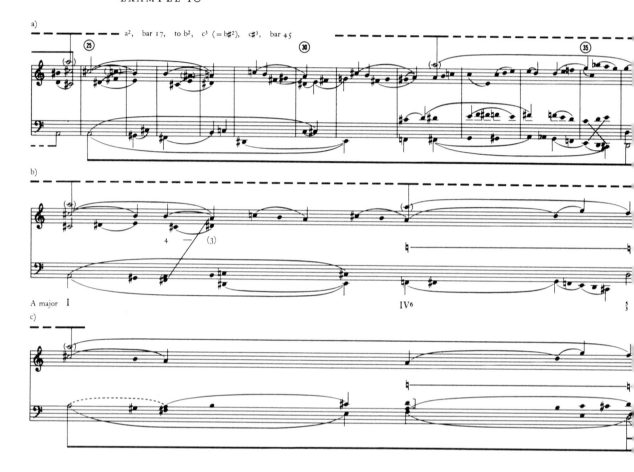

EXAMPLE 10 *(continued)*

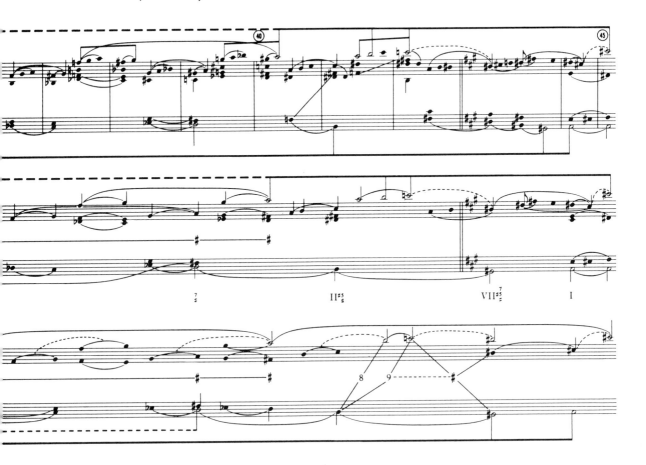

36–37 and 38–39) successively to f^2–g^2 and g^2–a^2 (Examples 10a and 10b).

As a result, the situation presented in bar 40 is a D-major–chord with a^2 in the top voice. The derivation of the linear-chordal relationships of bars 40 to 45 is sketched in Example 11. Under the pressure of increasing intensity and the shape of the motive, the top voice anticipates its normal accompaniment in such a way that a minor ninth, c^2, appears over the B-chord of bars 41–42. This is not a true chordal ninth, but an enharmonically written anticipation of the major third, b♯^{1}, of the G♯-chord of bar 43. It is this chord that presses on to the A-chord of bar 44 in an aroused transposition of the cadence of bars 16–17. Wagner's desired parallelism accounts for the chromatic color of the chord on G♯, rather than any putative flirtation with the key of C♯ minor.

EXAMPLE 11

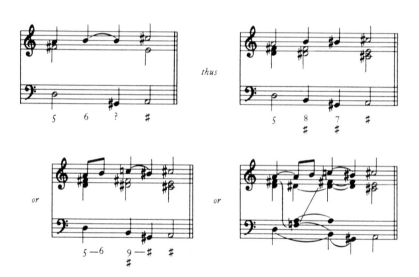

The upper voice of the cadence of bar 44 is literally b♯^{1}–c♯^{2}. But it is the c♯^{3} in bar 45, following the cadence, that is the tone sought after and prepared for by the transposition devices of the preceding bars. Note that it, too, is reached by an octave transposition of c♯^{2}. It is characteristic of the continuous nature of the music of the Prelude that $c\sharp^3$ should arrive one bar after the cadence. In fact, it should be noted that secondary factors add to the forward impulse of the cadence bar: the double basses and third bassoon retain A^1 and A^2 into bar 45; $d\sharp^2$ in the violas delays for three beats the arrival of $c\sharp^2$; the cellos press on by means of an $e\sharp$ to the $f\sharp$ of bar 45.

In summary of bars 1–24, 24–45: over two similar successions in the bass, the structural top voice connects a^1 with $c\sharp^2$ (bars 1–24) and then a^2 with $c\sharp^3$ (bars 24–45). A different kind of action ensues.

Bars 45–63. The A-chord, well established in the earlier sections, continues through bar 52, where it gives way to the subdominant harmony that prevails through bar 63. The dominant harmony of bar 64 is then prolonged in a manner that will be described in the following section. Above these harmonies, $c\sharp^3$ gives way in bar 53 to d^3, a structural neighboring tone. From each of these tones, downward motions are generated, $c\sharp^3$ to a^2 (bars 45–48, repeated in parallel fashion in 49–50, and twice in 51–52), and d^3 to a^2 to $f\sharp^2$ (filled in, in bars 53–62). These harmonic and linear prolongations are indicated in the illustrations of Example 12.

The motive employed in bars 45–52 is motive C, now an octave higher than its first statement in bars 25–32. However, the different continuations in bars 32 and 53 make an important difference in identifying the retained structural tone. While in bar 32 the action, carried out by motive B, emphasizes a motion picked up from a^1, the entrance in bar 53 of d^3 and its subsequent prolongation indicate that $c\sharp^3$ is its linear point of departure. For the rest, the reading of details for motive C is virtually the same as in its first statement (cf. Example 10).

A critical point is reached in bar 55 which can be settled only by study of the orchestral score. What is the structural meaning of $c\sharp^3$ in bars 54–55? Is it the completion of a neighboring motion, $c\sharp^3$ (bar 45), d^3 (bar 53), $c\sharp^3$ (bar 54)? Or is it to be regarded as a passing tone within the D-chord, as d^3 moves through this $c\sharp^3$ and b^2 (bar 57) to a^2 (bar 58)? The bass supports the latter reading, for the entire passage occurs within the D-chord, as indicated in Example 12. Furthermore, Wagner, by placing his accompanying voices above motive B, insures a retention of the proper register until motive B crosses over in bar 56 (Examples 12 and 12b). As noted earlier,

EXAMPLE 12

a)   Bars 45–63
      from a², bar 17

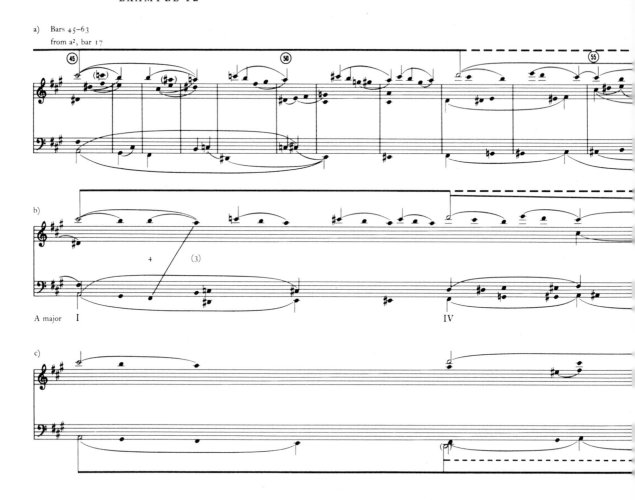

A major   I

IV

EXAMPLE 12 *(continued)*

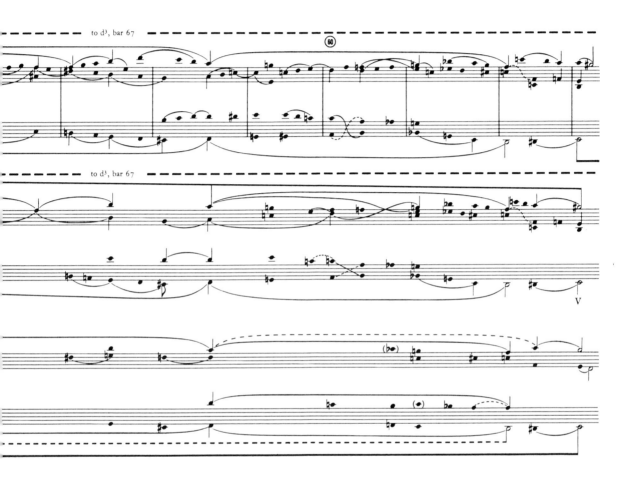

most keyboard transcriptions create a false misleading hiatus in these bars by abandoning the register so resourcefully retained by the composer. The same important crossing of motive B and its accompaniment occurs in bars 59–62 and for the same reason. The underlying sense of the entire passage is shown in Example 12c. Observe that the position of the sixth struck in bar 58 is not a "deceptive cadence," but a necessary reaffirmation of the D-chord which continues, as indicated, through bar 62, before giving way to the dominant harmony. It is instructive to compare the reductions of motive *B* in Examples 12b and 12c with the earlier reductions in Examples 9b and 9c, for the increased chromaticism and complexity of voice leading are reflected in the voice exchanges of Example 12b (bass clef) and in the four-part reduction of Example 12c.

Bars 63–74. Except for bar 74, these bars are property of the dominant harmony. From bars 63–70, it is asserted by a retention of E in the bass. In bars 70–73, however, Wagner uses the same arpeggiation technique that appears in the opening bars of the Prelude.

Above this prolonged harmony, new events occur. As indicated in Example 13a, 13b, and 13c, a stepwise ascent in bars 63–67 connects $g\sharp^2$ with d^3, already asserted in bar 53. The technique whereby Wagner achieves this connection is executed by motive G, a motive that lives its life in two registers (a^2–b^1, b^2–$c\sharp^2$, etc.). Its origin lies in 5–6–5 relationships as indicated in Example 13b. Motive *G* continues as an accompaniment through bar 72 of the section under examination, and in bars 73–74 it is brought down from its exploration of upper registers by a series of descending transfers, as indicated by slurs in Example 13a.

Once d^3 has been reaffirmed in bar 67, it is retained by the flutes and reiterated by the first and second violins as each of these sweeps upward. Below this, woodwinds and horns in increasing numbers sound motive A^2, carrying it upward, much in the manner of bars 1–17, but less protracted, from $g\sharp^1$ (bar 66) to a^2 in bar 74. Note that *Tr* has been modified in bars 66 and 68 by the necessity of retaining the structurally important d^3, as against the characteristic $d\sharp$. However in its following transpositions (bars 70 and 72), there is no need to modify the sonority, hence its original color remains intact. Specialists in the harmonic analysis of *Tr* would do well to observe and reflect on this modification brought about for structural reasons. However, beware of the run of piano transcriptions which modify the phrasing slurs.[9] Motive A^1 does not enter, except as aspects of it are incorporated into extensions of motive *G* in bars 70 and 72.

Bars 74–84. These bars, the dynamic and emotional climax of the Prelude, are organized around three prolonged harmonies, represented by the following bass tones: (1) f (bars 74–78) arpeggiated in the form of f (bars 74–76), c–A (bar 77), and F (bar 78); (2) B♭ (bars 79–82), the goal of descents from f (bars 80, 81, and 82); (3) e in bar 84, reached immediately from the neighbor f, and the basis of organization in most of the following section. These bass tones, f, B♭, e, representing the vi, ii (Phrygian), v of a minor, shoulder a feverish surge of the music. As noted earlier, the bass of bars 79–82, participating in this delirium, seems about to abandon all pretense of a relationship with the guiding tonality in favour of an excursion into other realms. The arrival of e, and the E-chord in bar 84, however, settles the issue in favour of a. Attention in these bars should be given to *Tr*, for its relation to the B♭-chord (bars 80–82), and its relation to the E-chord (bars 83–84), provide clear evidence that a♭ and the enharmonic g♯ are chordal elements rather than appoggiaturas,[10] as indicated in Example 14.

The prevailing motive in bars 74–78 is motive *B* in its most elaborate setting. Here again the orchestral score must be the analytic referent, for Wagner, as in the preceding instances, places his accompaniment above the motive initially to retain the proper register, as d^3 of bar 67 resolves ultimately to c^3 in bar 77. In essence c^3 is fetched from a^2 of bar 74 as indicated in Examples 14a and 14b. By comparing the present setting of motive *B* with earlier ones (bars 32–36), it can be seen that a new element is needed to carry the motion from a^2 through b♭^{2} (bar 76) to the desired c^3 of bar 77. Note that in the earlier settings the motion from a^2 has descended by step

---

9 As in the transcription by Richard Klein-michel.

10 Dr. Lorenz, who regards g♯^{1} as an appoggia-tura, writes (p. 20): "The appoggiatura, g♯, is present as a held tone up to the antepenultimate chord (bar 84) [83 according to the usual count] where it finds its normal resolution to a." Quite a feat!

EXAMPLE 13

a)   Bars 63–74

b)

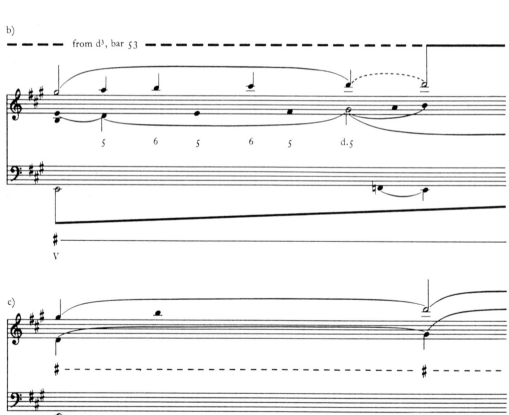

EXAMPLE 13 *(continued)*

EXAMPLE 14

a)   Bars 74–84

b)

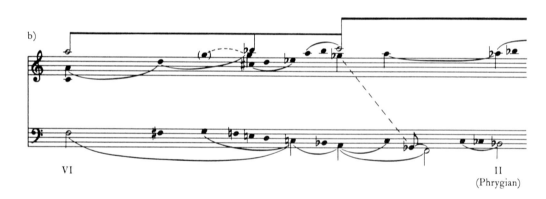

c)

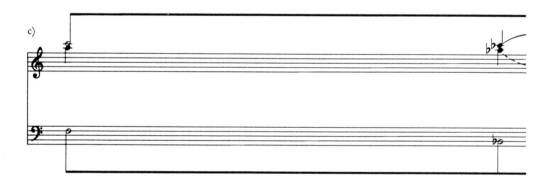

EXAMPLE 14 (*continued*)

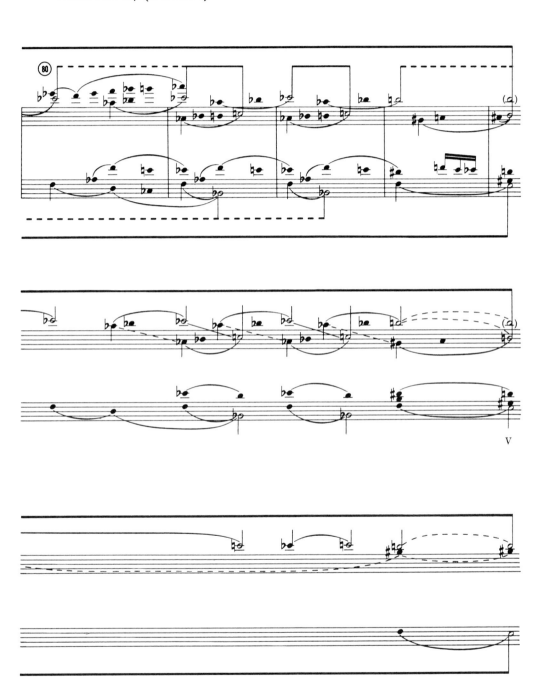

EXAMPLE 15

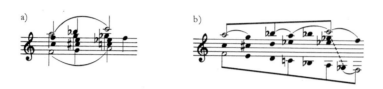

EXAMPLE 16

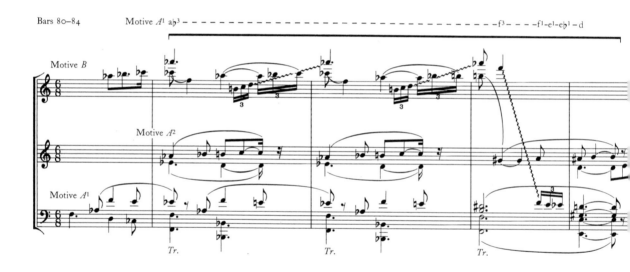

to f^2. Actually this earlier motion is still present, but above it Wagner places the new motion. The derivation of this complex passage is shown in Example 15. In 15a the bass moves upward in tenths with the top voice. However, 15b, with its downward motion, opens up new avenues of voice leading which create several additional chromatically inflected chords of detail.

Having reached c^3 in bar 77, the orchestra now spreads out to encompass an imposing range from $B\flat^1$ to $a\flat^3$. Within this vast tonal edifice, woodwinds, brass, and cellos secure the registers pertinent to the overall structure. The complexity of interwoven motives in bars 80 to 84 requires an additional illustration in short score. Example 16 indicates motivic derivations and the distribution of registers. Note that motives A^1, A^2, Tr, and B participate in the action, that motive A^1 is the agency by which the high point, $a\flat^3$, is brought downward to its proper register. The tones of motive A^1, $a\flat$ up to f^1, etc. (bars 79–84), become $a\flat^3$ (bars 81–83) down to f^3 to f^1, e^1, $e\flat^1$, d^1 (bars 83 and 84).

Example 14a incorporates most of the total activity of these bars. In 14b the coupling of $a\flat^2$ and $a\flat^1$, $c\flat^3$ and $c\natural^2$, are stressed. Finally Example 14c indicates the structural frame with the coupling brought into a single register above the broad march of the bass from f to $B\flat$ to e.

Bars 84–96, etc. As noted earlier, the present analysis will end with the beginning of Wagner's concert ending rather than with the transition to Act I, Scene 1. Hence we have been examining a Prelude, that is, a self-enclosed piece, rather than an Introduction leading to other actions. Wagner seems to have used both terms, Vorspiel and Einleitung interchangeably.

The structure of these closing bars is identical with a recurrent closing technique, represented in its generic form at the end of Example 2b. Specifically, b^2 of bars 83–84 connects with a^2 in bar 95, but with the help of a circling extension whereby b^2 moves first through a^2 (bar 92) to $g\sharp^2$ (bar 94) before its termination on the a^2 of bar 95, etc. Below this action, the prevailing structural bass, e, representing the dominant harmony, provides escort for the circling extension in the form of a (bar 90), d^1 (bar 92) and B, e (bars 93–94), before giving way in bar 95 to the terminal A. All of these relationships are shown in Example 17.

EXAMPLE 17

EXAMPLE 17 (continued)

The motives employed in the section are B, A^1, A^2, and the sonority Tr. Although these bars recall the opening bars of the Prelude as well as bars 36–40, the orientation is quite different. Each bass tone, e, a, and d^1, has its own extension. In bars 84 to 89, e is arpeggiated through the tones e (bar 84), g (bar 87), and b–b♭^{1} (bar 89). Next, a is similarly extended by way of a (bar 90), c and e♭^{1} (bar 91). The bass d in bar 92, however, drops down a third to B (bar 93) before moving on to the concluding and reaffirming e of bars 93–94. Note the quickening harmonic rhythms of these bars as e (six bars) passes on to a (two bars) to d^1 (one and a half bars) and to e (one and a half bars). Above these bass tones, the upper parts engage in an intermediate extension whereby b^1 (bar 84) moves to e^2 (bar 90) to connect with g♯^{2} (bar 92), as pointed out in Example 17b. Note the fine parallelism to the changes of register and the connection between g♯^{2} and a^2 in the concluding ascent (g♯^{1} up to a^2) of bars 92–94.

The beginning of the concert ending is included in the sketches of Example 17. Although its motivic content is related to the concluding bars of Act III, it nevertheless joins with the preceding music of the Prelude in an arresting manner. As indicated in Example 17a, the upper appoggiatura, b^2, has been featured throughout. However the suspension of f♯^{2} from the preceding music forms a strong transitional link. This tone has appeared earlier, in bars 10 to 16, and bar 73, as a prominent feature in the lengthening of g♯^{2}–a^2 into a motivically needed third, f♯^{2}–g♯^{2}–a^2. Its retention in bar 95 is heightened by the plagal support given to it by the bass.

THE FORM

VIEWED as a linear-harmonic entity, the form of the Tristan Prelude is a continuous, uninterrupted whole, subserved by a series of prolonged harmonies and an inclusive, descending melodic structure. The derivation of the broad harmonies and the extension of the prime melodic structure are sketched in the illustrations of Example 18. The purely harmonic elements are, as indicated, i–ii–v–i. The sketches of Example 18a and 18b, portray such a structure in A major, then in A minor, and finally in A minor with a lowered or Phrygian second step. Example 18c unites these modal variants in the manner of the Prelude and indicates the origin of the

EXAMPLE 18

a)

b)

c)

d)

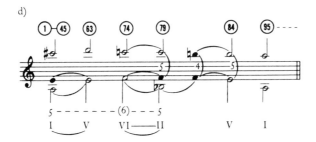

e)

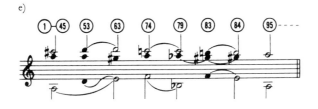

F-chord of bar 74 in an age-old 5–6–5 technique. It also shows the origin of the ninth over b♭ as a suspension. Example 18d illustrates the horizontalizing of I and II as first depicted in Example 18a. Out of this technique grow the v of bar 63 and the vi of bar 74. As a feature of this succession, the prime melodic structure acquires the neighbor d³. Note also the first suggestion of *Tr* between bars 79 and 84 in the working out of the linear technique 5–4–5. Finally, in Example 18e, a significant accompanying voice makes its appearance. It is the intervallic space created by this voice against the prime outer voice that is filled in by so many of the motivic elements, as already shown in Example 2b.

CONCLUSION

THREE POINTS remain to be mentioned as we bring this linear-harmonic analysis to an end. The first is the linking of the Prelude or, better, the Introduction, with the beginning of Act I, which hovers between C minor and E♭ major. The seeds of the modulatory transition are sown in bar 17, for the F-chord, which appears at this point and again in bar 74, becomes eventually the agent for the shift from A to C. Following its final appearance in bar 94 of the piece as usually performed, the music shifts its weight to the dominant of C, employing the F-chord, this time, as a subdominant. Note, in bar 107 and further, the imaginative way in which preparation is made for the ensuing solo of the young sailor. The ascending sixth is, of course, closely related to the similar interval of motive *A*¹.

The second point is concerned with the extraordinary difficulties that harmonic theorists have had in analyzing the chordal details of the Prelude in terms of one or another system of harmony. At best, chordal analysis provides only a one-dimensional view of a composition. Thus, even when some kind of agreement can be reached about chord names and functions, the resultant values are bound to be limited. However, in the case of the Tristan Prelude, even this kind of agreement over labels has not been reached, as can be discovered by a random sampling of available chord and key analyses.

The reason is not hard to find. There has been a preoccupation with each of the striking sonorities as individual sounds, or at most these have been related only to an immediate environment. This is, of course, not the only chromatic piece that has refused to reveal its harmonic meanings when its techniques are assessed on a chord by chord basis. It is axiomatic that the more intense the chromaticism, the greater the need to relate individual sonorities to a broad context. A simple case in point can be found in bars 32–40, where only a summoning of the inclusive frame provided by the D-chord can illuminate the meaning of the details. Without such a reference the analyst cannot help but record a confusing welter of chord labels and modulatory activities. With it, his problem shifts to one of assessing chords as elements of motion within a clearly marked area. Hence, the possibility of finding an insightful reading of detail becomes real and immediate.

The third and final point, to which the preceding considerations lead, relates to the attempt to find an embracing structure by means of linear-harmonic analytic procedures. Such an aim carries us well beyond the meaning of detail, for its ultimate problem is the relating to each other of the several pervasive frames with their contents. This can be a challenging and sometimes a despairing assignment. In the case of the Tristan Prelude, it has proven to be less formidable than in many another piece. For one thing, the harmonic pilings are strongly marked; for another, the broad contexts are easily found; and for a third, the controlling outer parts are always reasonably in evidence.

This does not mean, however, that there can be only one exemplary linear-harmonic analysis of a work such as this. Clearly, when so many diverse, often competing, factors await evaluation, when a desired objectivity is constantly menaced by the limiting slants of personal musical experience, a resolute effort must be made to reduce arbitrary readings to the zero point, to eliminate purely capricious judgments. When these hampering conditions are overcome, the success of an analysis can be measured by the degree of musical insight that it provides. Some will fall short of the mark; others will approach the heart of the work. It remains idle, however, to speculate on the most viable of all viable analyses, for in the end the analytic conclusions reached are individual judgments, however rarefied, rather than mechanical derivatives. This is a source of strength for linear-harmonic analysis, for it suggests a constant matching of the musical maturity of the analyst with the elusive essence of the work analyzed.

The Musical Language of Wozzeck

GEORGE PERLE

*T*HE SUBJECT of the present essay is neither the thematic material nor the formal design of Berg's opera *Wozzeck*, but rather those elements of pitch organization that generate the context within which themes and motives operate—that determine, in other words, the various pitch levels at which themes and motives are stated and the type and scope of modifications to which they are subjected—and that provide a basis for harmonic continuity and contrast. A description of these elements in the domain of the traditional tonal system may be reduced to a statement of the foundational assumptions of that system—the triad as the sole criterion of harmonic stability and the complex of functional relationships postulated in the concept of a "key center." No comparable generalizations regarding the musical language of *Wozzeck* are offered here, but a first attempt is made to describe certain means of integration and differentiation that are characteristic features of that language. Thematic and formal aspects of the work will be discussed only to the extent—in some instances considerable— that an elucidation of the central topic demands.

TONE CENTERS

THOUGH one notes the occasional presence of tonic functionality in this otherwise "atonal" work (explicitly only in Act III, Scene 1, and in the symphonic interlude between the last two scenes, but also more or less vaguely and transiently elsewhere, as in the *Ländler* of Act II and in the "folk song" episodes), the centricity of a given pitch or collection of pitches is no less unmistakable in many of the "atonal" sections of *Wozzeck*. In attempting to resolve the semantic contradictions that arise from an admission of the presence of "tone centers" in "atonal" music, I cannot hope to improve upon the introductory remarks of Arthur Berger's recent article, "Problems of Pitch Organization in Stravinsky."[1] Though Berger's observations refer to his ensuing discussion of Stravinsky's "pre-twelve-tone" works, the following quotations are explicitly relevant to the present study:

There are other means besides functional ones for asserting pitch-class priority; from which it follows that pitch-class priority per se: 1) is not a sufficient condition of that music which is tonal, and 2) is compatible with music that is not tonally functional. . . .

For purposes of non-tonal centric music it might be a good idea to have the term "tone center" refer to the more general class of which "tonics" (or tone centers in tonal contexts) could be regarded as a sub-class.

In the first scene of the opera, C♯/D♭ is unequivocally established as a tone center by "other means besides functional ones." The first musical statement after the curtain is raised is the unaccompanied leitmotiv of the Captain (Example 1).[2]

EXAMPLE I

Within this context, the priority of C♯/D♭ is established by its exposed position in the melodic contour (highest and lowest note), its exposed temporal position (last note), repetition (not only is it the only reiterated

[1] Arthur Berger, "Problems of Pitch Organization in Stravinsky," *Perspectives of New Music* (Fall-Winter, 1963).

[2] All citations from *Wozzeck* refer to the miniature score, copyright 1955 by Universal Edition A. G., Vienna. Examples reprinted by permission of the publisher.

pitch class but also the only one which appears in more than one octave position), and durational preponderance. The priority of C♯/D♭ is extended through Scene 1 as a whole by analogous means within the larger context. Throughout this scene, C♯/D♭ recurs as a spatial and temporal boundary and as an ostinato in inner and outer voices. The leitmotiv of the Captain, at its primary pitch level,[3] is a salient component of the formal design. The repeated D♭ of bars 5–6 becomes the recurrent monotone motive of Wozzeck's "Jawohl, Herr Hauptmann!" (bars 25–26, 67–69, 76–79, 87–89, 90–96, 136–137, 151). The series of perfect fourths that marks the Captain's ruminations on eternity descends to $D♭_1$, the lowest note of Scene 1.[4] Wozzeck's pensive reflection on virtue ("Es muss was Schönes sein um die Tugend") is accompanied by a passage in the solo violin that ascends to $C♯_8$, the registral climax of the second half of Scene 1.

The presence of more or less traditional functional relations in "atonal" and "twelve-tone" music has been asserted by some theorists. The basis for this claim is probably to be found in a tendency noted by Roger Sessions:

The intervals, and their effects, remain precisely the same; two notes a fifth apart still produce the effect of the fifth, and in whatever degree the context permits, will convey a sensation similar to that of a root and its fifth, or of a tonic and its dominant. A rising interval of a semitone will produce somewhat the effect of a "leading tone," principal or secondary, and so on.[5]

There is no question that an "atonal" melodic line, "in whatever degree the context permits," or in isolation from its context, will present a complex interplay of tensions and resolutions that are to some extent analogous to characteristic elements of melodic motion in tonal music. But it is precisely the fact that the intervallic "effects" to which Sessions calls attention generate a tone center in certain contexts but not in others that justifies the theorist in distinguishing between "tonality" and "atonality." The means by which C♯/D♭ is made to function as a tone center in Act I, Scene 1, of *Wozzeck* do not depend upon criteria of the sort mentioned by Sessions.

[3] The term "pitch level" refers to placement within the semitonal scale irrespective of octave position.

[4] The subscript refers to octave positions, with the "first" octave represented as C_1 to C_2 and successive ascending octaves correspondingly, named; e.g., "middle C" is represented as C_4.

[5] Roger Sessions, *Harmonic Practice* (New York, Harcourt, 1951), p. 407.

An unwarranted projection of these criteria, supplemented by imaginary implied notes, has led other writers to attribute tonic functionality to "atonal" motives. The leitmotiv of the Captain can imply not only a tonic of B, as has been conjectured, but also, with as much (or as little) justification, tonics of F♯, or A, or E (Example 2). (The assumption of tonic centricity requires that the composer's notated D♭ in bars 5–6 be replaced by C♯.)

EXAMPLE 2

The moment this music is considered in its vertical aspects, the distinction between centricity in an "atonal" and in a tonal context becomes doubly clear. Any inferences of tonic functionality that a tonally oriented ear may make will be dispelled by the dyads, F–B and G–D, that accompany the reiterated D♭ of bar 6. These are again associated with the linear tone center C♯/D♭ at salient cadential points of Scene 1. F–B is sustained throughout the first return of the leitmotiv of the Captain at the conclusion of the first number of Scene 1 (bars 26–30).[6] Here the additon of a second

6 Berg describes this scene as a "Suite of more or less stylized archaic dance-forms (such as Prelude, Pavane, Cadenza, Gigue, Gavotte with double-refrain)," as quoted in H. F. Redlich, *Alban Berg* (New York, Abelard-Schuman, 1957), p. 269.

tritone, A–E♭, produces, in conjunction with F–B and D♭, a five-note segment of the whole-tone scale, the significance of which in the total context
of the work will be discussed below. E♭ as upper neighbor to the tone center
introduces the second number (bars 30 ff.), at the conclusion of which both
dyads of bar 6 are sustained against the final note of the leitmotiv (Example
3).

EXAMPLE 3

At the conclusion of Scene 1 (bars 170 f), A is added to this collection
to form a simultaneity that serves as the principal referential chord of the
work as a whole (Example 4). This final cadential chord of Scene 1 subsequently demarcates only the largest formal divisions, the three acts. The
slow descent of the curtain at the conclusion of Acts I and III is accompanied
by a pedal on G–D and a tremolo figure of two chords, the second of which
consists of the remaining notes of Example 4 (Example 5).

EXAMPLE 4   EXAMPLE 5

The prelude to Act II opens with an arpeggiated version of Example 4 leading into the same tremolo figure (Example 6). At the conclusion of Act II, the cadential figure (Example 5) is dissipated by the elimination of

EXAMPLE 6

one note at a time, with the curtain falling in the ensuing bars of silence (Example 7). The final act commences with silence of the same duration as that which marked the conclusion of the preceding act, followed by a melodic figure whose initial notes are those of the sustained dyad of Example 5.

The concept of "centricity" in the context of the present discussion must be broad enough to encompass both the priority in Scene 1 of C♯/D♭ and the priority in the work as a whole of the chord illustrated in Example 4, and even of that chord plus its neighbor (Example 5), with which it is

EXAMPLE 7

invariably associated except in Scene 1. We shall designate a chord that is stabilized at a specific pitch level and that functions significantly as a referential detail by the term "compound tone center," as opposed to a "simple tone center" such as the C♯/D♭ of Scene 1. The term "tone center" is not intended to suggest any parallel with what is understood by "tonic" in the major-minor system, other than the quality of centricity within a given context.[7] In the traditional tonal system, centricity is asserted not only by the tonic, and by the tonic triad, but also by the dominant, which acts as a focal element in its own right in a definite functional relationship with the tonic. Various kinds of centricity may also be asserted in nontonal music. The simple tone center C♯/D♭ is the primary linear focal element of Scene 1 only, its priority expressed through repetition, durational preponderance, and prominence at registral and temporal boundaries. The primary compound tone center (Example 4), although it asserts its priority in terms of the largest formal components of the work, does not display, as a tone center, the variety of functions of the simple tone center of Scene 1. One of the dyadic constituents of this primary compound tone center, B–F, functions as a tone center in the context of *both* the largest and the smallest dimensions of the work.

By means of the dyadic tone center B–F, a referential pitch level is established for some of the principal leitmotivs whose intervallic content includes a tritone. Throughout Scene 1, the leitmotiv of the Captain is stated at the pitch level that will generate the adjacency B–F (Example 1). A leitmotiv associated with the Doctor, first heard at the Doctor's words, "Wozzeck, Er kommt in's Narrenhaus," in Act I, Scene 4 (bars 562–564), returns at the beginning of Act II, Scene 2, transposed so as to unfold the same adjacency, B–F, that defines the "home key" of the leitmotiv of the Captain, and stated concurrently with the latter (Example 8).

At bar 286 of Act II, Scene 2, a triple fugue begins, with the initial entry of each subject presenting the same fixed dyad. The first subject, the leitmotiv of the Captain, enters at bar 286, the second, the leitmotiv of the

7 I have borrowed the term "priority" from Berger, who, however, employs it only in reference to "simple tone centers." I use the term "chord" rather than "simultaneity" designedly in the paragraph above and elsewhere, in reference to recurrent, stable, or referential vertical structures. Such a structure is still a "chord" even when it is not a "simultaneity," that is, when it is a "broken chord."

EXAMPLE 8

Doctor, at the upbeat to bar 293. The third subject, representing Wozzeck, contains no tritone among its adjacencies, but its entrance at bar 313 is at a pitch level that generates the notes B–F as prominent components of the pitch content of this subject (Example 9). The initial appearance of this motive, at the same pitch level, occurs near the conclusion of the preceding *Fantasie*[8] (bars 273–274).

EXAMPLE 9

The priority of B–F (or F–B) is established in the first number of Act I, Scene 1 (bars 1–29). In the first three bars, this dyad appears only as an incidental detail, first as one of the linear intervals between the two chords with which the opera opens, and then as a vertical interval of the final chord of bar 3, which marks the conclusion of the curtain music. Thereafter it rises to prominence very quickly (bars 4, 6, 10–11, 26–29; note also that each of the first four vocal passages begins or ends on B or F). The importance of this dyad at certain cadential points of Scene 1 was discussed above. B and F frequently mark the outer limits of salient simultaneities, as

8 In Berg's outline of the formal design, this scene is entitled Fantasie und Fuge. Willi Reich, *Alban Berg* (Zürich, Atlantis, 1963), p. 113.

at bars 32–33, 59–60, and the ostinato passage for four trumpets at bars 93–96.

The priority of B–F is asserted again and again throughout the work, often as a means of reaffirming the dramatic, as well as the musical, "key-note" of the opera. The most striking instance is at the conclusion of the "Cradle Song" in Act I, Scene 3. Before the appearance of B–F, Marie is *in Gedanken versunken* as the orchestra plays the cadential chords of this number (Example 10). The open fifths express, according to Berg, Marie's

EXAMPLE 10

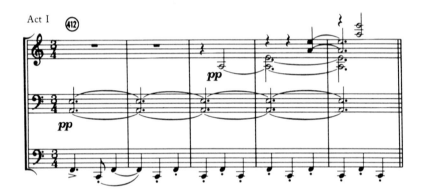

"aimless and indefinable attitude of waiting."[9] The pitch content of bars 412–416 is sustained to bar 423, where C is replaced by B. The concluding bars of the "Cradle Song" (bars 415–416) return at bars 425–426 (Example 11), but with the earlier pedal, F–C, converted into the basic dyad, F–B, a musical intimation of Wozzeck's approach.

Marie's reverie is interrupted when Wozzeck knocks at the window, at the 32d-note figure in bar 427 (Example 11). Bars 425–426 are recapitulated at the same pitch level at Wozzeck's exit (bar 455), an adumbration of Wozzeck's final leavetaking from Marie after he stabs her in Act III, Scene 2 (bars 106–107). There is a reference to the same music in the tavern scene that follows the latter (bars 152–153), now representing the

9 Redlich, p. 272.

EXAMPLE 11

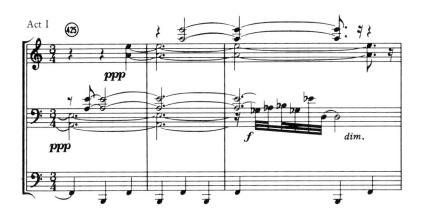

obtrusion of the thoughts which Wozzeck has come here to blot out. A last reminiscence of this music is heard in the concluding scene (bar 379), when one of the children calls out to Marie's little boy, "Hey you, your mother's dead!"

The primary dyad B–F is frequently associated with the rise or fall of the curtain. As a component of Example 5, B–F is part of the curtain music at the end of each act. Its inclusion in the chord that marks the rise of the first curtain at the conclusion of bar 3 was mentioned above. It returns at the fall of the first curtain as part of the final chord of the first scene (Example 4). As a component of the "fanfare" motive (Example 12), it is the first linear adjacency of Act I, Scene 3. The quick curtain that opens the final scene of Act I is accompanied by the inversion of the same dyad (Example 13).

EXAMPLE 12   EXAMPLE 13

EXAMPLE 14

The concluding melodic interval of Act II, Scene 1, is B–F (Example 14). The same two notes mark the extremes of the "white-note" collection in the orchestra at this point. A "white-note" glissando from B_6 to B_1 accompanies the quick curtain in the following bar. The importance of the basic dyad at the beginning of the next scene (bar 171) has already been pointed out (Example 8).

In the first bar of Act III, Scene 2, a sustained F joins the pedal B upon which the curtain rises (Example 15). When the curtain falls upon this scene, the repeated linear adjacency in the pedal, F–B, comes to rest upon its final note. B and F are components of the reiterated chord that accompanies the curtain that rises upon Act III, Scene 4.

EXAMPLE 15

Not only the means, but also the degree, of centricity varies throughout the work. There are extensive sections whose special character would seem to reside in the *absence* of tone centers. Even so, most themes and motives, including such as are not clearly orientated around a tone center, are stabilized at times at particular transpositions that have priority among the various pitch levels at which these themes and motives appear.

Act I, Scene 2, commences with a series of three chords which, at various transpositions, generates most of the tone material of the scene. Although centricity in the sense in which this term has been used above is not unambiguously present, the lowest note of the first chord of the series as initially given asserts a degree of priority in the scene as a whole, in consequence of the treatment of the bass line. With each return of the series of chords to its original pitch level (Example 16), C is heard as lowest note and point of departure in the bass line. In its principal thematic statement at T–0,[10] the succession of chords—x y x, x y z y x y x— gives priority to chord x, which serves not only as point of departure but also as destination. Thus, C functions as a goal of motion as well. C_1 is reiterated at bars 269–275 as the lowest note of the scene, and C_4 is the point of departure for a chromatic descent of the bass line to F_3 at bars 252–256, leading to a new permutation of the series—z x y z (bars 257 f).

EXAMPLE 16   EXAMPLE 17

X   Y   Z

Act I

Oh!   mei – ne   The – o – rie!

As a whole, the following scene (Act I, Scene 3) more or less suggests A as its tone center. The curtain rises upon a sustained chord whose lowest notes are the open octave on A; the "Cradle Song" begins with a neighbor-note motion from and to a chord whose lowest note is A (bars 372–373); the repeated open fifth in the cadential bars of the "Cradle Song," twice recapitulated in the same scene, is A–E (Examples 10 and 11); at the conclusion of the orchestral transition which follows this scene, A is sustained for seven bars, into the curtain music of Scene 4.

10 The level of transpositions is indicated by the symbol "T" followed by an arabic numeral representing the number of semitones counting upward from what is assumed to be the primary pitch level, indicated by "T–0," to the pitch level in question. Cf. note 3.

E♭/D♯ is the principal tone center of the latter. This scene commences and concludes on an E♭ pedal, and E♭ also acquires a certain measure of prominence through its position as the first note of the twelve-tone Passacaglia theme on which each variation is based. E♭ repeatedly occurs as an exposed element in the upper range of the Doctor's vocal line, culminating in the ecstatic solo with which the scene concludes (bars 620 ff): "Oh! meine Theorie! Oh mein Ruhm! Ich werde unsterblich! Unsterblich!" (Example 17). At bar 636, the bass line commences a chromatic descent from E♭ to the D♯ pedal which accompanies the fall of the curtain. The transition to the final scene of Act I opens with a pedal on G–D, in preparation for the pedal on the same notes in the concluding bars of the same scene (Example 5).

Though the dyadic tone center B–F far transcends in importance the simple tone centers whose priority is asserted only within the limited context of a scene, or merely part of a scene, the former is often, within that context, subordinate as a referential element. In Act I, Scene 4, for example the dyad is referentially significant only in association with musical reminiscences of earlier scenes. The twelve-tone theme of the Passacaglia (which, as a unit, is never transposed, though segments are elaborated at various pitch levels against the ostinato theme) comprises four tritones among its adjacencies, but none of them is B–F. It is interesting to note that in the two bars preceding the rise of the curtain upon this scene, the first statement of the twelve-tone series which forms the Passacaglia theme is anticipated by a passage that is rhythmically identical with and largely duplicates the pitch succession of the theme, but that comprises only ten rather than twelve pitch classes, since B and F are each stated twice. (This concluding passage of Act I, Scene 3, is a linearization of the symmetrical progression that introduces the "Military March" at the beginning of the scene. Compare bars 483–485 with the last two chords of bar 333 and the first chord of bar 334.) The revised restatement of this pattern, the series of the Passacaglia theme, expunges the basic dyad (Example 18).

The ultimate dramatic implications of the basic dyad are realized in the *Invention über einen Ton*,[11] Act III, Scene 2, in which an ostinato B symbolizing Wozzeck's obsession with the murder of Marie, is maintained in one

---

11 Berg's title. Cf. note 8.

EXAMPLE 18

form or another, culminating in the two crescendi on B in the orchestral interlude which follows. B had been charged with this meaning at the conclusion of Act II, where it appeared as the last element of the gradually dissipated cadential figure (cf. p. 209). Throughout the murder scene (Act

EXAMPLE 19

EXAMPLE 20

Den Him - mel gäb' ich drum und die Se - lig -

- keit, wenn ich Dich noch oft so küs - sen dürft!

III, Scene 2), F is employed as a complementary tone center—as upper limit of the first sustained simultaneity in the orchestra (Example 15); as recurrent goal of motion (Example 19); as first note, last note, or highest note of segments of the vocal line (Example 20).

The death of Marie (Act III, Scene 2) and the death of Wozzeck (Act III, Scene 4) are complementary climaxes of the opera. The principal leitmotivs linking the two scenes are visual: the locale, the murder weapon, and, above all, the red moon, which triggers both catastrophes, first rising "wie ein blutig Eisen" as the immediate incitement to the crime and later breaking through the clouds as witness and betrayer, its blood-red reflection in the pond as Wozzeck attempts to wash the blood from himself inducing the ultimate extremes of his derangement.

The musical links between the two scenes do not depend on motivic connections, but rather on the complementary relationship of the two members of the basic dyad. Compare, for example, the linear juxtaposition of the two tone centers at the moment of the murder (Example 21a) with the setting of the words "todt" and "Mörder" upon Wozzeck's return to the scene of the crime (Example 21b). The reiterated or sustained F in the top line of the orchestra part at salient moments in the formal design of Act III, Scene 4, and the prominence of F elsewhere in the scene as well, parallels the reiterated or sustained B of the earlier scene, and just as F played a subsidiary but complementary role within that scene, so B does within the later scene.

VERTICAL SETS

THE TERM "vertical set" as employed here will mean a collection of pitch classes that is defined solely in terms of its unordered content, of which any simultaneity within a given musical complex will represent an equivalent or transposed statement. To whatever extent horizontal details are generated by the linearization—rather than the juxtaposition—of such simultaneities, the set is the sole determinant of horizontal, as well as vertical, association. Such vertical sets were consistently employed by Scriabin

EXAMPLE 21

as early as 1911. The chord on which Act III, Scene 4, *Invention über einen Sechsklang*, is based (Example 22) conforms to the above definition of a vertical set.

EXAMPLE 22

Aside from a single exceptional statement of the set (Act III, bar 114), it is exploited only in Scene 4. In the orchestral interlude that follows the murder of Marie (Scene 2), Scene 4 is foreshadowed in the *fortississimo* chord that simultaneously marks the conclusion of the sustained unison on B and the inception of the rhythmic motive that is the basis of Act III, Scene 3. This interlude is thus a statement of the three *idées fixes* that respectively govern Scenes 2, 3, and 4 of the final act.

The principal form of the set (Example 22) is defined by its pitch level ("s-o")[12] and by the vertical disposition of its components. Act III, Scene 4, opens with reiterated statements of this "thematic" or "referential" version of the set (bars 220–222). The first section of the scene is bounded by these opening bars and their recapitulation, two octaves lower, at the midpoint of the scene (bars 257 ff). Within this section, the set is employed exclusively at its original pitch level, but in various vertical permutations and linearizations, and with octave displacements of segments of the set.

Almost all pitch elements through bar 266 are to be explained as components of s-o. The only exceptions are a few passing notes, a quotation of several motives from Act II, Scene 4 (at Wozzeck's words, "Hast Dir das rote Halsband verdient, wie die Ohrringlein, mit Deiner Sünde!"), a few passages in the vocal part, and a tone cluster (trumpets and trombones, bar 251) consisting of the notes that are not contained in s-o. At bar 267 the set is transposed to T-3, and following this there are overlapping set-statements at various pitch levels. The "drowning music" that begins at bar 284 returns to the primary vertical pattern and uses this form of the set exclusively, but transposes the set repeatedly along the twelve degrees of the semitonal scale.

The final section commences at bar 302, with a return to the initial sonority, transposed one octave down and sustained to the end of the scene. Against this final statement of s-o as a pedal, two passages that had appeared earlier in s-o, the "toad music" of bars 226 ff and the "moon music" of bars 262 ff, are recapitulated in s-7, a version of the set that is maximally invariant[13] with s-o. In the sixth bar before the end of the scene, s-7 is retired, so that the conclusion recapitulates the beginning of the scene in its exclusive use of the primary form of s-o.

---

12 Cf. note 10.

13 I.e., no transposition of s–o duplicates more of the pitch content of s—o than does s–7. The number of pitch classes that are common to sx and s(x plus y) is the same as the number of pitch classes that are common to sx and s(x minus y). Thus, except where the maximally invariant transposition is at the tritone of sx, there must be at least two maximally invariant transpositions. These are s–7 and s–5 in the present instance.

CHORD SERIES

A SERIES of chords which generates the principal material of Act I, Scene 2, was illustrated at T-0 in Example 16. In its formal design, this scene gives expression to two alternating ideas: Wozzeck's superstitious dread of the "accursed place" and Andres' lightheartedness, the former represented in the episodes based on Example 16 (bars 201–212, 223–245, 257–263, 266–309), the latter in the intervening "folk song" episodes. It is noteworthy that two of the three basic chords contain, at T-0, the primary dyad, B–F. There is a curious "rightness" about the progression, possibly a result of the linear connections between chords x and y—dyads moving in parallel motion against a semitonal inflection[14]—and the pitch classes held in common by chords y and z (Example 23).

EXAMPLE 23

The thematic version of the chord series is defined not only by the initial pitch level and initial vertical ordering of each chord as illustrated in Example 16, but also in the overall succession of the three chords as presented in the first eight bars of the scene (cf. p. 215). As the scene progresses, new material is derived from vertical permutations, transpositions, temporal displacements of chordal segments, and revisions of the thematic statement. As a source of pitch relations the chord series does not play the almost exclusive role of the set on which Act III, Scene 4, is based. Notes that are not

[14] Cf. pp. 243 ff.

components of the basic chords appear in association with these chords throughout the scene. The initial thematic statement of the basic chords, representing Wozzeck's estrangement from his physical environment in Act I, Scene 2, returns at the beginning of the barracks scene (Act II, Scene 5), in reference to his estrangement from his social environment. Other reminiscences and quotations from Act I, Scene 2, are found in this scene as well as in Act I, Scene 3 (bars 431–454), where Wozzeck, stopping to greet Marie on his way to the barracks, persists in his obsessions of the preceding scene, and in Act I, Scene 4 (bars 546–561), where he reveals his "aberration" to the Doctor.

The Trio of the *Langsamer Ländler* of Act II, Scene 4 (bars 456–480), is based, in the orchestra, upon a more extensive chord series (Example 24), the ordering of which remains inviolate except for certain modifications where one statement of the series is linked to the next. Within each restatement the chords retain the relative octave position and vertical structure of the original statement of the series in the bridge section between the *Ländler* and the Trio (bars 447–455). The Trio comprises two restatements of the series, the first at T-0, the second at T-1. In the former, a single rhythmic pattern is reiterated eight times, with the chord changes occurring

EXAMPLE 24

EXAMPLE 25

Act II (456)

at irregular points within this pattern (Example 25). In the second variation (bars 465–480), passing chords are interpolated to fill in the missing
semitonal degrees between the linear adjacencies of the series. At the conclusion of this variation, the concluding chords (bars 454–455) of the bridge
section return in a rhythmic pattern which is the retrograde of the rhythmic
pattern of the first variation. The reiteration of a single chordal pattern is
evidently intended as a reference to the chordal texture and strophic form
of the Protestant chorale, in analogy with the grotesque employment of
religious verbal motives in the text. Segments of the chord series return in
the *Choral* of the stage orchestra at bars 605–633, the original chords being
broken to form a *cantus firmus* against material not derived from the series.
The *Choral* is followed by a retrograde version of the series, with bars
641 (3d beat)–649 corresponding to bars 455 (2d beat)–447.

BASIC CELLS AND AGGREGATES OF BASIC CELLS

I HAVE CITED examples of extensive sections whose tone material is entirely,
or largely, derived from a single vertical formation or a series of such formations. A greater complexity and subtlety in the structural use of vertical
formations are occasioned by the imposition of the formal design of the
traditional sonata form in the opening scene of Act II. The formal components of this scene are characterized and coordinated by means that are
in certain respects analogous to those provided in the traditional tonal
system. A prerequisite is the possibility of defining and interrelating different harmonic areas. The latter are established, in the Sonata movement of
Wozzeck, by means of characteristic harmonic cells and aggregates of such
cells. Harmonic areas may be differentiated in two ways: (1) as to type, or
"mode," dependent upon the intervallic structure of the basic cell; (2)
within a given "mode," as to pitch level, or "key," as indicated by the
transposition numbers assigned to the basic cells and aggregates. Though
the basic cell occasionally generates the totality of pitch components within
a certain limited context, as in the Bridge Section of the First Exposition
(see below), this is not its function in general. It is therefore not to be confused with what was designated above by the term "vertical set." The
vertical set of Act III, Scene 4, generates the complex of pitch components

of that scene; the basic cells and aggregates of Act II, Scene 1, are characteristic harmonic details and focal elements *within* a given complex of pitch components.

As always with Berg, the text is arranged to delineate a formal design that parallels, in dramatic terms, that of the music.[15] Corresponding sections of the libretto and the musical design are indicated in the following outline.

FIRST EXPOSITION
Principal Section:
bars 7–24 (principal theme)

> Marie, the child on her lap, a piece of broken mirror in her hand, admires the earrings given her by the Drum Major.

bars 25–28 (transition)

Bridge Section:
bars 29–42

> The child stirs and Marie admonishes him to sleep or the bogey man will get him.

Subordinate Section:
bars 43–48 (subordinate theme)

> Marie sings a "folk song": "Maiden, close up tight! Here comes a Gypsy lad, will take you by the hand,

bars 49–54 (introduction to
　　Closing Section)

> away into Gypsyland!"

Closing Section:
bars 55–59

> The imagined entrance of the "Gypsy lad" terrifies the child, who has buried his head in his mother's lap.

SECOND EXPOSITION
Principal Section:
bars 60–80

> Marie again looks at herself in the mirror and admires the earrings.

Bridge Section:
bars 81–89

> The child sits up and Marie admonishes him to close his eyes. Still holding the mirror, she flickers

---

[15] See Berg's commentary on this scene, Redlich, pp. 274 f.

its reflected light on the wall. "There's the Sand-man running on the wall.

Subordinate Section:
bars 90–92 (subordinate theme
    in diminution)

Shut your eyes, or he'll look into them and make you blind."

Closing Section:
bars 93–96

Wozzeck enters, unnoticed by Marie, who is still watching the child.

DEVELOPMENT
bars 96–101 (based on
    principal theme)

Marie jumps up, putting her hands to her ears. Wozzeck: "What have you there?" Marie: "Nothing!" Wozzeck: "Something's shining under your fingers." Marie: "An earring. I found it."

bars 101–105 (based on
    closing theme)

Wozzeck: "I've never found anything like that! Two at one time!"

bars 105–108 (based on
    principal theme)

Marie: "Am I a bad woman?" Wozzeck, calming her: "All right, Marie, all right!"

bars 109–112 (based on
    Bridge Section)

He turns to the child: "How the boy always sleeps! Lift his arm, the chair is hurting him. The shiny drops on his forehead!

bars 112–115

Nothing under the sun but toil! Sweating even when we sleep! We poor people!

bars 116–125

Here is more money, Marie. My pay, and something from the Captain, and the Doctor." Marie: "God reward it, Franz!" Wozzeck: "I must go, Marie. Goodbye." Wozzeck leaves.

bars 125–127 (transition)

Marie, alone: "But I am

RECAPITULATION
Principal Section:
bars 128–139 (corresponding
    to bars 7–18)

a bad woman! I could stab myself! Oh, this

| | world! Everything goes to the devil, man and wife and child!" |
| bar 140 | Curtain. (From this point on the Recapitulation continues as Interlude between Scenes 1 and 2.) |

bars 141–149 (corresponding
   to bars 19–23)

Subordinate Section:
bars 150–161 (corresponding
   to bars 43–48 in augmentation,
   with *Hauptstimme* of principal
   theme continuing from bar 148
   as countermelody in bass)

Closing Section:
bars 162–166

Principal Section, Bridge Section, Subordinate Section, and Closing Section are each characterized by a special harmonic cell, and the movement as a whole is based on aggregates of the different cells. This dependence on a special cell is most obvious in the Bridge Section of the First Exposition. The cell, at the pitch level assigned to it at its initial appearance in the Bridge Section (T-11), is anticipated in the Prelude (bars 1–6) to the act (Example 26).

This cell, a diminished triad with conjunct semitone superimposed, will be designated as "cell B." The first six bars of the Bridge Section comprise four statements of cell B, in the order shown in Example 27. In bars 34–36, two new notes are joined to the cell (Example 28). The resulting hexad, marking the median cadence of the Bridge Section, is an aggregate of the four basic cells of the movement (Example 29). The transposition number assigned to this statement of the aggregate is T-10, for reasons that are explained below.[16]

16 Cell A is contained in the aggregate hexad at two different pitch levels. Each cell is shown in a characteristic vertical permutation. Cells and sets are primarily defined by their relative pitch content, however, and are cited in various vertical permutations in the examples.

EXAMPLE 26

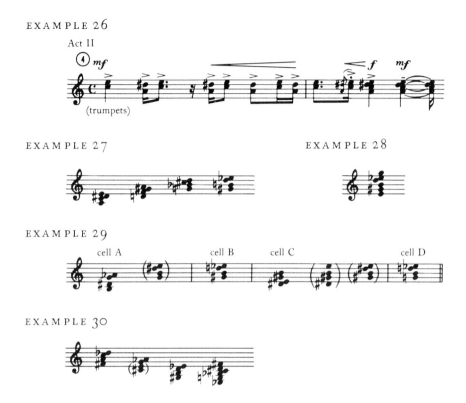

EXAMPLE 27   EXAMPLE 28

EXAMPLE 29

EXAMPLE 30

In the second half of the Bridge Section, the order of transpositions is inverted, with the fourth statement of the cell converted, as before, into the hexad illustrated in Example 28, now at T-9 (cf. Examples 27 and 28 with Example 30). A symmetrical inflection of a four-note segment of the concluding chord of the Bridge Section generates the initial chord and special cell (cell C) of the Subordinate Section (Example 31). In content, the concluding chord of the Bridge Section points toward the Closing Section of the First Exposition (given in its entirety in Example 32). Four notes of the aggregate collection of bars 40–42 are redistributed to form cell D, and the two remaining notes, G and E♭, outline the melodic component of the Closing Section.

The basic aggregate of the movement is the five-note collection that initiates the Closing Section (Example 32, bar 55). This basic pentad may

EXAMPLE 31

EXAMPLE 32

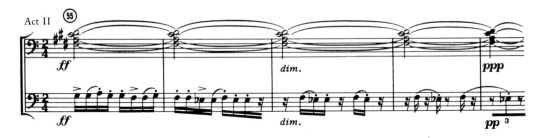

be regarded as a diminished triad with conjunct semitone not only superimposed (cell B) but also subimposed, or it may be regarded, more rele-
vantly in terms of the movement as a whole, as an augmented and a diminished triad sharing a common central tone. The basic pentad in its "home
key" (T-0) and its three component cells are illustrated in Example 33.
(The criteria that determine which pitch level represents the "home key"
of the basic pentad have been established earlier in the Principal Section of
the movement and will be discussed below.)

Both expository statements of the subordinate theme conclude with
ascending semitonal transpositions of the basic pentad from T-7 to T-11
(Example 34). In the Recapitulation, the same progression (bars 160–161)
rises by another semitone into the final statement of the Closing Section,
the latter thus commencing with the basic pentad at T-0 (Example 35).
The movement concludes with a restatement of the basic pentad at T-0,
with cell C—the only cell not contained in the basic pentad (cf. Example

EXAMPLE 33

EXAMPLE 34

EXAMPLE 35

EXAMPLE 36

33)—incorporated into the final aggregate through the addition of one new element to the basic pentad (Example 36).

The relevance of this or any other collection cannot be evaluated without some comprehension of the tonal resources from which it is selected. In terms of absolute pitch content, there are 924 different hexads[17] comprised within the material of the semitonal scale. The basic pentad at T-0 is a component of only seven of these, of which only the hexads shown in Example 37 can be construed as aggregates of all four basic cells.

Let us assume an additional requirement for the final chord, predicated on the fact that the irreducible referential sonority of the movement is the

17 Perle, *Serial Composition and Atonality* (Berkeley, University of California Press, 1962), pp. 117 ff. With the exclusion of transpositions the number of hexads are reduced to the 80 non-equivalent six-note segments of Hauer's 44 tropes. The tropes are given in Hauer's *Vom Melos zur Pauke* (Vienna, Universal Edition, 1925), and Karl Eschman, *Changing Forms in Modern Music* (Boston, Schirmer, 1935), pp. 84 ff.

EXAMPLE 37

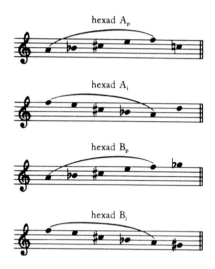

augmented triad on C♯, F, or A, the overriding importance of which will become clear when we consider the principal theme of the movement. Only the first and second hexads can give special emphasis to this component, by the containment of each within the minor sixth, the boundary interval of the augmented triad. Berg chose the first of these for the final chord of the movement (Example 36). Had he chosen the second, the aggregate of basic cells would have been the same except for cell C, which would have appeared as shown in Example 38. In the preceding bar, cell C appears at precisely this pitch level, as the climax of the final statement of the Closing Section (Example 39).

EXAMPLE 38   EXAMPLE 39

The hexads illustrated in Example 37 represent four out of eighty possible collections in terms of their *relative* pitch content—that is, with each hexad taken as a representation of the pitch content of any one of its twelve transpositions. If it is assumed that any two hexads that can be transformed into one another through inversion are to be regarded as representations of the same set, the total number of possible hexads is reduced to fifty. Of these, only the two whose mutually invertible forms are illustrated in Example 37 can represent aggregates of the four basic cells. The digression from the "home key" of the principal theme in the Bridge Section of the First Exposition is expressed through hexad B_p at T-10 (Example 28) and T-9 (Example 30). Thus, hexads A and B are both significantly exploited in the movement. Berg's compositional procedures in *Wozzeck*, however, do not appear to require, or to justify, the evaluation of complementary forms of a hexad as representations of a single set, though they do justify such an evaluation of smaller complementary collections.[18] It would seem to be appropriate, in the present context, to regard Example 37 as illustrating four nonequivalent sets.

The fact that cell C, where it is stated as the climactic chord of the final Closing Section (Example 39), coincides in absolute pitch content with cell C as a component of hexad A_i encourages one to speculate that this pitch content may be structurally significant and that hexad A_i may be present as an aggregate. Cell C at the given pitch level (Example 39) is found to be maximally related in pitch content with cell A at T-0, the compound tone center of the principal theme, restored as a component of the basic pentad at T-0 with which the final statement of the Closing Section commences (Example 35). The total tone material in the climactic bar of the final section (Example 40) may be construed as comprising: 40a, a linearization of the basic pentad at T-2; 40b, a series of passing chords; 40c, hexad A_i.

The basic cell of the principal theme, and indeed of the movement, is cell A, which may be conveniently defined as an augmented triad plus a conjunct semitone superimposed upon any one of its constituent notes.

---

18 The inversional forms of the basic cells play a subordinate role, however. Where the aspect—prime or inversion—of the latter is not specified by a subscript, "p" or "i," the name assigned to a cell is understood to refer to the prime, unless the context indicates that in the given instance it is to be understood as referring to either of the complementary forms.

EXAMPLE 40

The three forms thus generated are equivalent to transpositions of a single collection (Example 41).

EXAMPLE 41

The basic pentad, equivalent in content to an augmented and a diminished triad conjoined through a common central tone, shares cell A with the prime form of another pentad, equivalent in content to an augmented and a diminished triad conjoined through a common boundary tone. The complementary forms of this pentad will be identified as x_p and x_i. (The basic pentad is a symmetrical, that is, self-complementary, set, the same pitch content representing both prime and inversion.) Pentads x_p and x_i and the basic pentad, at their respective primary pitch levels, incorporate the complementary forms of cell A as illustrated in Example 42.

EXAMPLE 42

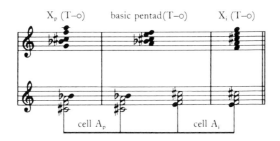

The augmented triad C♯–F–A is a pivotal harmonic center whose absolute pitch content is repeated at three different levels—T-0, T-4, T-8—of cell A, pentad x, the basic pentad, and the aggregate hexads. The same augmented triad is a component of the primary referential chord (Example 4) of the opera as a whole. As such it is prominently exposed in the Prelude to Act II and serves to introduce the "tonality" of the principal theme of the sonata movement. (The anticipation of the beginning of the Bridge Section in bars 4 and 5 of the Prelude was pointed out above, Example 26.) In fact, the characteristic pentad of the principal theme is completely contained, at T-4, in the principal compound tone center of the opera, and is thus an important component of the beginning and conclusion of the Prelude (Example 43).

EXAMPLE 43

That the chord on the initial downbeat of the Principal Section (bar 7) is to be interpreted as pentad x_p at T-0 with C♯ displaced by an appoggia-

tura may seem conjectural, but a comparison with the corresponding measures of the Second Exposition and with the transition into the Recapitulation confirms this interpretation (Example 44).

The harmonic material of the Principal Section is far more elaborately
organized and diversified than that of the other sections. The augmented
triad emerges as the most consistent harmonic feature of the principal
theme, within a complex which also includes pentad x and the prime and

EXAMPLE 44

a)

b)

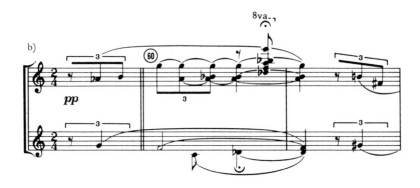

c)

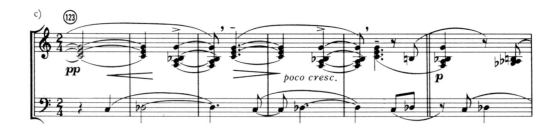

inversion of cells A and B. (The inversion of cell A is equivalent in content to cell D [Example 45], but in view of the harmonic character of the principal theme, it is more appropriate to refer to this collection in terms that stress the presence of the augmented triad.) These harmonic entities overlap with themselves and with other elements, some of which are of sufficient general importance to require discussion below.[19] Though pentad x is a

EXAMPLE 45

cell A_i cell D

characteristic feature of the principal theme, within which the basic pentad plays no explicit role whatever, the former is, within the movement, clearly subordinate to the latter. Whereas the basic pentad may be construed as an aggregate of the two forms of both cells A and B, pentad x_p and pentad x_i each incorporate one form of cell A only (Example 42). Moreover, the basic pentad, but not pentad x, is contained in the aggregate hexads whose all-important structural functions have been discussed above.

The structural role of the augmented triad in the principal theme of the Sonata is made clear in Example 46. Statements of the augmented triad are shown extracted from the simultaneities in which they appear and in their closest linear juxtapositions. Wherever the augmented triad occurs at its principal pitch level (T-0, T-4, or T-8), the basic cell or pentad of which it is a component is indicated. Each of these points represents a salient moment in the formal design of the principal theme. Bars 7–8 mark the beginning of the first period, bar 16 the parallel beginning of the second period, bar 22 the climax, and bar 24 the conclusion.

It is the augmented triad above all that differentiates the principal theme

EXAMPLE 46

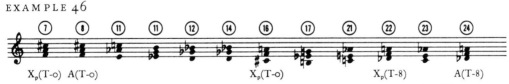

X_p(T-0) A(T-0) X_p(T-0) X_p(T-8)   A(T-8)

[19] These other elements are discussed, without special reference to Act II, Scene 1, under "Scale Segments" and "Symmetrical Formations."

from the other formal components of the Sonata. The augmented triad does not appear elsewhere in the First Exposition until the Closing Section (where it is a component of cell D), except as a component of an aggregate collection of basic cells (bars 34–36, 41–42, 48).

In the concluding bars of the Recapitulation of the principal theme, immediately after the curtain falls, the harmonic material is greatly simplified and the basic harmonic ideas clearly and emphatically exposed. Parallel lines generating successive statements of the augmented triad (bars 145–146) or of the basic cells (bars 147–149) supplant the various types of simultaneities that are found in the expository statements of the principal theme.

The dramatic significance of the C-major triad that is sustained in the final episode of the Development, as Wozzeck gives Marie his money and bids her adieu, has been much discussed, first of all by Berg himself.[20] In the prosaic relationship of Wozzeck to Marie and to their child—the "ordinary" plane of his existence, represented by this most commonplace of chords—there resides whatever is "sane" or "normal" in him, whatever measure he has of human dignity. (This "ordinary" Wozzeck has been musically characterized earlier, at the conclusion of the Second Exposition, where a prosaic version of the Closing Section supplants, at Wozzeck's entrance, the earlier version, that had represented the child's terror at the imagined entrance of the "Gypsy lad" and whose return is expected as a representation of the child's terror at the imagined entrance of the "Sandman.")

In the light of the present analysis of Act II, Scene 1, it can be demonstrated that the C-major triad is not only uniquely appropriate as a dramatic device, but that it is also an integral element in the purely musical context of the movement. The most characteristic triadic components of the Sonata are the augmented triad (principal theme), diminished triad (Bridge Section) and major triad (Subordinate and Closing Sections). In the concluding bars of the Development (Example 47), the major triad is sustained in the orchestra as the vocal line unfolds a diminished triad (bar 117), an augmented triad (bars 120–121), and cell B (bars 121–123). Voice and orchestra together present cell C (bar 118) and cell D (bars 120–121). In the transi-

[20] Redlich, p. 275.

EXAMPLE 47

tional bars that lead into the Recapitulation, pentad x_p returns at T-0 (bar 124) and is reiterated against a linear version of pentad x_i at T-0 (bars 126–128).

In the stability acquired by the note C as a pedal in bars 116–127 and the transformation of this note into an appoggiatura in the first bar of the Recapitulation, there is a parallel with the structural employment of C in the Prelude to Act II (Example 67) and its transformation into an appoggiatura in the first bar of the Sonata. Finally, the C-major scale, upon which the curtain of Act II, Scene 2, rises, associates itself with these elements of the Sonata, as well as with the "white-note" collection that accompanied the fall of the curtain at the conclusion of the preceding scene.

Examples of linearized basic cells and pentads that appear at formally strategic moments, other than those which were discussed in connection with Example 47, are shown in Example 48: 48a, the beginning of the

EXAMPLE 48

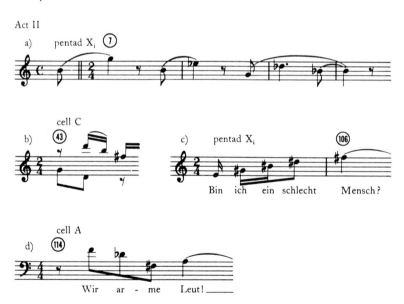

Hauptstimme of the principal theme; 48b, the beginning of the subordinate theme; 48c and 48d, two salient points in the Development.

SCALE SEGMENTS

THE TONE MATERIAL of numerous passages throughout the work may be defined in terms of three types of scales, or segments thereof—the whole-tone, the semitonal, and the diatonic scales. Associated with the last are collections that are reducible (as is the diatonic scale) to segments of the cycle of fifths. In Example 49, characteristic instances of each type are quoted from the first sixteen bars of the opera: 49a, a recurrent figure of Act I, Scene 1, which incorporates a permuted five-note segment— G–A–B–C♯–D♯—of the whole-tone scale; 49b, the basic dyad— B–F—encompassing a permuted segment of the semitonal scale; 49c,

EXAMPLE 49

overlapping "white-note" and "one-sharp" diatonic collections.[21] Collections derived from the three types of scale segments are qualitatively distinct sonorities, easily differentiated from elements not so derived. The quotations cited above in isolation from their original context define distinct harmonic planes within that context.

Example 50 illustrates a passage in which the complete gamut of twelve pitch classes is generated from the two distinct whole-tone scales. Whole-

EXAMPLE 50

tone formations are more significantly represented in mixed collections consisting of a five-note segment of the whole-tone scale preceded or followed by a single note that is not a component of that scale. Prominent melodic motives of this type that are found in Act I are illustrated in Example 51: 51a, the first linear motive of the opera and a prominent melodic idea of Scene 1; 51b, the initial motive of Andres' first "folk song" in Scene 2; 51c, the initial melodic phrase of the Doctor's ecstatic solo, the culminating and concluding episode of Scene 4; 51d, a prominent melodic idea with which the interlude between Scenes 4 and 5 begins, and which is literally recapitulated in the final symphonic interlude of Act III. The same collection of pitch classes—G–A–B–C♯–D♯—is shared by these most important self-contained melodic motives based on whole-tone segments in Act I.

21 If one could divorce such terms from extraneous associations, it might not be implausible, in view of the actual distribution of notes in Example 49c and considering the passage in isolation from its context, to describe it as "Phrygian-Aeolian." It is usually more convenient to refer such passages to the cycle of fifths of which every diatonic collection is a reordered segment. The overlapping "white-note" and "one-sharp" diatonic collections of Example 49c are equivalent in content to the following segment of the cycle of fifths: F–C–G–D–A–E–B–F♯.

EXAMPLE 51

One of the principal motives of Scene 5 commences with another collection of five whole tones (Example 52). At the climax of the movement, at
the moment that Marie and the Drum Major enter the house together
just before the curtain falls on an empty stage, a final statement of the same
motive appears, revised as Example 53 shows. In this form, this motive
restores the fixed collection of Example 51 and at the same time recalls a
salient motive from Scene 1, a variant of the first motivic element, Example
51a (Example 54).

An important motive of Act II, based, at T-0, on another five-note segment of the whole-tone scale, is first heard at Wozzeck's entrance in Act II,
Scene 2 (Example 55a). This motive clearly associates itself with the whole-
tone motive that accompanied Wozzeck's entrance in the preceding scene
(Example 55b).

Of the two discrete whole-tone scales that together generate the twelve

EXAMPLE 52

EXAMPLE 53

EXAMPLE 54

EXAMPLE 55

pitch classes, one (Example 56) has distinct priority over the other throughout the work. Each of the mixed collections illustrated in Examples 51
through 55a comprises one or another five-note segment of this scale.
(Example 55b comprises a four-note segment of the same scale.) The fact
that the primary compound tone center of the opera (Example 4) is such a
collection suggests the significance that must be ascribed to this scale in
the work as a whole. Outside of Act I, Scene 1, this chord invariably appears

in the context of a cadential figure (Example 5) which comprises, within a totality of eight pitch classes, the collective content of these whole-tone segments—the principal whole-tone scale of the work (Example 57).

EXAMPLE 56

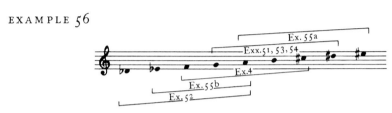

EXAMPLE 57

The most extensive exploitation of whole-tone formations occurs in the final symphonic interlude of the last act: the two whole-tone collections are explicitly unfolded in scale passages; segments of one or the other whole-tone collection are verticalized at a number of rhythmically stressed points, and the *total* content of the principal whole-tone collection is verticalized on the downbeat of bar 335; included among the motives that are recapitulated from earlier scenes are those illustrated above in Examples 51b, 51d, and 55a; the initial phrase of the special theme of the interlude presents a mixed collection (A♭–B♭–C–D–E plus A) of the type discussed above. The whole-tone segment of the last is, however, derived from the subordinate rather than the principal whole-tone scale. Unlike the earlier examples of these mixed collections, it is employed in a tonally functional context. An explicit linear statement of the principal whole-tone scale, in the top line, converges upon the recapitulated opening phrase of the special theme in the closing bars of the interlude (Example 58).

If the final symphonic interlude is a culminating episode in its explicit employment of whole-tone formations, so is the scene that precedes this

EXAMPLE 58

interlude in respect to the semitonal scale. Registral transfers effected by means of semitonal scale passages are so common throughout the opera that it is hardly necessary to cite specific instances. Where such passages occur simultaneously with other types of motion, they are heard on a separate plane, as in Act I, Scene 2, in which semitonal scale-segments are juxtaposed against the series of chords (Example 16) that generates the principal thematic material of the scene.

Explicit semitonal progressions are extensively employed to direct the motion of the bass line toward a specific goal. The semitonal descent of the bass line in Act I (bars 252–256) was cited earlier (p. 215). Coinciding with this bass line is a soprano line, marked *Hauptstimme*, that is reducible to its symmetrical inversion (Example 59).

EXAMPLE 59

Two focal elements outline the semitonal bass progression of the last thirty-three bars of Act I, Scene 4 (Example 60): the E♭ tone center of this scene and the G–D pedal of the orchestral interlude which follows (cf.

EXAMPLE 60

p. 216). The descent from G to E♮ in bars 623–636 is symmetrically inverted in the ascent from G♭ to B♭ in the top line. The semitonal scale
(bars 638–642) by means of which the E♮ of bars 636–637 is transferred
to the lower octave is aligned, note for note, with the final statement, in the
top line, of the twelve-tone Passacaglia theme (cf. Example 71). The music
of the orchestral interlude that begins at bar 656 is transformed into a
waltz for the stage orchestra in Act II, Scene 4. In this version, it is introduced by a descending semitonal scale to the pedal-tone G (bars 521–529).

The use of explicit semitonal scale segments to fill in the intervals between linear adjacencies of a chordal pattern in Act II, Scene 4, was cited
above (p. 223). The filling-in of a boundary interval with the *reordered*
content of such a segment, rather than with the explicit segment itself, was
illustrated in Example 49b. This is the principle that determines the modifications to which the initial motive of Act III, Scene 1, is subjected in the
quasi-canonic opening of the *Thema* of the movement (a set of variations
and a fugue). The initial motive is twice approximately imitated, the three
statements together outlining a G-minor triad in root position, with the
root doubled in the soprano in the octave above and the span between fifth
and octave melodically filled in by semitonal inflections of the initial motive
(Example 61). A telescoped version of the opening bars appears at the
beginning of the Second Variation (Example 62a) and another telescoped
version forms the subject of the closing fugue (Example 62b).

Movement by semitonal inflection permeates the texture of the entire
work, generating elements that range in scope from neighbor notes and

EXAMPLE 61

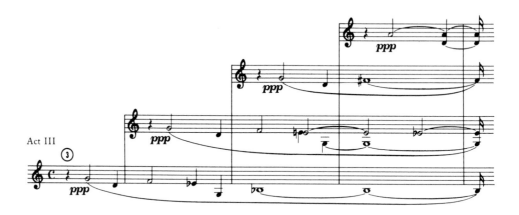

EXAMPLE 62

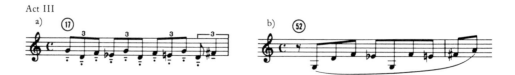

neighbor chords (Example 63) to the harmonic basis of an entire scene (Example 64).

A number of passages are based on special orderings of the *total* content of the semitonal scale. Berg thus foreshadows a concept that was subsequently generalized in the twelve-tone system. Examples of such passages include: the two whole-tone collections into which the semitonal scale is divided in Example 50; the three simultaneous diminished seventh chords into which it is divided in Act II, bar 115, and Act III, bar 364 (Example 65); the twelve-tone Passacaglia theme of Act I, Scene 5; the twelve-tone series that forms a segment of the *Thema* of Act III, Scene 1 (Example 73); the eleven-tone series against a sustained B that accompanies the rising

EXAMPLE 63

EXAMPLE 64

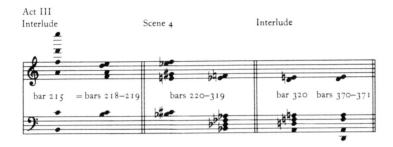

of the moon in Act III, Scene 2 (bars 97–100); a statement of the basic set of Act III, Scene 4, simultaneously with a tone cluster comprising the notes not contained in that set (Example 66).

EXAMPLE 65   EXAMPLE 66

Tonic functionality is more or less consistently expressed in Act III, Scene 1 (G minor), and in the final symphonic interlude (D minor). Key centers are explicitly represented by key signatures only in the latter and in the F-minor episode, bars 33–41, of the former. In neither section is tonic functionality associated with the employment of diatonic collections. Conversely, diatonic collections are found that do not, in their context, imply tonic functionality. An example is the "white-note" collection of Act I, bars 45–46.

Directed motion in the bass line sometimes proceeds along a series of perfect fifths, rather than a series of semitones as illustrated in Examples 59 and 60. The structural use of successive fifths in the bass line of the Prelude to Act II is shown in Example 67. The final cadential chord of this passage comprises a seven-note segment of the cycle of fifths plus one "odd" note (Example 68a). Verticalized series of fifths occur at other important points: the vertical set on which Act III, Scene 4, is based consists of a five-note segment of the cycle of fifths plus one "odd" note (Example 68b); the cadential chord of the preceding interlude consists of a six-note dia-

EXAMPLE 67

EXAMPLE 68

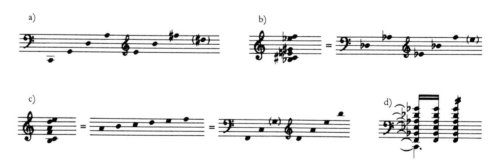

tonic segment, equivalent to a gapped seven-note segment of the cycle of fifths (Example 68c); the concluding chord (bar 379) of the first section of the "Cradle Song" of Act I, Scene 3, consists of a seven-note segment of the cycle of fifths (Example 68d).

The polarity of outer voices that is found in much of *Wozzeck* is a traditional textural feature, the absence of which in some other "atonal" music is one of the revolutionary characteristics of that music. A striking instance of this polarity is found in Act I, Scene 2. A series of fifths and a series of semitones are here simultaneously aligned in the outer voices (Example 69). The total simultaneous content is given at three points in the example, where vertical statements of whole-tone segments appear.

EXAMPLE 69

SYMMETRICAL FORMATIONS

SIMULTANEOUS voices moving by semitonal inflection are often symmetrically related to each other, as in Examples 59, 60, and 63. In Examples 59 and 60, this type of progression is presented in the outer voices only. In Example 63, *all* the parts are symmetrically disposed around the same axis, so that they are paired in parallel and contrary motion.[22] Such paired symmetrical formations are often presented simultaneously with nonsymmetrical elements, as in Example 70. (The symmetrical components are given in the two outer staves. The first and second chords, in conjunction with the vocal line, are each a five-note segment of a whole-tone scale.)

22 In Act II, bars 42 ff., a transposition of this symmetrical progression is enlarged to include three chordal components. Cf. Example 31.

EXAMPLE 70

OSTINATI

THE MOST PRIMITIVE means of achieving musical coherence is simple
reiteration. As Ernst Kurth points out in his *Musikpsychologie:* "Through
repetition an entire melodic unit becomes stable, in spite of its own movement. . . . That is, it acts in principle no differently from one repeated tone."[23]
In much of the music of the early decades of this century, the ostinato is a
primary structural device, occasioned by the increasing ambiguity of the
articulative means provided by a disintegrating tonal system. The surface
reiteration that is characteristic of certain works of Stravinsky, Bartók,
Varèse, and other composers is relatively rare in the music of the atonal
school, but the most extreme development of the ostinato principle is nevertheless to be found in the evolution of this school. In the twelve-tone system
of Schoenberg, a serial permutation of the semitonal scale is the ever-
present groundwork of each composition. The ostinato principle is represented here only in the assumed succession of pitch classes, not in their
relative octave positions and durations. The first examples by Schoenberg

[23] Quoted from Charles Warren Fox, "Modern Counterpoint: A Phenomenological Approach,"
Notes (December, 1948), p. 52.

in order of publication are the final movement of the Five Piano Pieces, Op. 23, and the Sonett of the Serenade, Op. 24, both completed in 1923. *Wozzeck*, completed two years earlier, presents some remarkable parallels with these movements in the Passacaglia of Act I, Scene 4. The ostinato theme of the latter corresponds to Schoenberg's "tone row," in that it is a fixed serial ordering of the twelve notes. If the twelve-tone movements of Op. 23 and Op. 24 are to be given precedence as "earliest examples" of twelve-tone music, it is because they are the first in which *all* pitch elements (with a few exceptions in the Sonett) are components of statements of the set.[24] This aspect of the twelve-tone system is foreshadowed in Act III, Scene 4, of *Wozzeck*, discussed above under the heading Vertical Sets, not to speak of still earlier examples, the Seventh Sonata and other works by Scriabin, in which all pitch relations are referable to an unordered collection of pitch classes and to transpositions of this collection. In each of these instances, however, the set, being unordered, can comprise only a partial selection of the twelve pitch classes.[25]

The function of the tone row in the Passacaglia movement of *Wozzeck* (Act I, Scene 4) is not comparable to that of the Schoenbergian twelve-tone set or the vertical set of Act III, Scene 4. The series in question is, rather, a special sort of "theme," special in that the only thematic property which it possesses is that of pitch class succession. No specific rhythmic pattern or melodic contour is sufficiently associated with this pitch class succession to function as a thematic component.[26] In illustrating the theme itself, therefore, a series of letter-names is more appropriate than staff notation (Example 71):

---

[24] According to Josef Rufer, *The Works of Arnold Schoenberg* (New York, Free Press, 1963), p. 45, Schoenberg's manuscript copy of the Prelude of the Suite for Piano, Op. 25, is dated *Juli 1921*. Basic concepts of Schoenberg's twelve-tone method—strict segmentation procedures and the employment of the row in its literal transformations (retrograde, inversion, and retrograde-inversion) and transpositions—appear here for the first time. In view of a more naïve employment of a tone row in the last piece of Op. 23, it is surprising to learn that "considering the date of the Prelude, it seems uncertain whether this or (as previously believed) the Waltz from Op. 23 . . . is the first twelve-tone composition."

[25] A totally unordered twelve-tone set is simply equivalent to the semitonal scale. A twelve-tone set may be defined either by partitioning its otherwise unordered content (Hauer) or by specifying the order of pitch classes (Schoenberg).

[26] It is interesting to note that Berg's treatment of the series in his later, "official," twelve-tone works is exceptional in the extent to which an explicit rhythmic pattern and melodic contour is associated with the series. See Perle, "*Lulu*: The Thematic Material and Pitch Organization," *Music Review* (November, 1965).

EXAMPLE 71

Salient harmonic details of the series are bracketed in the example: the augmented triad formed by the first three elements, the diminished triad formed by the last three, and the four tritone adjacencies.

In the penultimate variation, a special subsidiary motive and a segment of the series are employed in stretto at various pitch levels. Each of the other variations presents but one statement of the theme, at T-0. Segments, in particular the diminished triad, are independently reiterated, however. Two segmented versions of the theme are of exceptional interest in that they anticipate a basic procedure of the twelve-tone system, the verticalization of linearly defined relationships (Example 72).

EXAMPLE 72

Each of the five scenes of Act III is based on a different type of ostinato. In Scene 1, it is an aggregate of melodic details; in Scene 2, a single pitch class; in Scene 3, a rhythmic figure; in Scene 4, a chord; in Scene 5, a single durational value. The initial segment of the *Thema* of Scene 1 was illustrated, together with two of its variants, in Examples 61 and 62. The remainder of the *Thema* is in sharp contrast with the G-minor tonality of the opening, in that a twelve-tone series is unfolded in the bass line (Example 73).

EXAMPLE 73

This series, unlike that of the Passacaglia, retains the contour of its original version (except for an occasional octave displacement of the first and/or last note). Each statement of the series is shown in Example 74. In the Third Variation, the series is transposed down a semitone, except for the third and fourth notes, which are transposed down a whole tone, and the tenth note, which remains at the original pitch level. The original contour is thus maintained, but the size of some intervals is modified by a semitone and note repetitions and omissions occur. In the Sixth Variation, the series is not completed. In the Seventh Variation, the order of the first two notes is reversed.

EXAMPLE 74

EXAMPLE 74 (*continued*)

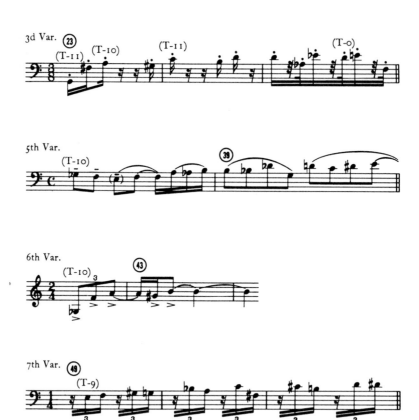

Another component of the *Thema* consists of two simultaneous linear details, marked X and Y in Example 75. At each restatement of X and Y they are juxtaposed in a new manner. The contour of X is repeatedly revised through octave displacements, but finally fixed as one of the two subjects of the fugue with which the scene concludes. (The other subject is quoted in Example 62b.) At several points the original intervals are modified by a semitonal inflection, and at one point by a whole-tone inflection. These points are marked by an asterisk in the example.

EXAMPLE 75

EXAMPLE 75 (*continued*)

5th Var.

X (T-10)

6th Var.

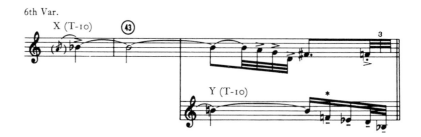

7th Var.

Fuge

Hei - land!___ ich möch - te Dir die Fü - sse sal - ben.

The ostinato as conventionally understood plays a negligible role in *Wozzeck* as compared with other music of the period. It is most significantly employed in Act II, Scene 4, the "Scherzo" movement of the "Symphony in Five Movements" which constitutes the formal framework of the act as a whole. In the recapitulation section of this movement, the *Langsamer Ländler*, which opens the scene, is given to the stage band and played against a basso ostinato derived from the initial melodic motive of the *Ländler* in the cellos of the pit orchestra (Example 76). Simultaneously

EXAMPLE 76

(bars 591 ff), in the upper strings of the pit orchestra, a chordal pattern commencing with and returning to an E♭-minor triad is progressively expanded in range and content, as illustrated in Example 77.

The focal elements of this first section of the recapitulation are the four-note ostinato motive of Example 76 and the E♭-minor triad. The incessant repetition of the latter against the first two statements of the basso ostinato (Example 76, bars 589–591) establishes the keynote of this section. There is a return to both elements in the tavern scene of Act III, at Wozzeck's words, "No! No shoes! One can go to hell barefooted!" (Example 78). Dramatically this music refers to Wozzeck's reply, in the earlier scene, to Andres' question, "Why do you sit by the door!" "I'm sitting all right here. There are people who sit by the door and don't know it until they're carried out of the door, feet first." The incorporation of the ostinato motive in the vocal setting of these words is shown in Example 79.

EXAMPLE 77

EXAMPLE 78

EXAMPLE 79

EXAMPLE 80

In the recapitulation of the *Walzer*, an ostinato figure in the pit orchestra accompanies the stage band (Example 80). The reiterated minor triad plus major seventh on E♭ associates this section with the earlier recapitulation of the *Ländler*. A single augmented statement of this figure, transposed two octaves down, is heard in the background of the music that accompanies the Drum Major's taunting of the fallen Wozzeck in the following scene (bars 798–804).

If I have not attempted to establish the coherence and unity of the work as a whole in terms of the interdependence and interaction of all the structural elements discussed in the foregoing survey, it is not because I am unaware of the importance and desirability of doing so. But the criteria upon which overall continuity depends cannot be determined apart from a fuller and more systematic presentation of such elements than can be offered here and now. Premature generalizations will not only fail to elucidate the larger relationships: they also ignore or distort the very details whose integration into the total work it is their chief business to explain.

A Glossary of the
Elements of Graphic Analysis

LINEAR-STRUCTURAL or voice-leading analyses are usually presented in the form of graphs that make use of elements of musical notation and a few additional symbols.[1] When these are meaningfully employed, the sense of an analysis can be presented with an unrivaled clarity, even when the musical judgments that prompt it are, perhaps, faulty. When carelessly or improperly employed they can easily create hopeless confusion, even when the musical judgments might be valid. In an attempt to eliminate as much obscurity as possible, a glossary of recurrent symbols is presented herewith. Our aim, it must be understood, is to suggest how analytic judgments can be presented graphically with definiteness and conviction, rather than to give instruction in the ways of reaching conclusions, or to justify conclusions that may have been reached. Variants of the symbols and abbreviations here presented are easily conceivable, as are additional symbols not included herein. Analysts have their own ways of presenting conclusions, and contrasting styles of composition often demand different graphing techniques (see the graphs of works by Perotinus and Wagner in this issue). The test of the validity of a symbol is its clarity, rather than its subservience to a fiat.

Before proceeding, it should be observed that structure, as conceived in linear analysis, is the interrelation of all musical factors as they subserve the inclusive character of an entire work. Structure, in this sense, exists on several levels, from immediately perceptible relationships to broad inclusive ones. In general, it is sufficient to construct separate but related graphs for three levels—immediate, intermediate, and remote. These are intended as equivalents of Heinrich Schenker's *Vordergrund*, *Mittelgrund*, and *Hintergrund* (foreground, middle ground, and background). At times, additional graphs of sections of a work are required for the explication of complex

---

[1] The content of this glossary applies to the graphing techniques employed in the articles by Peter Bergquist, William J. Mitchell, and Felix Salzer.

relationships. In the case of simple contexts, one or perhaps two graphs will prove sufficient.

Notes. Notes in various shapes are employed for the designation of pitches in the usual sense and also to differentiate among the various levels of structure. The different shapes have no fixed temporal or rhythmic value.

1. Unstemmed black noteheads are most universally employed to denote immediate levels of structure.

2. Stems added to black noteheads signify an intermediate level of structure. Within this level, further nuances of structural value are indicated by employing stems of different lengths.

3. Combinations of stemmed and unstemmed noteheads represent contexts in which a relationship of the stemmed notes is filled in or extended by means of the immediate values represented by unstemmed noteheads.

4. Half notes represent relatively remote structural contexts and should be employed for this purpose only.

5. To differentiate in a graph between various levels of structure, the three suggested shapes, unstemmed noteheads, stemmed noteheads (of which the length of stems may vary), and half notes, should be employed. Three levels of structural relations are illustrated in the marginal example. The half notes indicate a context on a remote level; the quarter notes on an intermediate level; and the noteheads on an immediate level.

6. Note values such as eighths and sixteenths designate immediate, at times intermediate, structural values. They are used sparingly and often mark a specific characterizing feature of a composition.

7. Parenthesized notes in various shapes represent notes that have been circumvented in a composition, yet form the underlying sense of a melodic or contrapuntal detour.

Other Symbols. Notes and noteheads by themselves represent judgments by the analyst about the various levels of structural significance. To clarify their specific contextual meanings, they must be used in connection with other symbols. Unattended notes can be a source of obscurity or they may reveal indecisiveness on the part of the analyst.

1. The slur is the most recurrent and useful clarifying symbol. It is employed to denote contexts and to subdivide them.

2. The dotted slur is used specifically to denote the return to or the structural retention of a single pitch.

2a. The dotted slur in the illustration signifies the return to or the structural retention of a single pitch, following an extension of the first notehead, as indicated by the solid slur in the upper illustration, or a motion back to the initial pitch, as designated by the solid slur in the lower illustration. Other combinations, often using superimposed solid slurs only, are of course possible, always being dictated by a particular analytic judgment with reference to a context. They are also employed with notes of intermediate and remote structural meaning.

or

3. Arrowheads added to slurs are used on occasion to denote the direction of relationships, such as the dependence of a dominant chord on a succeeding tonic (the upper slur), or on a preceding tonic (the lower slur). A straight arrow under the bass is used to indicate a prolonged transition from one point to another.

4. The beam often replaces the slur for the denoting of intermediate and remote structural relationships. As in the case of slurs, it is made solid if the pitches of the connected notes are different, dotted if they are identical.

4a. When the remote structure is formed by widely separated contexts, it simplifies graphing procedures to break the solid or dotted beam and interpolate a legend directing the reader to the relevant succeeding note.

5. Interchanged positions of notes are indicated by crossed lines.

6. Lines resembling an ess are employed to indicate structurally significant changes of register.

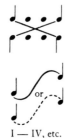

I — IV, etc.

7. Areas or points of harmonic significance are denoted by Roman numerals of different sizes which depend on the structural value of these areas.

(= I–IV–V–I)

8. Harmonic techniques of immediate or intermediate value are indicated by relatively smaller Roman numerals. To stress their subordinate character they may be put in parentheses.

I–IV–V–I
I
OR
(= I–IV–V–I)
I

I–IV–V–I
of V

5–6–5–6. etc.

9. The dominance of a single harmony over an immediate or intermediate chordal progression is denoted by a brace relating the detailed chords to an embracing harmony. This same technique can be indicated by a dotted beam connecting the bass tones of the beginning and end of the dominating chord.

10. The relationship of a modulatory technique to broader structural harmonies may be shown by the preposition "of" placed before the relevant harmony.

11. Thorough bass signatures or Arabic numerals are employed to point out techniques of voice leading or the linear or contrapuntal functions of a series of sonorities.

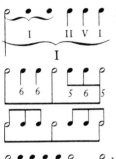

12. There are several ways of showing prolongations of the bass and the upper voice within a broader frame of reference. Some of these are shown in the marginal illustrations. They include the use of braces within braces, and beams within beams.

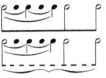

12a. A more immediate level of upper-voice or bass structure is indicated by the slurs that appear within a bracket or brace.

||

13. Parallel lines are used to indicate the location of the structural break in "divided" or "interrupted" forms, such as Suite movements or other less clearly marked designs, that are interrupted on the dominant harmony, and thereafter continue anew.

$\hat{3}$ $\hat{2}$ $\hat{1}$ also 3 2 1

14. Capped Arabic numerals are often employed in connection with the upper voice of the ultimate remote graph of a piece. They designate the scale steps of an embracing diatonic succession. Uncapped Arabic numerals fulfill the same function with respect to immediate and intermediate levels of structure.

Abbreviations

Cons. P

Consonant passing tone, a conceptually dissonant passing tone made into a consonance by its accompaniment.

CS	A contrapuntally derived chord of structural status.
D or Div.	Divider, a chord, usually V, that marks a section of a design.
DF	A chord of double function; one that exhibits structural as well as prolonging capabilities, or one that behaves as a harmonic as well as a contrapuntal element.
EM	An embellishing chord, as distinguished from a passing or neighboring chord.
M	A mixed chord, one whose elements are derived from the opposite mode, or through chromatic modification of, usually, the third.
VL	An element of voice-leading origin.

For the rest generally understood abbreviations are used, such as:

N, neighbor; IN, incomplete neighbor; P, passing; $\frac{\text{N}}{\text{P}}$, neighboring-passing; UN, LN, upper, lower neighbor; Phr., Phrygian. As with Roman numerals, the size of these signs indicates their structural level.

In order to demonstrate the employment of the various elements of this Glossary, Example 1 presents in four graphs a linear analysis of the Theme of the Variations Sérieuses, Op. 54, of Felix Mendelssohn. Examples 1a, 1b, and 1c are remote, intermediate, and immediate graphs, respectively, while 1d is an additional explanatory graph covering bars 4 to 12. In keeping with the illustrative purpose of the analysis, the accompanying text will be more extended than would be necessary ordinarily.

Before commenting on each of the graphs, a word is in order concerning a challenging aspect of the Theme. As a general rule, a double bar, such as that placed by Mendelssohn in the middle of bar 8, should act as a divisional guide for the analyst. In this case, however, the continuation through bar 12 is so tightly and persuasively related to the preceding music, that a broader, more inclusive reading is indicated. The double bar seems to be only a marking off of the midpoint of the Theme, rather than an indication of a structural division. Hence, no constructive analytic purpose is served by accepting it as a token of a two-part form. It should be noted that it reappears in only four of the seventeen variations. Furthermore, when Mendelssohn extends Variations 9 and 13 by repeating parts of the variations, he repeats only the final four bars, rather than the eight which represent the music that follows the double bar. In the case of Variation 10, the total of eighteen bars is achieved by extending the final cadence. Finally in Variation 17, which is greatly expanded, the beginning of the expansion makes use of material from bars 12–14 of Variation 16. In brief, it is apparent that the double bar in the middle of bar 8 is not to be regarded as a clear point of structural separation. On the other hand, a critical point in the graphs of Example 1, the regaining of f^2 in bar 12, is precisely the place that Mendelssohn turns to as he forms his extensions by means of repetition.

Example 1a expresses the remote structure and certain basic distinctions in structural values by means of half notes, as well as stemmed and unstemmed black notes. Observe that the bass is formed to indicate two ways of reaching f in bar 15: the first is through the ascent of a third from d to f; the other is through the descent of a sixth from d^1 through a facilitating b♭ (VI) in bar 12 to f. Both routes shape the structure of the Theme.

So far as the upper parts are concerned, a feature of the graph is the presence of a vertical bracket before the three upper parts. Its purpose is to point out a feature of the Theme, the reaching of f^2 by means of an arpeggiation of the tones of the d-minor triad. Because the technique that Mendelssohn employs in achieving this end is a complex one, as will be indicated in subsequent graphs, it is important to indicate its basis in the remote graph.

Example 1b superimposes intermediate structural values on the remote ones of Example 1a. Note that the vertical bracket of Example 1a has now become horizontal in its two appearances. The purpose is to point out a significant structural parallelism, the attaining of f^2 through two arpeggios, the second of which is partially filled in (from a^1 to d^2). The ascent from a^1 through b♭^{1} to c^2–c♯^{2} and d^2 (bars 4–12) is accomplished in such a way that b♭^{1} first satisfies its normal resolution by moving to a^1 before c^2 appears above. It is this complex detail that is graphed more particularly in Examples 1c and 1d. In the first arpeggio (bars 1–2), the technique includes a passing tone g^1 in the upper middle voice, as a^1 moves to d^2. The third, a^1–g^1–f^1, which includes this passing tone is represented here in the

EXAMPLE I

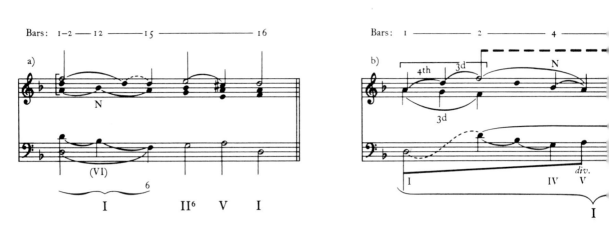

EXAMPLE I (*continued*)

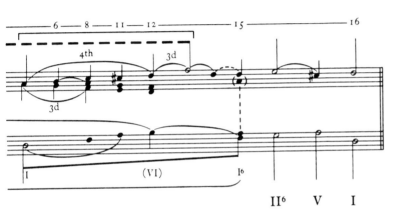

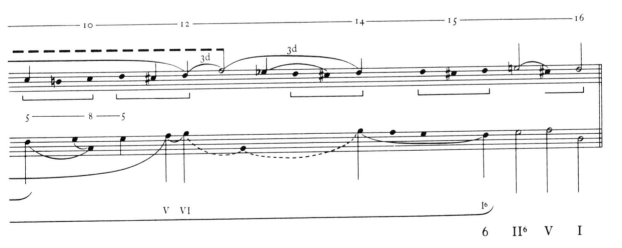

intermediate level, because it helps to explain the striking immediate technique of Example 1c.

In the bass, subdivisions appear. The first upper voice ascent to f² is accompanied by a change of register in the bass (d–d¹) which leads to a divider dominant (bar 4). The second, filled in ascent from a¹ to d² is accompanied by an arpeggiated bass, d–f–a, leading to b♭ in bar 12 and eventually f in bar 15. These bass motions are accompanied by slurs and beams which are intended to clarify the various levels of structure represented by each of the relationships. Note that half notes in the outer voices continue to represent the remote, inclusive structure of the Theme.

The structural level of Example 1c is immediate and detailed. Note that, in bars 1–4, the arpeggiation of the upper voice assumes a complex form which involves the upward transposition of inner voices (d¹ to d², g¹ to f²), indicated by ess-like dotted and solid slurs. The immediate motive that participates in the arpeggio is two-toned, consisting of a¹–g♯¹, d²–c♯². It is this motive that sets up the descending third of the middle voice (compare Examples 1b and 1c). The apparent repetition of this motive (bars 4–6) serves new ends. The descending third appears as the top voice, but it now connects a¹ with f♯¹. The accompaniment in the form of two neighbors, e and c, to the governing d is formed by transferred resolutions, indicated by oblique lines. The situation in the second half of bar 6 is an interesting one. Two b♭'s appear, b♭¹ and b♭, joined by a dotted double arrowhead. The upper one, as noted in Example 1b, moves on eventually to c², the lower one satisfies the impulse to resolve to a. A more generalized representation of this technique appears in Example 1d. The completion of the ascending fourth, a¹–b♭¹–c²–c♯²–d, follows as indicated in Examples 1c and 1d.

Note should be made of a second parallelism, also indicated by brackets. The first of these occurs in bar 1 as the upper voice descends in its two-note motive from a¹ to g♯¹. This is the germinal form of the neighboring motive that occurs in bars 8–10, 10–12, 13–14, 14–15, all indicated by brackets. At the very end an incomplete bracket underscores the final vestige of this prevalent relationship, now reduced to c♯²–d².

The remaining analytic symbols for this analysis of a remarkable Theme should be clear after a study of the Glossary.

Index